A SCANDAL IN BOHEMIA

Gideon Haigh has been a journalist for more than three decades, has contributed to more than a hundred newspapers and magazines, published thirty-five books and edited seven others. His work has won premier's literary awards in three states, two Waverley Library Prizes, seven Australian Cricket Society trophies and a Ned Kelly Award for true crime. Gideon lives in Melbourne with his wife and daughter.

A SCANDAL IN BOHEMIA

GIDEON HAIGH

HAMISH HAMILTON
an imprint of
PENGUIN BOOKS

HAMISH HAMILTON

UK | USA | Canada | Ireland | Australia
India | New Zealand | South Africa | China

Penguin Books is part of the Penguin Random House group of companies
whose addresses can be found at global.penguinrandomhouse.com.

Penguin
Random House
Australia

First published by Penguin Random House Australia Pty Ltd, 2018

1 3 5 7 9 10 8 6 4 2

Cover design by Louisa Maggio © Penguin Random House Australia Pty Ltd
Text design by Midland Typesetters, Australia
Cover image: *Sleep*, by Colin Colahan, private collection
Typeset in Adobe Caslon Pro by Midland Typesetters, Australia
Printed and bound in Australia by Griffin Press, an accredited ISO AS/NZS 14001
Environmental Management Systems printer.

 A catalogue record for this
book is available from the
NATIONAL
LIBRARY National Library of Australia
OF AUSTRALIA

ISBN: 978 0 14378 957 4

penguin.com.au

'I only caught a glimpse of her at the moment, but she was a lovely woman, with a face that a man might die for.'
Sir Arthur Conan Doyle, 'A Scandal in Bohemia', 1891

CONTENTS

INTRODUCTION

For one who spent so much time surrounded by sharp-eyed artists and writers, Mollie Dean would prove a challenge to describe. She was 'very, very attractive, very beautiful', thought the painter Colin Colahan, and 'knew her power with men'. She was 'not really beautiful but had a certain sultry charm', countered the playwright Betty Roland, being 'somewhat sullen-looking with a well-cut sensuous mouth'. Passing moods lit her face from within: one writer thought her 'plain in repose'; another evoked her 'dusky glow'. A solitary photograph, widely published, is grainy and flat, lent character only by the eyes' steady gaze and the jaw's slight clench. Newspapers made up for its deficiencies with expressive prose: 'Five feet, six inches [168 cm] in height, dark bobbed hair, dark complexion, well-set determined-looking features, little or no powder on face, slim to medium build'; 'A good conversationalist, she had a low speaking voice, an excellent thing in a woman. Her avowed preference was for

'Sultry charm': Mollie Dean

the society of men older than herself – a feeling that inevitably out-grows itself in time.'

The range of opinion reflected deeper ambivalence about Mollie Dean – a young woman resolved to get places, a young woman who when she got those places was not always welcome. Who was she? *What* was she? 'She was an exceptional girl,' the cartoonist Percy Leason told reporters. 'She had great vitality and charm and was par-ticularly interesting. She was deeply immersed in literary questions and was writing a novel. I do not know what the novel was about. She was the sort of girl who would make light of such a work and not talk too much about it.' Leason's confrère on *The Bulletin*, Mervyn Skipper, thought Mollie 'the first liberated woman' he had ever met; Mervyn's diarist wife, Lena, deemed Mollie a 'sex aggravator', 'a rum girl with plenty of that schoolgirl way about her' hiding 'in all her actions some monstrously selfish aim'. Roland complained that she had left 'a path of havoc in her wake'.

All that most came to know of her directly was how that wake trailed away. For in November 1930, a month after her twenty-fifth birthday, Mollie Dean was slain in a laneway two minutes' walk from her home – slain so sadistically that the press refrained from comprehensively listing her injuries. Intensified grief, idealised potential – these are the usual accompaniments of a tragically premature end. Not for Mollie. An investigation petered out that no-one, least of all the family from whom she was estranged, wished to revive; an inquest ensued, with an undertone of scandal it was in none of her friends' interests to prolong.

As for her life, a good deal of Mollie's adulthood had been spent in the fugitive role of the 'other woman', whose tracks are ideally self-obscuring. Her correspondence, purportedly racy, conveniently disappeared; likewise the manuscript for her novel, never finished. At Montsalvat, the Eltham art colony where many of her former circle settled, her name would be uttered only in muted tones. In art history, she has condensed to a curio. *Misty Moderns*, an extensive 2008 touring exhibition by the National Gallery of Australia, touched off a reappraisal of the artists with whom Mollie circulated – the quasi-scientific, objectively minded disciples of 'tonalism' such as Colahan, Leason, Justus Jorgensen, Clarice Beckett, Archie Colquhoun and, above all, their inspiration, the peppery controversialist Max Meldrum. Mollie was a line in the exhibition's genre chronology: 'November 1930: Murder of Colin Colahan's girlfriend, Mollie Dean. Impact temporarily disrupts Colahan's artistic trajectory.' No reflection was invited on the permanent disruption of Mollie's 'artistic trajectory'.

Mollie Dean's shadow lengthened by other means. She who had aspired to fiction inspired it instead – affirming Edgar Allan Poe's *aperçu* that 'the death . . . of a beautiful woman is, unquestionably, the most poetical topic in the world'. Generations of Australians have been unknowingly familiarised with her story through the pages of George Johnston's *My Brother Jack*. Johnston never knew Mollie Dean; rather, more than twenty years after events, did he fall in with the gregarious Colahan, who became a friend and familiar in addition to painting Johnston's wife Charmian Clift. The murder had by now become part of Colahan's extraordinary repertoire of stories; Johnston was transfixed. As his great novel took shape years later, he repurposed the relationship between artist Colahan and muse Mollie as the tale of star-crossed student painters Sam Burlington and Jessica Wray, who introduce Johnston's callow alter ego, David Meredith, to Melbourne's *la vie de bohème*.

It is an atmospheric telling. Jessica is first glimpsed hastily 'fastening the buttons of her blouse', fair hair suggestively loose. She reacts to Meredith's unexpected arrival at Burlington's bachelor pad by saucily withdrawing: 'The blonde girl went away soon after I arrived. She and Sam talked together for a while in the passageway in low voices, with a lot of smothered giggling on her part, and I heard her say, "But it's high time I went home anyway, after the way you've been carrying on, you devil."' Who is leading whom is rendered more ambiguous by Jessica's cavortings with other girls at an apartment party that further discomfits prim Meredith:

I remembered my alarmed revulsion at the shameless exposed way the girls sat on cushions on the floor, with their knees carelessly apart in their short skirts and the shadowy disturbing gleam of naked thighs above their rolled stockings. I was shocked by their casual acceptance of drinks and cigarettes, by the candour of their conversation, by their abandoned submission to kissing and petting.

The apartment is dominated by Sam's 'not quite finished but extremely frank' nude canvas of Jessica. Brother Jack, archetype of vernacular common sense, glowers at the painting disapprovingly when he arrives amid the bacchanal:

> 'Who did *this* thing?' he wanted to know.
>   'Sam,' I said.
>   'Cripes! It don't leave much to the imagination, does it?'
>   'Oh, stop this stupid business Jack,' I said.

Though Jack warily embraces the festivities, his curiosity has been pricked. 'You mean t'tell me,' he asks Sam, 'she strips off an' sits around starko and lets you paint her like that, without a stitch?' Sam's slurred reply betrays a deeper unease with female sexuality: 'Yesh, sir, thash my baby. Jesh. Look at her over there, eh. Jush *look* at her! Beau'ful girl. Talent too. No morals. Wassit matter? She'd sleep with you. Me. Anybody.'

When Meredith encounters Jessica and Sam next, their images are staring from the grey columns of the *Morning Post*, where tyro journalist Meredith is working. Jessica has been murdered in a park, and suspicion has fallen on Sam. The prurient turn of his hitherto 'conservative, old-fashioned' employer tips Meredith into crisis. He must bear witness to his trade's pandering to gossipmongers and breakfast-table moralists – including his own censorious father. He must reconcile Sam's travails with his own self-preserving instincts – a challenge he squibs in Petrine fashion, thrice denying his friend. He must even answer for his own titillation, with which a detective cannily confronts him: ('She was a very pretty girl, wasn't she? Did you find yourself attracted to her? [. . .] Didn't you ever wish it was *you* doing the canoodling and not Burlington?')

Ere long new evidence dispels the tension, and around the murder itself *My Brother Jack* ends up rather skirting, exploring it only in terms of the consequences for others. Like Colahan, Sam departs Australia; unlike Colahan, he abandons art; the experience turns Meredith into, by his own admission, 'a master of dissimulation', in ways that ramify through the whole trilogy. Yet, rereading the novel after many years, my own curiosity, like Jack's, was engaged. Didn't this book draw on Johnston's experiences? If so, to whom did he owe Jess and Sam? I consulted Garry Kinnane's life of Johnston, which sketches the original crime in a discursive paragraph; Kinnane's subsequent monograph on Colahan, which includes a helpful chronology; and in due course Kinnane, now retired in Geelong after a long career in academe, a memento on the wall entwining his two subjects: Colahan's large portrait of the handsome Clift.

Kinnane courteously rummaged his memory for impressions from the research he had undertaken, after all, decades earlier. The short Colahan book, he explained, had been written with the encouragement of the painter's third wife, after Kinnane had visited them in Italy while researching *George Johnston: A Biography* in 1983. He was not, in hindsight, entirely satisfied with it. His chief source of information about Mollie Dean had been research notes compiled by Eric Westbrook, director of the National Gallery of Victoria from 1956 to 1973, who had looked into the murder with a view to a book he had never written.

In fact, Westbrook had been severely disconcerted by the general paucity of material about Mollie, particularly the absence, when he inquired, of records of the police investigation and coronial inquest. In a 1991 interview with *The Age*, he had even inferred a cover-up: 'Let me be quite clear that I have no precise evidence. But the way in which I have been repeatedly blocked – I don't want to go into details – gives me the feeling that there is a reluctance to have these very unhappy circumstances brought into the light.' Under the head-line 'WHO KILLED MOLLIE DEAN?', writer Larry Schwartz wondered: 'Is this Melbourne's dark secret, a conspiracy of silence to protect not just those who might have been associated with Mollie Dean, but possibly her murderer?' Westbrook hinted to Schwartz that he thought so:

> 'In those days the idea of a girl who posed in the nude for painters . . . the implication was she must be an immoral woman, a loose woman. It seems to me, without overdramatising, I hope, that a message came down from something much [more] than the family in Elwood, from somewhere, that this was getting on dangerous ground, that once they investigated Mollie Dean's activities they . . . some rather . . .'
>
> Was he saying that details of the murder inquiry might have pointed to a link between Mollie Dean and certain men who did not want this exposed?
>
> 'Of course, but then a further echo of that, a kind of overtone of that, is would it have been convenient for somebody to have got rid of her? I mean, isn't that the inevitable follow-up?'

Some have agreed. Kinnane contented himself with noting that 'conspiracy theories thrive on stuff like this'. But in his recent semi-official history of the celebrated artists' colony Montsalvat, Sigmund Jorgensen drew innuendo to the brink of fact: 'The murder was never solved and all public records of the inquest and the police files have disappeared, thus fomenting another rumour of a high-level cover-up protecting perhaps a member of the establishment.' Kinnane also divulged something else before we parted: he had for several years been writing a novel based on Mollie Dean's murder, filling the historical lacunae with his own speculations. First Johnston; now his biographer: drawn to the same personality and mystery. We wished each other luck in our endeavours.

The nature of my endeavour I could hardly at this point have explained. I pored over the relevant art history and biography. I acquainted myself with the newspaper coverage of Mollie Dean's death, the lurid inquest, the nugatory investigation. It looked inviting. Yet it was also a subject previously raked over by two experts to little avail. Here was an attractive woman of whom there was one unprepossessing photograph and an aspiring author none of whose writing was known to survive; perhaps Kinnane, and Johnston before him, were correct in believing that the story better suited fiction's artifices and licences. Mollie had recently rematerialised, in fact, in the pages of Kristel Thornell's *Night Street*, a 2011 novel based on the life of Clarice Beckett, tonalist extraordinaire. She was here not Jessica but 'Jean', a 'new girl' who is 'famished for art', and who in her 'snug red jumper' exudes 'an extreme prettiness, a childish yet flowered femininity', with 'an irrepressible smile that seemed exaggerated and charming to Clarice'. A month later, Clarice learns from *The Age* of Jean's murder in circumstances mirroring those of Mollie's:

> Jean had gone to the theatre with 'artist friends' (was the journalist implying that frequenting artists was itself a dangerous activity?')

to see Bernard Shaw's *Pygmalion*. She went missing that night. After the play, someone saw her running for the train, giggling, and that was her friends' final view of her. She had been killed – a random inexplicable attack, apparently, no meaning to hang from her death. Her spark extinguished like that.

As with *My Brother Jack*, however, the effect of the murder was measured on others, the events causing Clarice to reflect on the death of her brother Paul in an asylum: 'She saw that Jean's death and Paul's were connected. They were the same, because one death is really all deaths – *is* Death . . . After learning about Jean, her body face down, one leg in the gutter, her handbag missing and red jumper askew – no doubt the same jaunty red jumper she had worn that day under her painting smock – Clarice wanted the details of Paul's death. She required them.' She does not, however, obtain them; curious, I decided to.

The numbering of the relevant series was tricky. Four separate visits to Melbourne's Public Record Office were necessary. Clarice's brother was, it turned out, not 'Paul', but Thomas Alfred Joseph Beckett, sixteen years old when he was admitted to Kew Asylum on 21 February 1899 at precisely '12.50 p.m.' Not '1 p.m.'; not '12.40 p.m.'; but ten minutes to one, as noted by an anonymous clerk, having perhaps flicked his fob watch open in the act of creating what became VPRS 7565/P1/Unit 2. *Night Street*, of course, was fiction, 'an imagining'. Yet the clerk's cool admission notes were somehow the more compelling: 'Is almost helpless by himself. Cannot speak. The mind is completely blank. Used to be uncleanly in his habits but is now improved in that respect. Is a congenital idiot. Constant dribbling from the mouth.' The sequel to these admission papers was then to be found in the coronial inquest at VPRS 24/P0/Unit 712 into Thomas's death from tuberculosis ten months later, which found him 'emaciated' but bearing 'no marks of violence'.

Where fiction diverges from fact is where art might be said to begin; and how readily, being so much more palatable and emollient, it substitutes for actuality's inconvenient randomnesses and contradictions, its jagged edges and stubborn silences. Far fewer readers, for example, know the Protestant Reformation by any factual retelling than by Hilary Mantel's *Wolf Hall* and Robert Bolt's *A Man for All Seasons*, even if each offers a decidedly partial slant. Historical fiction has undergone a vibrant rebirth in our generation, with a prestigious award named for its forefather, the Walter Scott Prize: no objections are raised to temporal appropriation as there are to cultural appropriation. Yet on reading *Night Street* a stubborn part of me objected to treating all deaths as 'the same', and to yielding in a decorous imagining of a murder that merely left a jumper 'askew'.

A paradox of true crime, meanwhile, is that it gains moral force from our revulsion of violence against the innocent, even as it often treats the innocent as marginal, recruiting them, as it were, chiefly to die, sympathetically but expeditiously; they should be *just human enough* so as not to delay our pleasure in vicarious detection. In extremis, when killing is serial, victims line up as if for sacrifice, no sooner introduced than despatched. Mollie Dean made an ill fit with these conventions. No killer was identified. No conclusions were drawn. The questions here were less obvious, more awkward: why she met her assailant alone, walking home after midnight, on a weekday, in a quiet city, in a conservative era, where the lives of the vast majority of young women were directed towards matrimony and motherhood; why she did not, quite, engage a community's sympathies, despite vigorously arresting their attention. Perhaps similarities *did* exist between Thomas's private death and Mollie's public one, relating to their failure, voluntary and involuntary, to fit period decencies. But these could be teased out only by following in her path, however vestigial it proved.

So how to approach a woman dead nearly ninety years, beyond the reach not only of firsthand but also second-hand memory? Long before, Garry Kinnane told me, he had come no closer than telephoning Mollie's younger brother. Ralph Dean had dismissed him tersely, and died the year after the publication of *Colin Colahan: A Portrait*. A will named his children: although none remained at the stated addresses, a son could be discerned not far away in the White Pages and a daughter traced via LinkedIn. In tactfully inquisitive terms I wrote both. Hearing nothing, I followed up. Their responses echoed their father's. The son put the phone down. The daughter claimed to 'know nothing of Mollie', and wondered why I could not respect 'privacy' and 'leave history to tell its own story'?

Fair questions. I also value my privacy. No law obliges anyone to assist a journalist – I am sometimes astonished how many do. Members of our trade are apt to overstate the therapeutic qualities of 'talking about things' – it suits our own purposes. In the daughter's response I heard pre-emption. If she knew 'nothing' what was there to protect? Clearly not the privacy of someone who died in 1930; something else, perhaps – some other family sadness or shame or taboo on which a stranger might obliviously trespass. But while I might feel myself to be a trustworthy confidant, the judgement was hardly mine to make.

At the same time, one thing an imagined history does not relate is 'its own story', particularly where events, as in the case of Mollie Dean, feature more gaps than facts. In those gaps instead accumulate the sediment of rumour, hearsay, assertion and, at length in some compelling cases, fiction. So I retraced my steps to the Public Record Office, just to make sure, one last time, that earlier researchers had exhausted every avenue.

On the face of it, they were confirmed – the inquest index contained no entry. Yet I was also aware that the gleanings of murder-related inquests became by convention the bases for criminal trial briefs, even if trials themselves did not proceed. And there, disarmingly fresh for its senior years, awaiting anyone prepared. to search a big calf-bound index and order a numbered file, was VPRS 30/Po, Unit 2383, Item 187: sixty-six pages of statements from thirty-nine witnesses that detectives had gathered in the course of their inquiries – neatly typed, double-spaced, and annotated by multiple unknown hands. The voices of friends, family, passers-by and police themselves spoke again – and much of what I had previously understood about the story of Mollie Dean was revealed as wrong.

I

HUMBLE IS MY PEN

'Shirley has too much to say to be thinking of men.'
– Lillian M. Pyke, *Three Bachelor Girls* (1926)

On 11 June 1928, Mollie Dean's mother, Ethel, posted a letter to a friend of her daughter's, another young teacher, Sadie Fields. The subject, as it would be repeatedly, was what she regarded as Mollie's misbehaviour. It struck what was, for Ethel, a routine tone: querulous, scolding, self-pitying. But most striking was the postscript, nodding to the date: 'This is the 13th anniversary of Mollie's father's death. A very happy day truly.'

Much in the various statements, I was learning, read as coded, in deference to proprieties. There was mention of 'friendships', when what was implied were relationships. There was reference to 'closeness', when what was at issue was sex. Respondents were straining to preserve a semblance of decency from the surveillances of law and order. This postscript stood out for its candour and its gratuitousness. Its deep feeling defied suppression. What kind of wife happily honours the anniversary of a husband's death? What kind of husband causes a wife to do so? In what kind of household had Mollie Dean been raised?

She was born Mary Winifred Dean on 14 October 1905, although she only used that name in formal communication: she was usually 'Mollie', spelling it that way herself rather than 'Molly'. She was 28-year-old Ethel's first child to George Edwin Dean. They had been married two and a half years, making their matrimonial home in Prahran's Oban Street.

George, thirty-six, taught at the Prahran State School in High Street, though was shortly to be relocated to Hawksburn State School, and at the time of Mollie's first birthday was serving temporarily as a relieving head teacher at a school in rural Cobram – taste of a seniority he patiently craved. Youngest of nine from Bendigo, he had commenced his career in education as a straitlaced fifteen-year-old pupil-teacher at Golden Square in October 1884. 'Good sensible boy,' wrote his first inspector. 'But he wants life, and to look sharper after his class.' Yet he had a good mind, matriculating through Melbourne's teacher training college, and completing a master's degree in arts at Melbourne University with an impressive variety of subjects: not only imperial history, political economy and English language and literature, but mental philosophy, natural philosophy, deductive logic, inductive logic, stratigraphical geology, paleontology and Latin. Afterwards George's inspectors were more laudatory: 'an earnest smart young man'; 'is energetic; has a manly and efficient style of teaching'; 'a very good disciplinarian, diligent, active, energetic'. The word 'vigour' recurred in reports of his work.

George's skills extended to what would now be called networking: he was successively secretary of the Teachers' Club, secretary of the Civil Service Club, and inaugural organising secretary of the Victorian State Schools Amateur Athletic Association. The last was his brainchild and his glory. Its annual carnival at the Melbourne Cricket Ground quickly became a firm date in the education calendar; George travelled widely through Victoria and interstate in its furtherance. He is unlikely to have enjoyed a prouder moment than when, in September 1908, 3000 boys and girls participated in an exhibition of athletic and calisthenic prowess for representatives of the Great White Fleet during their nation-stopping visit, with the governor-general and the Victorian governor and premier in attendance. For the months of intricate choreography gone into the running, rounders, word forming, club throwing, dumbbell lifting, maypole and Caledonian dancing, Victoria's head of education Frank Tate credited only George Dean by name. Dean's work, said Tate, was 'in the public interest'.

His teaching responsibilities remained heavy, however. Hawksburn had Victoria's largest school headcount: 1500 students in cold and dirty buildings equipped for only 1000. George was one of two men on a staff of twenty-nine otherwise composed of unmarried women: although teaching was a heavily feminised occupation, not for a further fifty years could women continue working after marriage as a matter of course. He taught classes regularly in excess of sixty pupils, where learning was rote and punishment corporal. Another recurrent theme in his inspectors' reports suggests he sometimes took standard practices to a fault: while George showed 'much strength and force of character', he was also deemed 'brusque', 'on the strict side', 'inclined to be a little impetuous', even 'somewhat wanting in refinement of manner'.

These may have been traces of frustration. For all his ample qualifications and extracurricular zeal, George was marbled into a heavily hierarchical system, taking seventeen years to advance from a Class IV to a Class III teacher, in March 1910. By then he was at Brighton State School, and would shortly bring his family to a newly built home nearby, at 25 Marine Parade, reflecting the birth of son Ralph in January 1911 – Brighton is also probably where Mollie commenced her education, although attendance rolls are long since lost.

Mollie's father would not become a permanent head teacher until March 1914, when he was appointed to the role at Sandringham State School. This was a relatively small school, albeit another challenging one, old and unsewered, alleviating its overcrowding by using a church hall, a drill hall and outdoor marquees. George Dean tackled the task with his trademark 'vigour' – and that seems to have been where his troubles began.

Few teachers cannot have had a nuisance parent; in the Dean household the name Ellen Bach must have been uttered as a curse. This 39-year-old widow had known great misfortune. In October 1908, her husband had been killed by a falling tree while clearing bush in Wandin South, leaving her to raise four children on her own; three years later, her six-year-old daughter had died of diphtheria. Ellen had moved to Sandringham, probably to be nearer relatives. But a month after George Dean commenced as head of the local school, she posted him the first of many letters complaining of maltreatment of her sons Jack and Eustace, which escalated into a correspondence first with the Education Department then with the education minister – all, she would undoubtedly have been gratified to know, scrupulously preserved to the present day in school and department files at the Public Record Office, interspersed with a selection of George Dean's high-handed replies. A parent who had lost a child, and sons abruptly deprived of a father, might now be handled with a certain sympathy; George treated the boys as sullen and stupid, and their mother as in need of unsolicited advice about the efficacy of the strap.

> Madame,
>
> Yours to hand complaining of cruelty etc. I fail to see any cruelty in making children do what they are told even if one has to use the strap. The cruelty often lies on the parent who brings their children up with false notions of their position and unfit for the stern duties of life.
>
> You admit your boy is a bad-tempered, idle youth. That is sufficient to warrant punishment. I dare say if you give him a little more strap at home and teach him that he must respect his masters and do as he is told you will find that in 12 months he will be an entirely different youth. You talk about taking measures to put a stop to the strapping – you can take any measures you please – no necessity to notify me – only first be sure you have something real to complain about . . .
>
> Your advice about how to manage the school is not required as I have had 25 years of experience teaching boys in Melbourne so know a little about it. Suppose I talk to you in the same strain and tell you that if you would spend more time doing your work, and not looking around for every little fault on the part of the teacher, you would get along better – at any rate your children would. You talk of humanity so practice a little of it on the teacher.

'*Cruelty etc.*': Ellen Bach was not so easily deflected. By the end of 1914, she was consulting lawyers, gingering other parents, even writing to the premier, revealing some depth to her anxieties: 'My little girl's head was banged with force against another little girl and ever afterwards she suffered from an ear ache + shortly after she died + up to her death she always complained of her ear = when I visited her the last time she could speak to me in the hospital she complained of the same + now I am very much afraid.' So frequently was her five-year-old now being strapped by the infant mistress, she claimed, that his hand never healed: 'He is continually beaten until the whole story is getting on my nerves.'

At last, the department reluctantly asked the district inspector to convene a hearing – noisy, protracted and marred by an 'amount of irrelevant speech that could not be suppressed'. It was by now not only the strap at issue, but George's whole demeanour, as he grudgingly conceded under questioning: 'I admit calling Jack Bach a "pig". Very likely "blockhead" too. I may have called him a "lunatic", but not a "maniac".' The inspector was not enamoured of Ellen Bach: she clearly placed her boys 'on a pedestal', and they had not after all suffered a 'severe thrashing'. But he concluded that there were 'some just grounds for complaint'. Not only should the head teacher 'consider carefully whether he has shown a tendency to rely unduly upon the use of the strap', but his communication with Ellen had shown a 'want of tact and judgement', involving the use of 'expressions to pupils to which objection could properly be taken'. George was reprimanded – and infuriated.

At first, George purported to rage on behalf of his colleagues: 'I think it is simply heartbreaking for teachers to be unable to punish a child in any way without being assailed by threats of the department and to a nervous teacher these threats hang like the sword of Damocles constantly over his head.' But as Ellen Bach found further grounds for complaint in 1915, his pushback grew more personal. George had entered into the cause of the new war with his usual 'vigour'. Not only was he issuing badges of commendation to children who made the biggest contribution to the Patriotic Fund, but he barred non-contributors from swimming classes: if they could bring their pennies to swim, they could jolly well 'bring money for patriotism'. When the education minister upheld Ellen's complaint that this might 'cultivate national rivalry in helpless children', George was apoplectic: his least favourite parent, he now claimed, was 'a member of the Socialist Party', made a practice of 'unsupported and nonsensical charges', and should be aggressively prosecuted, even jailed:

I think in these times of danger any honest endeavour to assist the Empire and inculcate patriotism should be employed and there is nothing derogatory or humiliating in the methods I have employed. My idea of the matter is that Mrs Bach's letter should be sent to the military authorities and the woman's antecedents and actions looked into as she is evidently anti-British. I think there is a clause in the new act now before Parliament that anyone doing or saying anything calculated to raise dissatisfaction or stir strife may be imprisoned.

We are at war and my ideas of war are to fight for one's country and not to knuckle down to every paltry complaint hurled at us by unpatriotic people. You said to say nothing of the matter. Do you think Mrs Bach will say nothing of the matter? The very next meeting of her clique she will narrate with great glee how she bowled the headmaster out. She recently laid down some practically false charges against me and, as there was a scintilla of truth among them, for that I received a mild but undeserved reprimand. However I let the matter drop. But

Mrs Bach's friends knew I was to be reprimanded although I never told anyone . . . Unless I receive a written order from the department instructing me to discontinue I shall proceed as before.

In fact, George was now keeping the outgoing mails busy himself. Here he was, for example, still a Class III teacher after thirty years. What, he demanded, did he have to do to advance to Class II? The department advised that regulations required him to apply to a new school; on his reading of the law, George countered, promotion was automatic, and if a regulation overrode this then 'Parliament is not worth twopence'. Other pettinesses detained him: bureaucratic quibblings, local frictions. His irascibility might have had physical cause: George was suffering the onset of uraemia, a consequence of kidney failure, whose classic symptoms include mental fluctuation in addition to weakness, fatigue and loss of appetite. His health deteriorated rapidly. Three weeks after first consulting a doctor, George died – seemingly to Ethel's lingering relief.

Explanation for this relief, of course, is incomplete. Martinet teachers can be solicitous husbands and parents. But the glimpse of George Dean's pedagogical convictions suggest rather a prig at home – and perhaps, as a self-confident man travelling widely in an occupation full of young women, footloose away. George's well-attended funeral at Brighton Cemetery left Ethel a widow like Ellen Bach. The latter now fades from view, although she remained a local, and outlived her nemesis by fifty years. It was the Deans, including nine-year-old Mollie and four-year-old Ralph, who moved, and into diminished circumstances.

*

In November 1915, Ethel Dean bought a semidetached cottage in Milton Street in the growing seaside suburb of Elwood, probably spending the lump sum from George's life insurance. Existence henceforward would be precarious: an annuity provided £50 a year, but there would no longer be an Education Department pension to look forward to.

The Deans were followed to the locality by the Blyths, George's sister Emily and her husband, Daniel, a coach builder. Previously near neighbours in Marine Parade, they moved in round the corner at 2 Addison Street, with their teenage children, Norman and Jean. They had had their own sorrows, having cost an infant son, while Norman was plagued by tuberculosis. One of George's older brothers, Peter, died a month after him, from empyema of the gall bladder; another, William, was shortly to enlist. Abruptly, life seemed a good deal less secure.

Mollie had taken after her father in at least one direction: she was, by all accounts, precociously articulate, reading omnivorously and writing in a firm hand. And thanks to her father's old boss, Frank Tate, there existed new possibilities for her: under the *Education Act* of 1910, Victoria had opened almost fifty new secondary schools. The reform-minded Tate was resolved to extend teachers' remit beyond the three Rs, to satisfy 'not only the intellectual and moral interests of the child, but also his aesthetic and constructive interests' – or, indeed, hers. Even the look of Victorian classrooms was to change in the next little while, from long continuous rows to two-person fliptop desks, with new tools like Cuisenaire rods, and new classes such as 'free reading'. Not a few years earlier, Mollie would probably have been working, as a shopgirl or seamstress, by the age of fourteen. Instead, she gained entry to Carlton's University High.

University High was a remarkable school, perhaps especially for a child fathered by George Dean. Head teacher Matthew Sharman was a liberal educationalist who prided himself on knowing all

250 of his students by name. He shunned corporal punishment and deprecated examinations, fostering cultural activities instead, including theatre, debating, music and literature: a lively school magazine, *The Record*, ran essay and poetry competitions. He gathered around him a noteworthy staff. Art mistress Miss Bertha Merfield was a widely exhibited landscape artist, trained at the National Gallery School and London's Slade School. Her mural of 'dawn in the Australian bush' adorned the banquet hall of Walter Burley Griffin's Café Australia in Collins Street, popularly deemed 'the most beautiful café in the world'. English mistress Miss Isàbella Marshall had taken honours in history at Oxford at a time when the university would not confer degrees on women. So adored was she that children would flock from all over the yard for the privilege of pushing her motorcycle underway. For a generation of impressionable girls, then, University High offered glimpses of lives of calling.

Mollie was also exposed to influential peers. Her University High year included two other literary girls, also being raised by widows. Clara Behrend was the eighth of nine children in a sophisticated Jewish family who lived not far from the Deans. Her late father Albert had spoken fourteen languages, played violin to orchestral standard, and sung bass in the Melbourne Liedertafel with Nellie Melba. Her older brother Phillip, a gifted engineer, had unselfishly stood aside as Labor candidate for Balaclava in favour of a young John Curtin, and run sacrificially in Toorak instead – in the end, both had lost. Her mother, Minni, had been keen to educate Clara at prestigious Presbyterian Ladies' College; it was at the insistence of Phillip, who believed his sister had a lawyer's makings, that she successfully sat the University High scholarship examination.

Joyce Pyke had spent most of her first seven years on railway construction camps in the Queensland bush, where her father worked as a paymaster. In November 1914, Dick Pyke had levelled allegations of corrupt behaviour at an engineer. To his dismay, these had been dismissed. A few weeks later, Dick rose from the family breakfast table, walked into a back tent, and was heard to ask wife Lillian if she had packed his lunch, then after a pause to shoot himself in the head. 'Run and get help,' Lillian told Joyce. 'Daddy is ill.' Dick was dead by the time Joyce returned with the constable and storekeeper. 'He was a good husband and very fond of his children,' Lillian told the coroner loyally.

Relocating to Melbourne, Lillian Pyke commenced to support the family by her pen. In the next decade she churned out dozens of books: from nursery-rhyme collections to etiquette guides, three novels for adults, sixteen for young adults. One series was set in a boys' school, St Virgil's, explicitly modelled on Wesley College, where son Laurence was educated; another was set in a girls' school, Riverview, implicitly inspired by University High, where Joyce was enrolled, and Lillian was a popular parent, one year writing the school play. A good deal of the wholesome action at Riverview was centred on the school magazine, *The Exciter*, whose plucky editor Shirley declares in *Three Bachelor Girls* she has 'ink in her veins instead of blood' and a heart 'in tune with the throb of printing machines'. United by similar enthusiasm, Mollie and Joyce stand together in photographs of *The Record*'s editorial staff, fresh and trim in their navy-blue skirts, white blouses and dark ties – it may have been a wink to the Deans that Lillian Pyke's characters included namesakes in sensible Molly Lindsay and her dependable brother, Ralph.

Mollie Dean fully imbibed the University High motto, *Strenue ac fideliter* ('With zeal and loyalty'). She won the essay and poetry prizes in her age group in three consecutive years. She peppered *The Record* with fiction, poetry and other cameos. Much of it is cheery juvenilia

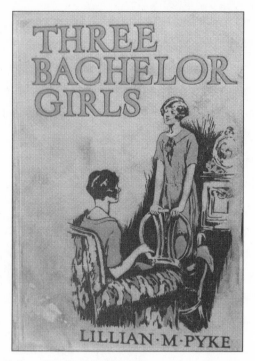

'Ink in her veins': Pyke's *Three Bachelor Girls*

rooted in the day-to-day of education. In the story 'A Dream', a sleeper is visited by apparitions of historic figures intersecting chaotically, Napoleon burning cakes, Brutus promising to save England, Friar Tuck singing 'La Marseillaise' and Queen Victoria quoting Cicero in Latin. In the verse 'Elegy (written on the Flight of the Form-Notes)', by contrast, the speaker's mind is mock-tragically blank:

> Oh, cruel Muse! Thou comest not
> Unto mine aid; this tangled knot
> Of would-be wondrous form-notes, I
> Cannot unravel; hear my cry!
> I bow to thee, Oh, Muse! And lay
> My spirit low; if on my way

Thou wouldst, with all thy train

But leave thine impress on my brain

And give to me an inspiration,

That I might write, although my station

Is low, and humble is my pen.

Oh! Muse of Form-Notes, come again!

What! art thou fled? Oh. Cruel Muse!

For ever more I'll abuse.

All hope is gone; and now despair

Hangs on my brow, and settles there!

Yet Mollie could also turn her hand to the more metrically formal and aesthetically lush. For a girl barely sixteen, in fact, 'The Spinning Wheel' is surprisingly accomplished:

In the pure and holy air of the mossed stone-cottage there,

Sits a figure, 'twixt the dawning and the dusk,

And her golden hair is shining, though the gentle soul is pining

'Mid the faint, sweet scents of lavender and musk.

For the silken lashes never on the quiet eye-lids quiver,

The drooping head is never upward raised,

Although everyone that passes through the lush, green, unmown

   grasses,

Is astonished at her beauty and amazed.

And she sits there, turning, turning, while her riven heart is

   yearning

For the love, the smiles, the sunshine, scarcely known,

And she sits there spinning, spinning, while her youthful days

   are thinning

And through the vine leaves over her the low winds softly moan.

For she does not see the flowers, and all the lonely hours
Are spent in darkness, terrible and blank:
In the hardness of her duty and the pathos of her beauty,
Oh, she has cursed the bitter cup that once she drank!
And the little children playing, when comes the month of
    maying,
Steal round, and whisper, point from behind,
At her black dress, old and worn, and the pale, still face forlorn,
'She cannot see the flowers, for she is blind.'
And the small, sad slippers press with accustomed weariness,
And so the wheel goes turning, turning on:
And the scents of unseen flowers fling defiance in fragrant
    showers
On the bruised heart that is yearning, yearning on.

Not all art is autobiographical, even at sixteen, but there is a sense
of identification here with a path that is solitary, and a heart that is
'yearning, yearning on'. In the company of friends also being raised
by widows, in classrooms taught by capable spinsters, Mollie Dean
caught glints of life possibilities beyond matrimony and motherhood,
and was also introduced to the sway of luck. Clara was to spend only
eighteen months at University High, after losing her beloved brother
Phillip to a stroke in October 1919, then being stricken with hepa-
titis – rather than the law, she trained in office skills, and joined the
mail-order department of a Prahran store as a correspondence typ-
ist. After she and Mollie completed their intermediate certificates
in June 1921, Joyce went on to a further year at PLC, where she was
dux. Yet the bonds of these three bachelor girls lasted: a decade
later, Clara and Joyce would swear statements for the inquest into
Mollie's murder.

2

MOULE DENE, M. DEAN, M.

'Clippings,' I said. 'I've written some poems, quite dreadful, but a paper might take them . . .'

– Dorothy Cottrell, *The Singing Gold* (1928)

In the early 1920s, Melbourne was Australia's capital, its population of nearly a million spreading into gaps left by its initial disorderly sprawl: much of Elwood, where the Deans lived, was reclaimed swamp, at first prised open by a canal. Austerities of depression and war were abating, with taller commercial buildings beginning to intersperse the city's familiar domes and spires. From the subdued tints of suburbia now and again emerged foreshadowings of a new youth and style. Stanley Melbourne Bruce, with his flamboyantly patriotic name and fashionable spats, was not forty when he became Australia's prime minister.

Optimism was reinforced by technological accomplishment. Cars were starting to outnumber horsedrawn vehicles, bulk electricity to replace gas; if films for the time being remained silent, the air hummed with transmissions of the new wireless radio; if the daily newspapers stayed starchy, they were being gingered along by a perky new tabloid, the *Sun News-Pictorial*. That new symbol of modernity, an aerodrome, had opened in Essendon; from the railway station nearby Bruce's imposing St Kilda birthplace, Melbourne's first suburban tram line stretched as far as Brighton Baths, stopping en route in Elwood.

In the day-to-day, Melbourne remained culturally homogenous, religiously observant, socially buttoned-down. Tastes were modish rather than modern. Six o'clock closing was securely entrenched. Suppression fell on illegal totalisators and industrial unrest alike. When Victoria's policemen went on strike over their entitlement to trade union membership, three-quarters were peremptorily sacked. When rioters took advantage of their temporary licence, the *Sun*'s headline brooked no argument: 'OUR UNLEASHED SCUM'.

No city could have seemed so securely British, even in Britain. The young were schooled in the Norman conquests, Runnymede and the Roses; the mature chorused 'God Save the King', saluted a British Red Ensign, and saw British sea power as the guarantor of national sovereignty: vast crowds lined the Elwood foreshore to see the visiting battle cruisers HMS *Hood* and HMS *Repulse* in March 1924. With her writerly yearnings, Mollie Dean could hardly have found a more auspicious address than near the corner of Milton and Addison streets, Elwood, all three names honouring poets. Streets within the surrounding triangle likewise celebrated Shakespeare, Marlowe, Dickens, Wordsworth, Tennyson, Dryden, Browning, Cowper, Spenser, Burns, Thackeray, Southey, Byron, Goldsmith, Scott, Shelley, Coleridge, Keats, Bronte, Rosetti and Meredith, with an Australian leavening from the names Daley, Gordon and Lawson. Arrivals from the United Kingdom felt quickly at home – and for the Dean family some were imminent.

The Grahams, widow Bella and three children in their twenties, arrived in Melbourne from Cowdenbeath, a coal town in Scotland's

West Fife, in April 1921. They were hosted first by Daniel and Emily Blyth, Ethel Dean's nearby in-laws. When the Blyths' daughter Jean married her fiancé Alex Stevens, however, the Grahams again had need for lodgings, and it was arranged that they should move in with the Deans in Milton Street. Ethel would have welcomed their incomes, for daughter Catherine was working as a seamstress, sons John and Adam as a hairdresser and a mechanic respectively.

Of this period, virtually nothing is known. But for Mollie, seven souls beneath the one semidetached roof can hardly have conduced to privacy at an age when its value is appreciated. Of the new arrivals, Adam was closest in age: five years her senior, a tall, taciturn figure who had never known his father, killed in a mining accident in December 1900. The two, however, built no rapport. For the next year, girl and boy seem to have circled one another awkwardly. Adam grew closer to Ethel, whom like his siblings he called 'Auntie', and remained a regular visitor when his family found their own small house in nearby Gordon Avenue. Rather than an interlude in Mollie's life, in fact, the Grahams would prove to be a factor.

For the moment, events seem to have sharpened Mollie's determination to lead something like the life she had glimpsed at University High. Friends would later say that Ethel disapproved of Mollie's choice to become a pupil-teacher, combining contin-ued study with classroom responsibilities at Brighton Road State School. But if she was not to marry it was a logical path, providing a small but instant income of about £100 a year, with the possibil-ity of progress. In fact, she took naturally to teaching. Over the next four years, she was praised by each of her four district inspectors: 'is intelligent and promising'; 'is a capable and promising teacher and organiser'; 'is intelligent and bright and capable of doing very good work'; 'is making good progress as a teacher and displays a

very good amount of ability as a student'. Perhaps with her father's
example in mind, she insured her life, taking out a £200 policy with
City Mutual in December 1922. She duly completed her education
also, obtaining her first-class Leaving Certificate with honours in
English and French in April 1924. Most importantly of all, work did
not preclude her writing.

George Steiner has argued that access to literature began women's
'inner emancipation', offering 'an access they could not have socially
or politically, or of course economically'. It proved so with Mollie
Dean. According to later chroniclers, her early tastes were suitably progressive: the romance of Keats, the naturalism of Moore, the
realism of Ibsen, the social criticism of Shaw, the swooning lyricism
of Swinburne. Of what she wrote in response, however, no trace was
known to remain. A writer in *Smith's Weekly* reported her as having
'had some stories published'. But where, I wondered, were they to
be found?

Even in days when a mere scuffling of keystrokes qualifies as
'research', there remains no substitute for simply turning pages over
for long days at a time. No survey of this kind can be comprehensive.
Indeed, I arbitrarily narrowed the search to half-a-dozen 1920s
periodicals publishing short fiction and serialisations: *The Bulletin,
Stead's Review, Australian Journal, The Triad, New Triad* and *Romance*.
There was the further consideration that, according to that *Smith's
Weekly* scribe, Mollie regarded her works as only 'amusing experiments
and used to laugh at them and at herself'. But the biographical incentive
was that what we put behind us can sometimes point at where we are
headed. It was a lengthy search that produced only three possibilities –
and in the end possibilities is all I could call them, nothing so helpful

as the modern 'author bio' existing in the 1920s. For all that, they were striking.

The healthy girth of the September 1924 edition of *Australian Journal* heralded the literary debut of 'Moule Dene' – pen names were standard at this popular-fiction monthly, Lillian Pyke contributing regularly as 'Erica Maxwell'. 'The Eternal Sameness', published when Mollie would have been eighteen, conforms to accepted formulae of 1920s romance, contrasting male stoicism with female sensitivity, admitting the possibility of feminine restlessness while upholding the marriage bond. Former city typiste Ena Waynor is married to hardworking farmer Frank, but sick at heart from numerous mundane maternal duties, mirrored in the Mallee's monotony: 'The very sameness of the scene beyond the open window served to irritate Ena afresh. The same paddocks sloping away to the horizon – the same scanty fringe of trees bordering the creek to the west of the homestead – the same shabby old barn, the same sheds, the same everything.' Frank is similarly weary, but determined to press on – in order, he says, that he might return his wife to the city that she so clearly hankers after. 'We'll live in a fashionable suburban villa, with neat squares of lawn in front, situated close to the tram track and within sound of the rush and toot of the electric trains,' he promises. 'Now, what do you think of my sweet daydreams?'

As Frank adjourns to fell 'the gaunt old gum tree in the entrance paddock', Ena watches him recede 'with tears of gratitude in her eyes', and slips into a soothing reverie. At length she is disturbed by worried farmhands. 'We're afraid there's been rather a bad accident, Mrs Waynor,' they admit reluctantly. 'The tree fell the wrong way.' When they return with Frank's maimed body, the scene assumes a pained stillness: 'The distant lowing of cattle, the cluck, cluck of a mother hen calling to her little brood, the faint whinnying of a horse, the screech of a parakeet. Vaguely she wondered how such usual sounds could continue when the master of the farm lay shattered and suffering.'

With seemingly his dying breath, Frank tells his wife to wait no longer: 'Go to – the city – til the boys – old enough – to manage here. Don't grieve – dear.' Ena, feeling complicit in the accident, prays for deliverance: 'Spare him! Oh, spare him! And I shall care not whether I live forever in this monotonous sameness or in the long-wished-for rush and bustle of the city.' And it is, like Mollie's earlier story in *The Record*, a dream: Ena, fallen asleep over her sewing, is awoken by her husband's return from the paddock. 'Oh, thank God!' she exclaims, gratefully willing away her 'vision of green lawn, a modern suburban villa, and streets and streets of gloriously arrayed shops and business houses'.

A prentice work, 'The Eternal Sameness' is nonetheless painstakingly done – coincidentally or not, the imagined misadventure is the same as befell Ellen Bach's husband. And if the concluding tone is of relief and redemption, there is an unillusioned admission of Ena's struggle to reconcile with 'this horrid, grim, eternal sameness'. Ena loves Frank – *Australian Journal* would hardly have welcomed a story suggesting otherwise. But she is also allowed affection for her days as 'a happy, irresponsible young woman' in 'the busy life of the office' before she had been 'bound hand and foot to the homestead, and the captivity palled'.

I continued turning pages in *Australian Journal*, but the rest of the decade threw up no more that was honestly suggestive, a task complicated by the screen of pseudonyms, from 'Snowberry' and 'Chilternite' to 'David Powerful' and 'J. K. Waterjugs'. Perhaps Mollie had work among the scores of stories rejected each month in the *Journal*'s 'Declined with Thanks' columns, the titles now all that remain of their authors' fond hopes: 'A Humpty Bang Romance', 'Romance of Lonesome Shack', 'Constable Reilly, Troubadour', 'The Mysterious Malady of Margaret Ingham', et al. In June 1925, 'M. D.' was advised that a contribution was 'meritorious, but not required'. Was the comment addressed to 'Moule Dene'?

That same month, there appeared in *The Triad* a shorter, sharper offering by 'M. Dean'. 'Three Years' came with a strong editorial recommendation: 'If ever a story fitted the description "true to life", then here it is. Not a word is wasted, yet the writer has created a pathetic picture full of significant details.' The 500 words read at first like a fairytale: a little girl skipping past a clear pool in a cooling glade encounters a 'hideous wreck of a man', seemingly a forest-dwelling gargoyle. In her innocence, she discerns his inner soulfulness. They become playmates: 'He knew stories without end, and every day used to bring pockets filled with strange objects – coloured matches, miniature houses and tents, and every tale was played out on the soft earth. He worked in the evenings indefatigably, constructing pygmy cities and villages, and he sent to town for a supply of celluloid animals.'

It was hard here not to hear an echo of Mollie's poem 'The Spinning Wheel', with its lonely blind heroine whose 'riven heart is yearning/For the love'. Offered the chance, the man proves capable of a 'beautiful dream of friendship'. With a 'peculiarly trusting blue glance', the girl reciprocates: 'When I grow up we'll always be pals.' Announcing one day that school now awaits, she pledges to meet him in their usual rendezvous three years hence. But by their reunion, experience has changed her:

> Obviously she had not expected to see him there, and quite as obviously she had no recollection of him at the moment. But the man saw in her eyes that which made him wince – a frightfully

visible, swiftly repressed look of repulsion, and, quickly, following that, a faint hint of recognition. But of the pleading in the
man's eyes she took no notice, merely averted her glance and
walked on.

The man's gaze falls on the pool, and the readers' on his reflection:
'There he saw only too adequate reasons for her aversion – a distorted
mass, with the grafted skin only too apparent, and the staring artificial
eye. Why had he not died? Had fate preserved him, a relic of the war,
for this?' The story ends with his motionless figure merging into the
falling shadows.

Shadowy fates awaited the overwhelming majority of World
War I's injured, disfigured and traumatised. The medical science so
successful in containing the death rate made this a proportionally
huge number: 150,000 Australians returned as casualties of their service, compared to the 60,000 killed. But after only ten Anzac Days,
there remained the acutest reluctance to acknowledge war's ongoing
human toll, as distinct from the idealised 'fallen', while the first wave of
'anti-war' fiction would be another five years reaching Australia. 'Three
Years' is not self-consciously in this vein. Like the 'pygmy cities and villages', it scales reality down to the level of a child's comprehension, and
so reduces the warrior that he is merely a 'man', vulnerable at last to a
girl's disdain. Yet it is a strikingly sensitive, even daring story. Perhaps
Mollie Dean saw the stricken at the consecration of St Kilda's new war
memorial on Anzac Day 1925; perhaps she wondered what her loyally
jingoist father would have made of the spectacle.

'M. Dean' returned to *The Triad* on 1 April 1926 with another brief
but distinctive tale. 'Aboriginal Nights' was no less ambitious than an
Indigenous romance, in which Lurna and Kadu, totem-crossed teenage lovers of the Arunta, elope in spite of the superstitious taboo on

their relations. The story opens with Lurna awaiting Kadu, growing 'colder and colder with fear':

> She was not afraid of her kinsmen. They might kill her if they caught her, Lurna, running away with an enemy; or they might drag her back and marry her to one of the young men – or, worse still, to one of the old men of the tribe. Then, perhaps, the kangaroo spirit would pass into her body, since she herself belonged to the kangaroo totem, and she would bear children. But it was not all this which made her afraid. No; the cold terror came when she remembered the love that had lured her from her tribe and safety, and in the sinking dread that her love had not been strong enough, and the Arunta had done as they threatened, and killed . . .
>
> Far away, a dingo howled . . .
>
> She longed, with an animal's dumb longing, for the touch of the youth she loved: her thin body – she had not eaten for two days – quivered with her passion as though a whip had struck it. The sweet dark mouth trembled, and now and then great tears fell from the soft black eyes, splashing on her bare breast and limbs.

If the 'sweet dark mouth', 'animal's dumb longing', passionate quivering and dingo howling now read as kitsch, 'M. Dean' does seem to have made an effort to familiarise with a culture known to Melbourne mainly by the Arrernte ceremonial robes and slabs in the museum's display cases. A likely source was *Across Australia*, the popular ethnography of the interior by Baldwin Spencer and Francis Gillen, which documented restrictions on relations between the tribe's various 'moieties': 'If a Panunga man, say, wants to marry a Bulthara woman

he knows perfectly well that it means certain death to both of them.'
It recorded only one successful defection: 'A Panunga man eloped
with a Kumara woman where his proper wife was Purula: parties were
sent out to kill them, but by his strength and watchfulness the man
managed to outwit his enemies.' Lurna and Kadu are less lucky. They
journey three days and nights, until Kadu persuades Lurna that they
are beyond the reach of the kangaroo totem, and can make their love
nest in a bark hut:

> 'Kadu,' said Lurna, sighing softly, 'the fear is gone.'
> The boy laughed joyously as he clasped her close.
> The Arunta trackers work silently, and Kadu and Lurna were
> still smiling when the spears slew them in the little hours.

Though barely 800 words, 'Aboriginal Nights' is another unusual story.
Where they thought of it at all, Australians tended to see Indigenous
love and sex through their fearful fascination with miscegenation. It
would be interracial rather than intraracial relations that Katharine
Susannah Prichard explored in *Coonardoo* and Vance Palmer in *The
Man Hamilton* and *Men Are Human* later in the decade. Slight and
naive as it is, 'Aboriginal Nights' has the youthful boldness that might
spring from a twenty-year-old breast.

There is no proving or disproving that Mollie Dean lay behind
'Moule Dene' or 'M. Dean'. Nobody else laying claim to 'The Eternal
Sameness', 'Three Years' or 'Aboriginal Nights', they are the literary
equivalent of lost property or unclaimed laundry. Yet I could not escape
a feeling that the stories rather suited Mollie. They were unafraid to
push into unexplored subjects; they made breaking away appear both
desirable and dangerous; they presented love as a survivable ordeal,
as a fragile hope and as a blissful doom; and like the transports of a

blossoming imagination, they blended familiar emotions into lives far beyond her experience.

Too brief to leave deep traces, Mollie Dean's life drew one unavoidably into such realms of conjecture. For most bureaucratic filters, she was too fine a particle, eluding even the Public Record Office's assiduously maintained files of Brighton Road State School, at VPRS 795/Po/2238 and VPRS 796/Po/262. Was she to the forefront when the inspectorate surveyed the school, documenting classes by unnamed teachers in spelling, mathematics, geography and needlework, instruction in the uses of a compass and of a State Savings Bank passbook? It could be said only that she formed part of a staff 'regular and punctual in attendance' setting 'a praiseworthy example to the children'.

There existed one other school relic, rather less official. The years of teenage teacher Mollie overlapped almost exactly with the years of boy pupil Sidney Nolan, enrolled from January 1922, just short of his fifth birthday. 'We were well taught,' he recalled, 'and when released, ran wild at playtime, the boys trying to be masculine with feats of glory like hanging from the football scoreboard.' Those playtime sensations, he said, even imprinted themselves on his work: 'The playground was a mass of dispersed activity and that's how I still activate my paintings.' One painting in particular commemorated his alma mater: *Brighton Road State School*. And in the asphalted foreground, surrounded by larking children, is a head-and-shoulders sculptural bust of a young woman to whom Nolan referred as 'my teacher' without ever identifying her by name – nor, it being one of the artist's less celebrated works, has anyone troubled to do so since.

Nolan painted *Brighton Road State School* in December 1944. For some months he had sequestered himself in a Parkville loft after deserting his post as a military sentry in the Wimmera, at weekends repairing to 'Merthon', the Baillieu family mansion of his charismatic lover Sunday Reed, and reacquainting with boyhood haunts in St Kilda, which feature in paintings like *Diver, Bathers, Under the Pier* and *Giggle-Palace. Brighton Road State School* also reprises earlier motifs: the 'curious shadows', Nolan explained, 'came out of the Wimmera where I made them often more solid than trees'; two children hold hands like the lovers in *The Sole Arabian Tree*, which adorned the cover of the fabled Ern Malley edition of *Angry Penguins* in May 1944. The bust invites comparison with *Head of a Soldier* and *Head (Max Harris)*, also painted round the same time, but perhaps above all with *Ballarat Cemetery*, where the graveyard is festooned with pale memorial statuary. Did the bust in *Brighton Road State School* have a similar funerary association? Nolan would have been an impressionable thirteen years old when Mollie Dean died, just two years out of the school where she had taught. Might this have been his tribute?

I invited the art historians Nancy Underhill, Kendrah Morgan and David Rainey to dismiss this speculation: best to be disabused of one's fancies before they get out of hand. But as they noted, nothing ruled it out. Rainey reflected further that the road to 'Merthon' passed Brighton Cemetery, where the plots of both the Baillieus and the Deans are located. Sunday Reed was devoted to the memory of a brother who had died of pneumonia in 1926. Joining his lover's pilgrimages to the grave of 25-year-old Kingsbury Baillieu, Nolan might well have encountered the grave of 25-year-old Mollie Dean. Additional layers of association lay in the decades of friendship between Nolan and George Johnston, both sons of tram drivers, students of Brighton Technical and the National Gallery schools, and mutually supportive escapees from Australian philistinism, Johnston the inspiration for

Nolan's Gallipoli series, Nolan the chosen cover artist for *My Brother Jack*. In the end, perhaps, all it exemplified were the tight swirlings of a city that had more socially in common with a town. But these were real too – for some, stiflingly so.

In January 1926, probation complete, Mollie Dean started a year's studies in primary teaching – following fully, as it were, in the family trade. Melbourne Teachers' College in Parkville's Grattan Street presented quaintly – a building with Queen Anne facade and Gothic flourishes, heated only by open fires, lit in many corners by candles, and recycling newsprint for toilet paper. Professor John Smyth, the donnish Presbyterian who had been the college's principal for a quarter of a century, gave a daily inspirational address on the dot of 8.35 a.m. at which attendance was compulsory and morality strict. Yet in common with Mollie's old headmaster at University High, Smyth's philosophy was holistic. 'Play, to children, is life,' he maintained. 'It is, like food, one of the necessities.' Students felt part of a vanguard movement, personified by Smyth's new offsider George Browne, a decorated 35-year-old ex-serviceman who had studied education at Oxford and the University of London on a military Rhodes Scholarship. Browne had recently returned from travels in the USA fired with enthusiasm for a new kind of project-based teaching, the Dalton Plan, and was editing the first national pedagogical survey, *Education in Australia*. A student cartoon of staff in the college magazine, *The Trainee*, accented his patrician profile and cerebral air.

Women like Mollie remained the backbone of the teaching services, outnumbering men almost two to one. College offered a foretaste of a system skewed against them. Women's studentships were smaller, their activities restricted, their etiquette policed. Dormitories

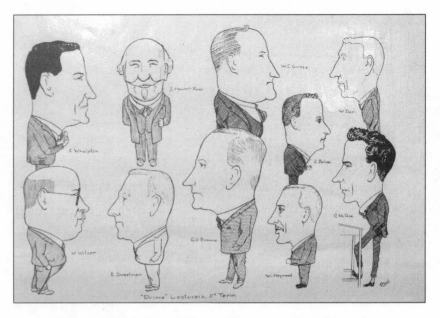

'True epitome of man': George Browne and teaching peers

and lecture rooms were segregated; young ladies could not leave the college without gloves and hat, and their hair chastely up. They could expect in due course poorer prospects and smaller salaries, calibrated as they were for a male breadwinner and an unmarried woman living at home. Even their main textbook, James Elijah's *The Principles and Technique of Teaching in Elementary Schools*, referred to the teacher only as 'he'. Yet Mollie unmistakably flourished. Her reports are a succession of golden opinions: 'Academic results strong and teaching very promising. Original and of very strong personality, should do very well'; 'Academic work very good – teaching ability outstanding. Marked proficiency in athletics and social activities. Excels in literary work. An exceptional student.' At the end of her studies, she was judged the college's outstanding primary teaching student, accepting the Gladman Prize, named by Frank Tate for his own esteemed mentor.

MOULE DENE, M. DEAN, M.

Mollie benefited, above all, from Browne's paternal interest. Browne had known George Dean before the war – his career in education had begun as a hall monitor at Hawksburn State School. It is tempting to ascribe to Mollie an ode to Browne in *The Trainee* by 'A Primary Student' with its cheeky antistrophes, rhyming 'Thou true epitome of man!' with 'He'll drop me to C minus, that's his plan'. Mollie was certainly one of four first-year representatives on the magazine's editorial staff, and probably the prolific contributor 'M.' who chronicled student life in such causeries as 'On Poverty', 'On Study' and 'On Swotting for Examination':

> I have decided that the motto in all preparation is, 'Never put off till tomorrow what you can do to-day – after midnight'. The place of preparation is a rudely furnished room in the remotest part of a building, preferably one provided with electric light. The furnishing consists of a bare floor, a table, a chair, piles and piles of books of every species, some well-used, some as yet unused, a fountain pen – full, and an eyeshade. The hosts are characterized by dark rings under the eyes, a listless manner or a short temper, and a set do-or-die expression about the face. They are able to snatch several fitful hours of rest, but may frequently be heard to start up in their sleep muttering, 'Was Hamlet really mad?' or 'Is Henry IV a dramatic unity?' or 'What is the derivative of arsin?'

Like Mollie at University High, 'M.' inclined to whimsy and pathos. A poem, 'The Ballad of Avon', enumerated the grisly ends of the bard's tragic heroes: 'When Shakespeare's plays are at an end/ How many are alive?/But few? Well, then, I've this to say:/With him men do not thrive.' An essay about second-hand bookstores was charmingly wistful: 'It is infinitely more sad than a cemetery, which harbours but man's mortal remains; men's very souls lie buried here, buried in those old, musty volumes with pasteboard covers, which are tied up in bundles of about eight, and marked "1/- the bundle". Just think of it!'

The college had a well-developed social calendar, of clubs and concerts, of mountain hikes and country picnics, of Palais (dancing) and Yaffles (pie nights). Mollie made other friends: Sadie Fields, a nineteen-year-old born in Scotland; Edna Johnson, a twenty-year-old with parents from Wales; Mollie's old schoolmate Joyce Pyke enrolled in the college the following year, although her studies were interrupted by her mother's death in August 1927, and her studentship cancelled due to 'ill health'. By then, Mollie had returned to the system, having, like Edna Johnson, joined the staff at a primary school in Faraday Street, Carlton. But she was already not one readily contained by systems.

3

A KINK IN HIS BRAIN

'Pausing in her ministrations to her own loveliness, Mary gazed
for a reflective moment at a framed photograph which stood on
her dressing table. It was of a young man, well-bred, pleasant to
look upon, totally uninteresting.'
— Molly Keane, *Taking Chances* (1929)

Sometime in the mid-1930s, *The Bulletin* journalist Mervyn Skipper
sat down to commence a long-contemplated *roman-fleuve*. *A Press-*
man's Soul would be narrated by his alter ego David Ferling, writer of
one mildly successful book of verse and one failed play, now a semi-
distinguished journalist at a well-known magazine ensconced in an
old office where the smell of printers' ink 'hangs like mist in a gully'.
Ferling's first encounter in his day's work is to be from 'a young woman
whom I already know quite well':

> A year or so ago she brought me an article on physical culture
> in which she declared, with ardour and sincerity, that the trou-
> ble with the country was that its youth were growing up without
> a knowledge of the Greek ideal of *mens sana* and that with-
> out such knowledge the nation would degenerate and lay itself

open to conquest by some foreign power. I knew whose lines
these were. They were the stock in trade of the principal of a
well-known school of physical culture, a man of gigantic size,
of perfect physique but with a double chin and the face of a
spoilt child.

And later she came to me with an article which said that the
nation's degeneracy was due, not to neglect of its body but to the
neglect of its ear; she put her case with charm and facility but
in a certain vagueness of diction, a timidity and lack of logical-
ity where I recognised the hand of our most eminent musician,
a man of great vivacity and sensitiveness, but lacking, in my
opinion, steadfastness of character.

This time she has brought a fresh bundle of manuscript.
She draws her chair up to mine so that our knees nearly touch.
I am conscious of a pretty, oval face, of a firm figure, of the dis-
turbing fragrance that emanates from her clothes. Laying the
article before me she looks at me with challenging eyes and says:
'I think you will like this.'

The character, never named, is palpably modelled on Mollie Dean.
A Pressman's Soul would be populated with thinly veiled renderings of
real people, some named, like Penderton (inspired by Colin Colahan),
Erikkson (Justus Jorgensen) and Lupin (Percy Leason), others not,
such as Clarice Beckett and Skipper's wife Lena, who were nonetheless vividly wrought. It's possible that the foregoing is the way Mollie
first encountered Skipper, bouncing up to his office at *The Bulletin*
to pitch her wares. The playwright Betty Davies introduced herself
similarly, seeing the magazine's nameplate by a doorway and decid-
ing on the spur of the moment to ascend to the first floor and thank
Skipper personally for a laudatory review, finding him 'a slender, rather

rumpled figure seated at a table on which sat an ancient typewriter, a clutter of press cuttings, papers, books and an overflowing ash tray'. Whatever the case, Skipper conveys a strong sense of Mollie's aura of youthful physicality – near-touching knees, near-shocking scent, near-scandalous reputation and all.

Ferling is impressed with the article, noting that 'since I saw her last she has developed an amazingly logical mind, her language is crisp and epigrammatical and she uses words that are unfamiliar even to me'. The reservations he expresses are that she could be better off transacting in her own ideas rather than those of others. Disagreement flares quietly between them: she is 'angry'; he is irritated by her bumptiousness:

> I feel a tremendous urge to tell this young woman what I think
> of the modern generation which imagines it has attained free-
> dom and independence simply because it no longer respects the
> sanctity of the marriage bond, to ask her what this freedom and
> independence actually amount to, as concerns herself, since it is
> obvious that she has been the mistress of her physical instruc-
> tor, and then of her musician, and now is, apparently, the mistress
> of some artist of whom I have not yet heard. Without, however,
> acquiring a soul that she can call her own.

In the end Ferling backs off: 'Instead I tell her that I will read her article at my leisure and ask her to call again and she goes out with a self-confident smile on her face leaving behind some of the faint fragrance which entered when she came.' What to make of what else lingers from the exchange – Skipper's seeming bequeathing to posterity of Mollie's liaisons?

*

Mervyn Skipper was a better journalist than he knew: no less than Keith Murdoch once called him 'Australia's best'. He had come to the craft via the roundabout route of Morse code, with which he dealt for twenty years as an officer of the Eastern Extension Company in New Zealand, Borneo, the Malay States and China – it was in the last that he married Lena, at the altar of Shanghai's Cathedral of the Holy Trinity before a Yangtze honeymoon. To *The Bulletin*, which he joined aged forty in 1926, he brought a crackling telegraphic prose, a cosmopolitanism reflected in his mastery of Malay, Dutch and Mandarin, and a constitution left morbidly sensitive by his eastern sojournings.

The Bulletin itself was drifting into a staid middle age, rivalled now by the cheeky *Smith's Weekly* and the discursive *Stead's Review*, but still suited Skipper's broad-gauge mind: he could write incisively of imperialism in Asia, coolly appraise fiction in China, knowledgably interrogate Bronislaw Malinowski's ethnographies, wipe the floor with Marie Corelli's memoirs. He covered the Melbourne stage caustically – 'a miasma of melancholy'; 'a doddering nuisance'; 'all the dramatic fury and intensity of a 40-acre paddock' – and every so often would even pastiche Lorelei Lee as 'The Melbourne Office Flapper':

> I mean, it shows how a girl can grow up and know nothing at all about the country. I had no idea before I saw *The Newlyweds* that the population of an Australian township consisted of one (1) hero, one (1) heroine, one (1) villain, one (1) dear old mother, and four (4) low comedians with names like Anastasia Culpepper suffering from mental deficiency. So I asked the girl who went with me if the villains, the sane people and the lunatics were always in that proportion and she said yes, she had seen several Australian players and she had never seen the ratio any different.

In his U-shaped family home on Outlook Drive, Eaglemont, designed by Walter Burley Griffin, Skipper was more the *homme sérieux*, always either denouncing something he had just read or toiling over the well-regarded juvenile fiction to which he also turned his hand. Between times he lay rigid in the dark with his numerous aches and maladies, during which his children would take pains, such as fitting a sock to the doorknocker, not to disturb him. Lena ministered pityingly throughout – rather too pityingly for some. To Betty Davies, Lena 'seemed to revel' in her husband's disabilities, 'finding her reward in his dependence and devotion'.

Around Mollie, Skipper was more than a little fascinated. Davies wondered if she slept with him – as, indeed, Betty later would. And Skipper's interest in her history was reflected in *A Pressman's Soul*, which closely followed the contours of Skipper's thinking if not always his life. While we'll revert to the aforementioned 'musician' and 'artist', the 'physical instructor' of 'gigantic size' to which Skipper referred would in the 1920s have been unmistakable.

Clarence Weber was Australia's foremost disciple of the body-building creed called the Sandow method – his legendary contemporary Georg Hackenschmidt called Weber 'the best figure of a man I have seen'. Hailing from Brighton, he was a formidable wrestler before and after World War I, but above all an entertainer and educator. In 1904, aged twenty-two, Weber gathered a company of vocalists, musicians and magicians to support him on a touring show in which he gave displays of physical prowess – one-handed jerks, tearing decks of playing cards into four, and party pieces like 'The Span of Life', where he formed a bridge across two chairs with an anvil on his chest on which a blacksmith then broke a piece of cold iron. He later pioneered *poses plastiques* inspired by classical statuary like Myron's *Discobolus* and Leighton's Laocoön; when he modelled for painter Nelson Wood, *The Boomerang Thrower* drew exhibition crowds in the tens of thousands.

Thousands also attended the annual shows of Weber's physical culture college, quickly expanded to include women. An erudite correspondent of *The Bulletin* in March 1915 reported how 'six wrestling amazons' struck a male audience dumb by how they dealt with 'the Insulting Hound':

> It appears that the way to handle a man who puts his arm around your waist is to administer a brisk push to his face. He either has to abandon the Marcus Superbus business or have his neck broken. The girls demonstrated the way to do it. Guffaws rose from the stilled youths. Clarence invited any one of them to step up and be experimented on; and then, lo and behold, there was a dead silence. Another dainty trick is to throw the licentious one with a shin kick, and then grip him round the neck with your leg. The pose is hardly ladylike, but the shock of the proceeding is said to be enough to turn a Heliogabalus into an Anthony.

In fact, women found Weber magnetic. He was often accompanied by a retinue of female show pupils, enjoying their 'hum of admiration', and maybe more. Wife Louisa bore him six children in nine years, then died delivering a seventh in May 1918. Within nine months he had married one of his students, Ivy Mitchell, widow of a lieutenant killed at Bullecourt, who quickly bore three further children. And here, effectively, Weber's problems began, for the families did not blend, and the crowd round the dinner table of his Mont Albert villa was swelled by in-laws to sixteen – all more or less financially dependent.

By the mid-1920s, Weber's hair had thinned and silvered, but he remained on a treadmill of fighting, writing, teaching and talking. He even vaunted his masculinity by promoting the wrestling silent *The Beloved Brute*: 'Women love strength more than anything in a man. Deep in their heart lurks the joy that possessed the prehistoric woman when carried off by her brawny captor.' But the unpublished memoirs of his daughter Lois relate considerable domestic tension, especially antagonism between high-strung Ivy and the children of Louisa. Weber felt helpless when his three older daughters could stand it no longer. 'He cried, which upset us a great deal, but we still insisted on leaving,' Lois recalled. 'Dad admitted that Ivy would only transfer her animosity to the boys. We agreed she would, but still kept insisting that we would leave.' Lois's daughter Gillian Breth remembers family talk of her unhappy grandfather having 'several' affairs.

Whether one of these was a seaside tryst with Mollie Dean, her having perhaps been a show pupil, is unprovable. With Weber's grandson Graeme, a keen genealogist of his far-flung family, I spent some hours poring over group photographs of Weber's light-footed, white-clad girl students striking stances of beauty and strength. Graeme was sure he saw her; I could not honestly say; what it proved was moot in any case. What *A Pressman's Soul* testified to instead, perhaps, was how readily Mollie inspired rumour and innuendo, and how she may even have enjoyed it. 'When she said goodbye to a man, she preferred the shadow of a tree to the light from the street lamp,' Lena Skipper wrote decoratively. And the mystery of her death would render more mysterious her life.

Carlton State School in Faraday Street, whose staff Mollie joined in January 1927, was a regular posting for newly minted graduates, and experimenting at that stage with aspects of the Dalton Plan that Browne so favoured. Again, Miss Dean was consistently lauded: 'sincere and alert'; 'pleasant address and proper outlook'; 'has a pleasing manner with pupils'; 'exerts a pleasing influence'; 'well-tested methods of instruction'. Whether it involved Clarence Weber or not, Mollie's social world was also expanded. At Teachers' College, no young man could invite a young woman out without the principal's permission; a young woman would, of course, never have asked out a young man. With a job and an income, Mollie enjoyed greater freedom. Although not at home.

Ethel Mary Dean was now a fifty-year-old widow. Of her only one identifiable newspaper photograph survives, face shaded by an unfashionable hat tugged low, mouth a mirthless slit; one pictures her battleship figure pushing through crowds, scolding unruly boys, tut-tutting noisy girls. Though increasingly a martyr to rheumatism, she was determined to wield absolute power in her household – and in this had an unlikely confidant, Adam Graham, now in his mid-twenties. Graham would visit Milton Street virtually every evening after dinner with his family, for 'a cup of tea' with 'Auntie Ethel'. Whether it involved more, as police would allege, is muddied by accusations and denials. Bella Graham, Adam's mother, let slip one glancing detail: that for the years after leaving their former host-cum-landlady, all the Grahams had paid regular visits on the Deans; that except by Adam those visits ceased after 1928 due to 'a small family difference'. It might have been over a pound of sugar; it might have been over the tightness of Adam and Ethel. Whatever the case, theirs was a relationship with peculiar undercurrents, as a young man, Teddy Sell, was to discover.

Fresh-faced twenty-year-old Sell was a clergyman's son born in the Indian town of Coonoor and pursuing law at Ormond College.

Warned off: young Teddy Sell

He met Mollie in the second half of 1927, and 'occasionally took her out' until the middle of the following year. As he would later tell police, it was a courting plagued from the first by worsening tensions in the Dean household. Mollie described her mother to Sell as vindictive and violent, determined that Mollie and Adam Graham should marry, and so opposed to her socialising with any other man that the pair were in the habit of stalking her. Sell found it disturbing. One night when they met at St Kilda's Victory Theatre, Mollie informed Sell that she had seen Graham's car in a nearby laneway. When Sell was en route home afterwards, a car drove alongside his tram for a distance while a driver he took to be Graham stared at him before peeling away. Another evening Sell was on the tram to the university and met Mollie, who told him that her mother and Graham were in pursuit.

As they alighted at Tin Alley, a narrow university entrance near the end of their journey, Sell heard a car stop, and the scuttle of footsteps in the darkness: 'I did not see who it was at the time but the next time I saw Molly she informed me that it was her mother and Adam Graham who had followed her on this night and that her mother did not believe that she should go through Tin Alley to the university.' Mollie confided in Sell that Ethel routinely searched her clothing and belongings in search of correspondence, and that Ethel had steamed open a letter Mollie was planning to send him. Soon after, Sell received a letter direct from Ethel 'warning me not to go out with Molly' – reiterated, Clara Behrend stated, by a visit Ethel paid to Ormond. It had its effect. Sell 'did not afterwards go out with her' although he 'ran into her on one or two occasions'.

Mollie's other friends absorbed her opinions and stories of home: Clara, who seems to have been the most frequent visitor at Milton Street, described Ethel as 'more or less always morose' but also possessed of a 'violent temper'; Edna Johnson told of Ethel pulling Mollie's hair out; Joyce Pyke told of Ethel throwing 'a quantity of butter' at Mollie; Sadie Fields reported instances of Mollie arriving at school in tears, bearing a 'bruised lip', and still shaking from being threatened by her mother with a carving knife; all four mentioned Mollie's reports of Ethel's regular self-dramatising threats to do herself in by drowning. As for Graham, Mollie told Clara that she had rebuffed a marriage proposal from him, and told Sadie of feeling so uncomfortable in his company that she left any room he entered.

When police taxed Ethel about her behaviour, she admitted regular quarrels 'owing to her [Mollie's] wilfulness', and that 'on several times Mary exasperated me with her conduct and I was very annoyed with her'. She conceded also having on one occasion physically restrained Mollie from leaving; to having on another occasion seized Mollie's evening frock and put it under the copper; and to having on several occasions threatened to 'end the lot' and 'throw myself in the sea', although she never intended 'doing any such thing'. She also admitted to following Mollie on 'four or five occasions', but only because she 'told me lies' about where she was going. For his own part, Graham recalled following Mollie with Ethel 'on four occasions into the city', and that 'Mrs Dean told me she wished to follow Molly because she thought that Molly was going out with men'.

The chronicle of abuse and harassment collected by the detectives reads almost as chillingly as the statements later concerned with the murder. Even minor exchanges became fraught. Clara told of an occasion when she was waiting with Mollie to catch a tram home from the corner of Dickens and Mitford streets, and Graham pulled up in his car:

> He saw us, stopped, backed to where we were and said:
> 'Can I drive Clara home?'
> Molly said: 'No, thank you.'
> He said to Molly: 'If you would like to come I can drive you back.'
> I said: 'No, thank you, I can get home quite quickly by tram.'
> Graham drove away, before doing so looked most annoyed and muttered something to himself.
> Molly said: 'In a way I am sorry we did not go with him.'
> I said: 'Why?'
> She said: 'He will only go carrying tales to mother.'

In a tiny house where secrets were impossible to keep, every involvement became suspect. And in the case of a figure who drifted in to Mollie's life as Teddy Sell drifted out, grounds existed for supposition.

*

'A short wiry man with a white mane of hair, a beak of a nose, a bright eye and a voice like buzzing bees': so did the boy Graham McInnes remember Fritz Hart, a family friend from the 1920s. Hart had many friends, and even more admirers: in Melbourne, he *was* classical music. A graduate of the Royal College, a peer of Gustav Holst and Ralph Vaughan Williams, he had arrived from London with his wife Jessie on a contract for the production company J. C. Williamson in 1909, then stayed, a largish fish in a shallow musical pond, serving as director of the Albert Street Conservatorium in the Victorian Artists' Society building, as music critic of *The Age*, and later as chief conductor of the Melbourne Symphony Orchestra.

World War I consolidated Hart's influence. Sensitive to anti-German prejudice, he anglicised his name to 'F. Bennicke Hart' and abolished German classes at the conservatorium in favour of English locution. He became an ardent proponent of the so-called Celtic Revival, a rummaging in the literature, lore, music and motifs of Anglo-Irish folk tradition that flourished in the atmosphere of jingoist imperialism. In 1915, too, he received a telephone call from a figure with similarly extravagant pro-British sentiments. 'Fritz Hart,' said Nellie Melba. 'What would you do if I offered to come to the conservatorium and teach singing?' The answer was anything in his power. Musicians and students flocked from the conservatorium's rival at Melbourne University for the opportunity of working on 'Melba Days', when the grand old lady instructed in the VAS building's upper galleries as reverent reporters looked on. A journalist from *The Age* described a scene in August 1927 evocative of the mutual affection of prima donna and director:

The south gallery of the Albert Street Conservatorium has rarely been the scene of a more dramatic incident than that which took place yesterday morning, when Dame Nellie Melba leaned down from the stage and, suddenly and unexpectedly, kissed Mr Fritz Hart soundly on the forehead. For a barely perceptible moment he looked surprised; then he smiled and handed her a bunch of roses, while the students applauded in high good humour.

But Melba came back at once to the twentieth century.

'Heavens!' she cried. 'Are there any journalists here?'

'One or two,' Mr Hart replied, a little apprehensively.

She laughed happily. 'Oh, don't tell the people that I kissed Mr Hart,' she said, but it was impossible to believe she meant it seriously.

In fact, Mr Hart rather enjoyed kissing. By the mid-1920s, his marriage to Jessie had curdled, she devoting most of her time to breeding black-and-tan cocker spaniels. Divorce, with embarrassments unseemly for a public figure, was not really an option: besides, the Harts' son, Basil, a law graduate, had been gravely injured in a shooting accident, and lived at home. But Hart remained suave and vital, temptingly surrounded as he was at the conservatorium by comely young singers. There were rumours, always rumours – of assignations, of mistresses, even that he had had a love child, as would his louche friend Philip Heseltine, fellow traveller in the Celtic Revival. But as a character argued gaily in his musical farce *The Fiancées*, Hart believed that some men were innately flirtatious:

One never can tell what a man will be doing
When he is born with a kink in his brain;
From morning till night-time he'll ever be wooing
Dark girls or fair girls or pretty or plain.
From twenty to thirty he's gay and he's flirty,

Yes! Till he's forty he'll be just as naughty;
Even at eighty he will not refrain
If he's born with a kink in his brain,
And they're more to be pitied – I take it – than blamed!

In only one area had Hart's magnetism not availed him. When the
university's Ormond chair of music fell vacant in September 1925,
he applied. His appointment made sense: it would have healed the
rift between the rival institutions; it would have united Melba with
the university where her name already adorned the hall of its conservatorium. But Hart was outmanoeuvred by the shrewd Bernard
Heinze, whose skill in cultivating powerful allies contrasted with his
rival's seeming flightiness and flippancy. Certainly, Hart was never
lost for an opinion. On art, he was a spirited egalitarian: 'A nation
that looks upon Art as a luxury, as an embroidery upon the skirts of
life, is a nation . . . in spiritual twilight.' On music, he was defiantly
anti-modern, deploring popular music as 'rubbish', canned music as
'a terrible expedient', talking pictures as 'essentially bad', and jazz as
'the work of the devil', stemming 'from a very unhappy negroid influence'. Soirees at his East Melbourne home on the first Sunday of
every month drew together a creative community, contemporaries at
the conservatorium and musicians with the Melbourne Symphony
Orchestra mingling with familiars in the worlds of art and literature.
Women too. If he was an old-fashioned charmer, he was a new-
fashioned gender thinker, encouraging female composers in a fashion
quite radical for his time: students such as Peggy Glanville-Hicks,
Margaret Sutherland, Linda Phillips and Phyllis Batchelor flowered
under his influence.

Mollie first joined these gatherings as a guest of another Hart
composition protégé, Hubert Clifford, a school science teacher who

had become a viola player with the MSO: Hart conducted the first performance of Clifford's *A Pageant of Youth* at the town hall in October 1928. How Clifford met Mollie is unclear, although he had earlier taught music at University High. Whatever the case, Clifford quickly grew infatuated with her, and she flattered by his attentions. She showed him her poetry, a sample of which he undertook to set to music. He squired her to the theatre, even if he made the mistake afterwards of accompanying her back to Milton Street – Ethel Dean burst from the front door and dragged her daughter inside by the hair. But Clifford was altogether keener on Mollie than she on him. To Lena Skipper she later confided that Clifford was 'not brainy enough for serious thought'; he was also, like Teddy Sell, roughly her age. Mollie hankered instead for someone older, more worldly and seasoned – for a man, in fact, of 'great vivacity and sensitiveness'. Mollie revelled in the heady drafts of Swinburne; Hart had written a vocal and piano setting for 'The Winds'. Mollie adored 'Ode on a Grecian Urn'; Hart had recently composed a version to be sung by a female choir. Neither, moreover, was looking to be tied down.

Hart's relations with Mollie became public at the inquest when Sadie Fields produced Ethel's letter of June 1928 whose postscript was quoted at the beginning of Chapter 1 – its context being that Mollie and Sadie had colluded in a secret visit to Hart, but that Mollie had let this slip under Ethel's questioning. The letter is short but informative: it suggests both that relations had existed for some time, and that Sadie herself was vaguely disquieted by carryings-on with a married man.

Dear Sadie,
Mollie tells me, after telling me a deliberate lie about going to Miss [Edna] Johnson's to tea, that you are going with her to Fritz

Hart's place tonight. I must say I am disappointed in you. You have known for a long time what I thought of her friendship with him and I know what you have said about him doing her no good etc. I just feel I cannot live like this much longer. The fact of what I have in front of me with my rheumatic trouble nearly drives me crazy sometimes – and with this underhand business going on – I feel the best thing is to get out of it some way or another. I hope you will reason with Mollie for I can't. I feel I will never trust her any more.

Yours etc.,

Ethel Mary Dean

Anxious at being named at the inquest, Hart presented the smallest possible target, leaving town for the coastal retreat of Rosebud rather than attending, and providing no statement – or at least none that survives. Instead, he strove to head gossip off with an interview in *Smith's Weekly* a week later, citing 'certain statements that have recently been made in connection with the inquest on Molly Dean, so far as they relate to my family and myself', and the need to 'remove any misconceptions that might have arisen'. Gatherings at which Mollie had been a guest, he stressed, had 'consisted of men and women of eminence in their circle and profession'.

Yet while Hart made light of his connection with Mollie, he also suggested someone who'd studied her closely and charitably. Hart revealed that he had at her invitation read all her poetry and prose over two years – indeed, her two longest poems had arisen from his suggestions. 'Personally, I considered that her literary gifts showed very great promise,' Hart said. 'She would work with unremitting care and was not only tolerant of but eager for criticism.' In this sense, she appealed to Hart's conviction that an appreciation of art lay within every compass: 'I would like to make it very clear that she was no mere celebrity hunter. She had a genuine love for all the arts, and was always endeavouring to improve her knowledge of them. She was one of those to whom self-education was the most important thing in life.' Seeing her as 'a young woman of experience' who 'knew exactly what she wanted and what she was doing', he expressed further respect for her 'great ambitions' and 'quick, eager, alert, and analytical brain'. Nor could Hart help revealing that he had shared in her personal confidences:

> The breaking-off of her affair with the University student had wounded her *amour-propre*; but she seemed to see the ridiculous side to it. Discussing it afterwards she had remarked to him [Hart], 'Just imagine my being turned down by a student – me, who have all my life been turning other men down!'

Twelve years on, in private, Hart laid down more intimate reflections inspired by Mollie Dean. By then he was in Honolulu, and had taken up writing fiction for his own amusement. In *James Goes Home to Dinner*, the temptress is a 25-year-old schoolteacher, Eileen Coote, who seeks distraction from a bare suburban existence by exercising her sensual allure:

> Her small nose was well-shaped, and her rather full lips were inviting when she did not drag them down at the corners with a kind of self-mocking bitterness. Her eyes were beautiful, dark and liquid; and her chin had just enough character to make it worth painting, he thought. He liked the way in which her hair grew at the nape of her neck . . . He had always been aware of her lissom figure with its promising curves.

Glimpsed at home, Eileen gives her crabby mother and idle brother, Wally, as good as she gets:

> 'You little fool, you have been getting yourself mixed up with some man,' said her mother accusingly.
>
> 'It is about time I did, isn't it? I'll be twenty-six next May . . . It is no good looking at me like that, either. I have my own life to lead and I'll lead it in my own way.'
>
> 'Leading your own life means only one thing, Eileen – and a very wicked thing!'
>
> 'Luckily there are two opinions on that matter . . . I am not an undutiful daughter; and if I am occasionally bad-tempered it is because I have so much reason to be. I've never had the life most of my friends have had, because I've been a household drudge, and – what is more – I have never had a thank you for it. Oh, you think I do not know I am getting warped, sharp-tempered and bitter? But who is to blame?'

The exchange ends with Eileen threatening to move out, and a flash of violence that reads as if it must have been originally narrated by Mollie:

> 'So you want a room where you can entertain your married men!'
>
> 'Yes, mother, and where I can sleep with them if I feel so inclined.'
>
> Eileen had had no intention of saying anything quite so outrageous, but the sight of her mother's angry face, and her knowledge of her extreme selfishness, stung her to utter the first words that came to her tongue. Mrs Coote caught hold of the first thing that came to her hand, which happened to be a pair of

scissors, and flung them at Eileen, who – throwing up a hand to guard herself – was severely gashed on one of her fingers.

Both of them looked at the other in consternation. Their tempers died down under the shock of violence, but each of them was as implacable as ever. Eileen put her bleeding finger between her lips, and then, wrapping a handkerchief around it, said quietly: 'You see the sort of home I live in. Do you wonder I want to live my own life? I am sorry this has happened, but you have been driving me towards something like this for a long time. You might have blinded me – and what would have happened to your precious Wally then?'

Mrs Coote was crying, angrily and impotently, and Eileen was trying desperately hard not to feel ashamed of her own share in the altercation but – in spite of herself – there were scalding tears in her eyes as she said: 'I think we must both be careful in future to avoid any recurrence of anything so horrible – and so ridiculous. I am sorry. Goodnight, mother.'

The debt Eileen Coote owes Mollie Dean is unmistakable – we shall return to it. Yet their lives also diverge in noteworthy respects. For example, Eileen is no writer. And Mollie, as Hart knew well, assuredly was.

4

THE AMIABLE MUSE

And the best and worst of this is
That neither is most to blame,
If you have forgotten my kisses
And I have forgotten your name.
> – Algernon Swinburne, 'An Interlude' (1866)

While inquiring into lives of long ago, there are inevitably phases where the individuals seem unreachable – as though they hardly lived at all, were phantoms of imagination, characters of fiction. With her solitary photograph, missing detail and reticent family, Mollie Dean felt at times like the chalked outline of her body in that Elwood laneway. Was she the 'M. Dean' whose name appeared in the membership rolls of the Athenaeum Library in the late 1920s? Was she the Faraday Street teacher noted by a school inspector teaching nature writing by reading a short story and poem about a mighty oak: 'Incidents in the life of the tree were made to dwell in the mind. Teacher then read the poem sympathetically and expressively.' I liked to think so, but could hardly say.

Yet there were also moments of unexpected clarity, and one awaited among the stacks in Victoria's State Library when I checked

Versifier: Percy Serle

a mention from the *Cairns Post*, of all newspapers, that Mollie Dean had been a contributor to *Verse*. This short-lived literary periodical had been run by two friends of Fritz Hart's: Percival Serle, scholar and bibliographer, and Louis Lavater, poet and composer. Serle was a tireless patron of Australian writing in unsympathetic times. He was responsible, for example, for badgering the Commonwealth Literary Fund, a starveling body that occasionally awarded pensions, into providing the destitute poet John Shaw Neilson with a pound a week. For his own part, Serle subsisted on dividend income, by running a second-hand book stall and by growing his own vegetables. Lavater lived a similarly precarious existence, having published four minimally successful selections of his own poetry, although his recent anthology of Australian sonnets had enjoyed critical favour at least.

Mollie seems to have been introduced to Serle and Lavater by another in Hart's circle. A. E. H. Nickson had spent more than two decades at the conservatorium teaching organ, piano, harmony, counterpoint, and the history and aesthetics of music – the last involved his marching up and down classrooms proselytising about fine art as sacrament, plucking quotes from Ruskin and the Book of Common Prayer. His tall, spare figure would often be seen striding between Albert Street and St Peter's, where he was for decades the organist, identifiable by his homburg, capacious black coat, unfashionable wing collars, well-worn leather case initialled 'A. E. H. N.' and habit of conversing with statues – he once interrupted a walk in Westminster to remonstrate bitterly with Thornycroft's sculpture of Oliver Cromwell. The walls of his Wattletree Road home were heavily hung with medieval religious art.

Nickson's earliest surviving letter from Mollie, which he passed to Lavater, is undated. But it seems to be from the second half of 1928, and obviously followed their meeting, perhaps at one of Hart's East Melbourne soirees, and his sending her copies of his monographs *The Mind Beautiful* and *Christ in Art*. It is worth quoting substantially, for in it can be heard a most distinctive voice – the voice of a young schoolteacher addressing an accomplished man twice her age almost if not quite entirely undaunted, engaged by his ideas but not content to be a mere acolyte.

Dear 'A. E. H. N.'
I want to thank you for *Christ in Art*, which I have been reading, and pondering over . . . If I may be honest with you, I shall tell you that I am not religious, that I never go to church, and that Christ does not mean a very great deal more to me than Buddha, for instance. After this confession, you will understand why *Christ*

in Art puzzled me where *The Mind Beautiful* delighted me. I have been thinking over the Beautiful, the Good, and the True: and wondering what Beauty really is, and whether you would think beautiful the things I love best in poetry.

I cannot conceive anything more beautiful than Keats' 'Ode to a Grecian Urn' [sic], and though I (I) could love a less sensuous form of beauty equally, I could not place it higher than Keats. So it is difficult for much of *Christ in Art* to find an echo in me. Material and visible beauty does not seem to me merely 'the golden bridge that stretches from the finite to the Infinite', but a perfect end in itself. Nor can I agree that 'what delights the sense is false and weak'.

I can realize, of course, the logic of regarding the outward world as a mass of obstructions to the spirit that would see into the heart of things: but I can't <u>feel</u> the sensuous beauties of earth to be obstructions

. . . Daffodils

that come before the swallow dares, and take

The winds of March with beauty

. . . mean more to me than a whole book full of philosophy, not because they are symbols, or because I am not interested in philosophy.

But I can understand, of course, the inner world as well as the outer, although the outer world is in itself perfect at times: I can feel with AE the breathing of earth, and the mysterious life it holds, as well as the force of Deity, the 'Magician of the Beautiful', behind it.

I shall read and re-read both your books, though I don't expect I shall ever feel that in the conquest of mind over matter, the 'matter' <u>doesn't</u> matter. Thank you again for sending them to me, and for the beauty they have given me. They will both be read and understood, and loved, in spite of my paganism, which is perhaps one of the follies of youth.

Very sincerely,

Mollie Dean

Much is packed into these few lines: familiarity ('A. E. H. N.'), deference ('*The Mind Beautiful* delighted me'), candour ('*Christ in Art* puzzled me'), self-disclosure ('Christ does not mean a very great deal more to me than Buddha') and self-awareness ('the follies of youth'). It is green with youth – the tiny solecism of 'Ode *to* a Grecian Urn' and the excited erudition of the lines from Perdita in Act IV of *A Winter's Tale* prelude a hesitant postscript:

I have kept this letter until I could write out for you some of my poems. They are full of faults and weaknesses, and have been written under great difficulties, and I feel anything but satisfied with them. You will perhaps think they contain too much 'matter' and too little mind: if so, I must try and write a more spiritual one that will please you, in return for your kindness to me. Not that I ever write what I can't honestly <u>feel</u>: but I should like you to be able to like <u>something</u> I have written however weak it may be. I hope these will not bore you and waste your time.

Although these poems are no longer attached, one of them was almost certainly 'Merlin', a 130-line lyric in blank verse, beginning with an ambitious metaphor for evening: 'Once more the hounds of dusk do turn, and yawn,/And shake themselves awake: once more begin/Their gloomy pacing through the tired earth/While day lets fall her last low westward gold'. The echo is explicitly of Swinburne's chorus in *Atalanta in Calydon* ('When the hounds of spring are on winter's traces'); the mysticism and spiritual imagery are pure Celtic Revival, whose canonical works included Spenser's *The Faerie Queene*, Tennyson's *Idylls of the King* and numerous rebootings of Arthurian legend as well as lush artistic imaginings like Edward Burne-Jones' *The Beguiling of Merlin* and *The Last Sleep of Arthur in Avalon*. It's also almost certainly one of the two poems Hart claimed to have inspired – he had himself just written a comic opera in a Celtic vein, *The Woman who Laughed at Faery*. The poem should by rights have been cause for jubilation. But the 'great difficulties' to which Mollie had referred were shortly to worsen.

In January 1929, Mollie Dean accepted appointment to a new school, in Queensberry Street, North Melbourne. It also involved a new challenge: as a 'temporary assistant', she would be taking over one of Victoria's thirty 'opportunity classes', for children with learning difficulties. This involved an adjusted curriculum, the three Rs broken up by games, music, physical exercise, carpentry, leatherwork, broom weaving and brush making. As the Teachers' College's resident expert explained it with his period's customary lack of euphemism: 'According to usually accepted definitions about one per cent of school age children can be classified as mentally deficient, but a much larger group, perhaps four or five per cent, can be classified as "dull". The opportunity grade is an effort to cater for the education of this "dull" group.'

Why did Mollie, otherwise so averse to dullness, make this move? Special teaching offered a slight incremental increase in pay, even if it could slow promotion; the appointment also had the effect of anchoring Mollie in the city, preventing her relocation to the 'eternal sameness' of a rural posting. In any event, it was a commitment for which she again showed aptitude. 'Interested in her special class,' said an inspector at the end of her first month. 'Has already made useful aids. Shows good to very good teaching and organising methods. Has good controlling influence. Very promising teacher with further experience.' It was a shift she would hardly have made without the encouragement of her old teacher George Browne – which became an issue.

On 20 March 1929, Browne was surprised to be bailed up in his Grattan Street office by an argumentative woman who introduced herself as Ethel Dean. Mollie's mother, it seems, had been reading their occasional letters. As Browne recalled her complaint: 'I am very worried about my daughter Molly and I think that the friendships she made at the Teachers' College have been a bad influence over her. They have heightened her desire to go on with artistic and journalistic work and they have given her too great a conceit of herself. I intercepted a letter from Molly to yourself and I object to her correspondence with you.'

Browne explained that he had occasionally written Mollie with advice and news, but deferentially agreed to 'terminate the correspondence' if Ethel objected. 'I believe that you drove Molly home from a dance at college,' Ethel alleged further. Browne insisted that this was untrue:

> Mrs Dean said there is a Mr Fritz Hart whom I must also go and see regarding his friendship with Molly.
> I said: 'If you are so worried about Molly's conduct, why not let her take a small school out in the country for a year? This would free her from the influences you think are harming her.'

Mrs Dean said: 'That would never do because then I should lose the amount of money she is able to pay me as a contribution towards the home.'

To propitiate Ethel, Browne wrote a letter for her to deliver to his former star pupil, streaked with an anxiety not to offend either.

Dear Mollie,

Your mother came to see me yesterday and was very distressed. I felt very upset about the whole business and did what I could to heal the rift between you and her, but not very successfully, I am afraid.

She strongly objected to the existence of any correspondence and I gave her my word that it should cease. I also said I would write to you, sending the letter to her and asking her to hand it to you after perusal. In this letter I shall try to help your relations with her, and you will realise from it what I am trying to do.

I am very sorry that I have thoughtlessly involved you in considerable trouble at home. Please forgive me for this. I have been distinctly inconsiderate of your situation, I am afraid.

Meanwhile let us remain good friends. I still think there are great things ahead of you if you walk warily and do not lose your enthusiasm.

Yours very truly,

George Stephenson Browne

Why did Browne strain for such a placatory tone? What was 'the whole business'? Had the relationship gone beyond the professional? Not necessarily: it was enough in the straitlaced college for married Browne to have endangered his reputation by corresponding with an unmarried female student, however innocently. But the loss would have come as a bitter blow to Mollie, to know that her mother's surveillances were so sweeping. In fact, this invasion would have been among the reasons that Mollie, in the next few months, left home to stay with Joyce Pyke, who had been sharing a flat near the university with her sister, Phyllis, since their mother's death two years earlier. For two weeks, they lived a version of Lillian Pyke's novel, as three bachelor girls – at least until Ethel traced Mollie to Parkville.

When Ethel went to her address, Mollie was out; so she was the next evening when Ralph called. Mollie voluntarily visited the garage where Ralph was apprenticed as a mechanic the following day, her brother presumably conveying that their mother was contrite and subdued: without Mollie at home, Ethel had only her annuity and her valetudinarianism to rely on. Comforted by a few concessions, Mollie agreed to return to Milton Street. On their next meeting, Mollie told Browne that she and her mother were getting on better. To him she never mentioned Adam Graham.

Nickson, meanwhile, had taken Mollie's remarks in good part – indeed, he had thought enough of 'Merlin' to pass it on to Lavater, then preparing the first edition of *Verse*. Mollie's next letter to 'A. E. H. N.' was bashfully cheerful about this new editorial scrutiny: 'I am not at all satisfied with anything I have written + feel rather diffident about seeing any of it in irrevocable black and white, so I won't be too disappointed if Mr Lavater agrees with me. On the other hand, I expect being printed would be rather exhilarating.' She concluded buoyantly: 'The muse is very amiable just at present.'

Lavater was impressed, and wrote Mollie a letter of acceptance, commending the obvious effort. She received it uneasily, suddenly feeling all her twenty-three years at the prospect of formal entree into the circle of Australian poets: '"Merlin" is quite free and I only wish I were more satisfied with it. I don't feel confident enough of its worth to feel altogether happy at the idea of seeing it set down beyond hope of repair: in fact I feel distinctly nervous, so if you should reconsider your decision I won't be heartbroken!' She offered her services in other ways too:

I have been wishing for a long time for such a magazine as *Verse*, and hope fortune will smile on it. The infant mortality in this direction has been enormous in the past. I think I can collect a dozen or more annual subscriptions, which I shall send along to Mr Serle + I can probably dispose of quite a lot of copies of the November issue – not much to do, but I expect better than nothing.

Thank you for realizing the 'spade work' in my efforts – so few people do: and it's very stimulating to have hard work recognized and appreciated. I am afraid if it were not for Fritz Hart, I should still be believing that a poem must be born easily or not at all.

I shall do my utmost for *Verse*, and I wish it every success.

Thanking you again,

I am,

Very sincerely yours,

Mary Dean

The more formal 'Mary' hints at a new seriousness; likewise a post-script suggesting she call on Lavater in order to take a final glance at 'Merlin' 'before anything happens to it'. When she did visit Lavater's home in Alma Road, Mollie seems to have exerted her usual effect. At sixty-two years old, Lavater was a lonely man, marooned in a loveless second marriage contracted quickly after the death of his first wife.

Beatrice, formerly a nurse, had several times moved out after quarrels
with her husband and with neighbours; in a rage, he would recall, she
'completely lost control of herself'. Mollie, brimming with vim and
verse, must have been a tonic. They went line-by-line over 'Merlin';
they discussed other favourite poets; she left with Lavater's prized
copy of *Ballad and Lyrical Poems* by John Shaw Neilson, for whose
welfare Serle had striven so tirelessly. Alas, the visit also further aggravated Ethel's suspicion of Mollie's literary 'friends'. Mollie's next letter
referred to Lavater having received a frigid welcome at Milton Street,
and to renewed discontent at home: 'I am unhappily conscious that
I did not do justice to your kindness in calling, and must ask you to forgive any lack of cordiality. As a matter of fact, my mother is extremely
antagonistic to almost everything I do and everyone I know, especially to my writing and any people connected therewith. So I am on
continued pins and needles at home – not a happy state of affairs.'

The 'pins and needles' had not prevented her copying 'Merlin'
afresh, or appreciating the 'beautiful lyrical qualities' of the Shaw
Neilson. The letter unfolded into a consideration of the 'sound-versus-
sense question', a contested area of poetry since Pope's 'Essay on
Criticism', and her delight in Swinburne, whose 'Laus Veneris' she cited:

> At school one is taught Browning's 'Grammarian's Funeral' as
> great poetry. I think much of it is doggerel: it's certainly great
> stuff but to me it's not poetry. Swinburne is, I think, the sheerest,
> though not the greatest, poet of them all.

> Ah yet would God this flesh of mine might be
> Where air might wash and long leaves cover me,
> Where tides of grass break into foam of flowers,
> Or where the wind's feet shine along the sea.

Also the famous Huntsman's chorus from 'Atalanta', one of the most perfect lyrics ever written [see above]. I think it surpasses in music anything I know + I suppose a lyric, from its name, should be musical.

Fortunately, perhaps, Swinburne, though he acts on me like a drug, doesn't inspire me to imitate him. I <u>try</u> to try usually for the right sense of a word first and sound afterwards, and as women are not supposed to be overburdened with brains, I don't expect to achieve too intellectual an atmosphere by this method. Don't you admire the naivete with which [one brackets] Swinburne and oneself in the same sentence? [. . .] Perhaps I should call sometime with Shaw Neilson and hear something about your own work? At any rate I will bring the book up and leave it in a week or two.

Thanking you very much for your kindness, and hoping you are not thinking too badly of me . . .

Sincerely,

Mollie Dean

'Mary' has become 'Mollie' again, although the confidence in the literary judgements competes with a desire not to seem too forward or 'too intellectual' in the eyes of a gentlemanly older editor. It is possible to picture Mollie Dean, two weeks from her twenty-fourth birthday, bent low over a lamplit desk, putting aside piles of her pupils' papers to copy stanzas from a book of poetry she could not afford, and thrilling to such as 'You, and Yellow Air': 'Out of your eyes a magic/Fell lazily as dew,/And every lad with lad's eyes/Made summer love to you.' Mollie might already have had a lad in mind too.

*

'Sweet-voiced': Vi Colahan (middle) in *The Woman Who Laughed at Faery*

A day or two before writing, Mollie had enjoyed a night at the
theatre courtesy of Fritz Hart: in her letter to Lavater, she refers to
having attended *The Woman who Laughed at Faery* at the Playhouse,
which she found 'too magical for words'. Based on an Irish folktale,
essayed by Melbourne's musical man-about-town, played by students at the Albert Street Conservatorium who had benefited from
Melba's tutelage, the fey tale of an old woman warding off a sprite's
spells with her merry laughter met widespread acclaim. A repeat season was scheduled at the Playhouse, a broadcast arranged on 3AR and
2BL, and reviewers chorused praise for Dawn Harding, as mocking
Mrs Murphy; Kathleen Goodall, a 'miraculously uncanny goblin';
and as a 'sweet-voiced and tenderly human colleen', Violet Colahan.

Violet, too, was such a fortunate woman, being married to that dashing young artist Colin Colahan . . .

Whose eyes met whose? For lives were shortly to cross, including that of another present. In his playful *Bulletin* notice, reviewer Mervyn Skipper called on Hart to offer show-goers 'a really up-to-date fairy':

> Instead of casting an old-fashioned spell over the earth maiden, the modern fairy could lure her with the offer of a ride in a new sports model Chrysler, the petrol would run out, the maiden would be obliged to walk home in the small hours, her mother would interview the fairy's parents and insist on him doing the right thing by the damsel, the marriage would be unhappy owing to the girl's cooking disagreeing with fairy's stomach, he would fall into the habit of being unavoidably detained at the office, and the injured lady would call in the services of the Fairy detective agency, which would obtain a photo through the office keyhole. The Court would refuse to accept the fairy's statement that it was necessary for him to have the blonde typist on his knee while he dictated an order for 300 gross of purple fireflies; so she would get a *decree nisi* with costs and marry her human lover. Mr Hart is free to use the above plot without acknowledgement.

What transpired would be thoroughly up to date but no fairytale.

5

THAT SELF-OPINIONATED SECT

The followers of Meldrum
Paint but seldom
They are chiefly employed
In the study of Freud.
         – Cyril Pearl

She called him 'Shiny' – such was his surface glow, and also his capacity for dazzling reflection. He had always possessed an artist's eye, although perhaps no image he produced was more vivid than the one Colin Colahan made of himself. He was a diminutive figure, hair swept back from a high forehead, the gaze of his pale-blue eyes accentuated by spectacles. Yet he was a ball of energy, mischief, passion and contention, with what Mervyn Skipper called an 'inexhaustible flow of ideas', and a sense that no time was 'unsuitable for an exposition'. Men were no less sensitive to his effect on others. 'Mine were not the only eyes that followed him,' noted Skipper. 'Their models, their wives and their women friends who sometimes came in with them hung on his lips with the same pleasure, even when they themselves became the objects of his amusing ridicule.' Colahan deferred to one man only: his sage, Max Meldrum. Otherwise his life resembled a ceaseless flit, between paintings, proclamations, amusements, amours. Mollie Dean, whom he met when he was aged thirty-two, in a sense combined all four.

Born in Woodend soon after his family's arrival from South Africa, Colahan was the fifth of six children. His mother, in her girlhood an accomplished pianist, died of pneumonia when he was two. His father, an Irish-born surgeon major general retired from the British Army, was a classically distant Victorian paterfamilias – Colin and his siblings were raised mainly by their maternal grand-mother at 'Kangatong', St Kilda. Their Catholicism was strong. The girls were educated by the Loreto nuns at St Mary's Mount in Ballarat, the boys by the Jesuits of Xavier College before mostly enrolling in the family trade of medicine at Melbourne University. This last Colin detested. From boyhood he had drawn with uncanny facility, including waggish illustrations for *The Xaverian*. But these were serious times: his brother John enlisted and was killed by a gas shell in Belgium in October 1917. Colin had to content himself with lobbing cartoons into *The Bulletin*, suitably patriotic. One of his first, which enjoyed the signal honour of reproduction in Chicago's venerable *Cartoons Magazine*, featured the Kaiser as Herod, mil-itarism as Salome, and Germany's head as the sacrifice; he later contributed the images to Eustace Boylan's novel of public-school sacrifice and post-conscription referenda Catholic loyalty, *The Heart of the School*, in which Xavier boys enlist enthusiastically and die like Christians ('Australia – and Xavier – may well be proud of a son like him').

Colahan then had a lucky break. By his own account, editor Samuel Prior offered him a sought-after staff position on *The Bulletin*. He lasted, he would joke, a week – politics, he realised, was not his forte. But the major general was sufficiently impressed to allow his son to 'throw down the scalpel and pick up the brush'. Colahan was a compulsive burnisher and embellisher of stories – the veracity of this one is unascertainable. But when his father died in November 1918, he and his son seem to have been on good terms. Colahan was left an annuity worth £4 a week, not to mention an eclectic collection of personal effects: *inter alia*, an Ionian Island crest ring, a set of the International Library of Famous Literature complete with revolving stand, a host of cameras, lenses, shutters and darkroom lanterns, a yellowish-brown portmanteau, and a revolver. Colahan and another medical school dropout, Jim Minogue, enrolled at the National Gallery Art School, and quickly made lasting friends including Justus Jorgensen, John Farmer and Archie Colquhoun.

The school was Australia's most prestigious but, under the sway of the mandarin Bernard Hall, hewed tightly to the orthodoxies, with painstaking instruction in draughtsmanship, composition, perspective and anatomy. Colahan chafed, to the extent that he and Jorgensen soon found themselves at the *atelier* of Max Meldrum in Hardware Chambers at the corner of Elizabeth and Little Bourke streets. Awarded one of the gallery's triennial travelling scholarships in December 1899, Meldrum had divided his time between Paris and the village of Pacé in Brittany, gradually turning against the 'academic painting' taught by Hall. Intense study of his heroes Velázquez and Corot had convinced him that art was a science of optical analysis, and depictive art no more than the reproduction of what the brain registered through the eye, unenhanced by prior knowledge, emotion or memory. When he returned to Melbourne, Meldrum's smokily dark *A Peasant of Pacé*, belatedly submitted in completion of his scholarship, seemed like a repudiation of all the exaltations of Australian light and national landscape then in vogue. As Heysen was painting his monumental *The Three Gums*, craggy

'Indomitable Max': Meldrum, guru

eucalypt castles bedded deep in the earth, Meldrum was producing the austerely minimal *The Three Trees*, a glance at an Eltham glade that seemed to hover in space.

Compact, bearded, austere, proud to call himself a 'fourth-generation free thinker' without a Christian in his family, Meldrum's tirades were somehow the more uncompromising for his Doric burr. Ever packing a pipe or gesticulating with a shinbone, he was immortalised by his contemporary Norman Lindsay as 'the MacQuibble' in *A Curate in Bohemia*:

'Are there such things as lines in Nature?' demanded the MacQuibble.

'The line—,' began Limpet sententiously.

'Is there a line around my nose?' shouted the MacQuibble, thrusting that organ prominently into the discussion. 'Does it not tell against the rest of the face solely by reason that the tone is deeper, and the high light stronger?'

'The line—,' said Limpet, evidently about to propound a crushing rejoinder, but he was not allowed to finish.

'How are you going to differentiate your half tones if you whack a line round everything?' roared the MacQuibble, thrusting the point home on Limpet's stomach with the shin bone . . .

'I say,' said the MacQuibble loudly, 'that a man who draws by line is no better than a primitive savage!'

Setting up as a teacher, Meldrum soon attracted a tiny sect of students, including Clarice Beckett, Arnold Shore, Richard McCann and August Cornehls, and he had not long been president of the Victorian Artists' Society than they had a name. Reported a supporter signing herself 'Jean S' in *The Bulletin*: 'The Meldrumites, headed by the indomitable Max himself, have declared war on the Potboilers who want to turn the Victorian Artists' Society's annual show into a bargain sale.' The alleged Potboilers were not to be marginalised, and accused Meldrum of leading artists away from 'the true ideals of a National Australian School' and of creating 'a grave of artistic reputations'; an anonymous hand, additionally enraged by Meldrum's open pacifism, even slashed a penknife across Meldrum's *A Peasant of Pacé* in the National Gallery. Among voices calling for calm amid the aesthetic trench warfare was Mollie Dean's art teacher, Bertha Merfield: 'Now, with the world in this awful upheaval, when artists above all others were feeling the inharmonious conditions, and it was so difficult to produce work at all, is the time that artists should stand together, and at least try to keep the tiny flame of art alive in this part of the world, and do what little they are able to under the stress of circumstances.' The cry went unheard.

When the mild-mannered sculptor Douglas Richardson was nominated for the presidency to 'bring together the opposing sections which at present were so bitterly at variance', Meldrum's supporters advertised their happiness with variance on a banner: DOUGLAS RICHARDSON AND PEACE, OR MAX MELDRUM AND ART. And what Meldrum lost when Richardson won, he gained in anti-establishment credibility. A decade-and-a-half *drôle de guerre* commenced. Others followed Colahan and Jorgensen to Meldrum's side, Farmer within days. Hall banned casual visitors from the gallery school, wary of recruiting agents from that 'self-opinionated sect'; gallery trustee Sir Baldwin Spencer inveighed against the 'mud and chocolate style' of that 'conceited little megalomaniac'.

The Meldrumites, more technically grouped as 'the tonalists', were tightly bonded by principles: a reliance on raw umber and white, followed by black; the use of a large palette enabling a mixing of tones; a gradation of these tones into four from lightest to darkest; a preference for round brushes to minimise brushwork; a comfort with painting in artificial light, and further partiality to the mellowness of mornings and evenings in the unkempt bushland of Eltham and Olinda and on the foaming coasts of San Remo and Anglesea; a custom of evaluating work through half-closed eyes or dark glasses, or from a distance of 6 metres, with Clarice Beckett the first to improvise a trolley that relieved all the toings and froings. Yet they were almost as defined by what they rejected: not just the sterilities of academe but also the bombast of modernism, whose buffetings of representational art Meldrum deplored as a 'pathological symptom of the diseased condition of modern civilisation'. His denunciations were always memorable. Asked to evaluate a stark chunk of stone at an exhibition of modern sculpture, Meldrum replied: 'I can't answer that. I'm not a geologist.'

Ironically, Colahan was shortly tasked with preparing an essential accoutrement of any modern movement: a manifesto. Colahan's introduction to *Max Meldrum: His Art and Views*, a 120-page monograph based on Meldrum's public lectures about the 'Scientific Order of the Impressions', positioned him as first among equals in his teacher's salon. 'A very great deal of the hostility towards Meldrum is caused by the unflinching attitude adopted by his students, in their outspoken propagation of their master's principles,' Colahan opined, and proceeded to demonstrate same by assailing 'the cult of technique', 'the ring of mutually helping criticism', 'art's state of gaudy stagnation', 'the ravings of the colour maniacs, the puzzles of impressionists, the inanities of the academicians' – all at age twenty-four. One mordant denunciation followed another, such as: 'The impressionist who insists on breaking up a flat tone into a heterogeneous mass of spotty colour is just as scientific as the surgeon who would insist on removing the appendix through the back of his patient simply because he likes to show his individuality.'

On the country's gallery walls, there was suddenly all to play for. In August 1919, Roy de Maistre and Roland Wakelin held the 'Colour in Art' exhibition at Gayfield Shaw's Art Salon in Sydney, claiming a similar scientific basis for their work by aligning the seven colours of the spectrum with the notes of an octave – a key date, it is now felt, in the coming of non-depictive painting to Australia. A month later at the Athenaeum, Colahan, Jorgensen, Farmer, Minogue, McCann, Colquhoun, Cornehls, Beckett, Shore and Polly Hurry exhibited alongside Meldrum in the inaugural tonalist exhibition, the movement proclaiming its unity and creed by scorning to provide titles in the catalogue and using uniform black frames.

Bliss it was in this artistic dawn to be alive, and to be young, like
Colahan, was very heaven.

To continue his emulation of Meldrum, Colahan would need to
travel overseas, although he was to marry first – the last of his siblings
to do so. His Catholicism still bore on him: he seems to have courted
26-year-old Violet Lester, educated at Loreto Abbey in Ballarat,
mainly because it was the only way to bed her. It was a registry wedding, Meldrum and Jorgensen acting as witnesses. But by the end of
1921, the newlyweds were in London, proceeding from there to Paris,
settling in a Montmartre studio. At last Colahan felt 'an artist like
others', a full-fledged aesthete and epicure. The couple would remain
away almost six years, not half as long as 'the indomitable Max', but
just as intensely, joined after a time by Colquhoun, Jorgensen and
his new wife, Lil, and, briefly, Meldrum *en famille*. Colahan travelled
widely, painted ever more expansively and indulged his Francophilia,
helped by Britain's restoration of the gold standard. 'Those were the
days when the Franc was low and the Pound was resplendent,' he
recalled. 'We ate splendidly.'

The Colahans never seem to have been particularly compat-
ible. Vi was musically gifted, a singer and pianist. But for Colahan's
torrential eloquence she struggled to be an adequate foil, and on a
group trip to Spain warmed to the handsome Colquhoun and vice
versa. Tensions worsened until Colquhoun, incensed at Colahan's
impatience with his wife and half in love with her himself, at last
sheered away. Vi thought that her conceiving a child would heal the
rift; if anything, differences deepened. Colahan would willingly have
stayed where he was. But when David Michel was born in October
1926, Vi grew keener to return home, cajoling her husband into it

Aesthete: Colahan in Paris

by organising an exhibition of his works at the Fine Art Society's Galleries in Exhibition Street.

Back in Melbourne, Colahan inevitably courted the jealousy of indigenous critics, who had neither forgotten nor forgiven his insolence. *The Herald*'s blimpish J. S. MacDonald scolded him for 'diluted Meldrumism' with 'erroneous ideas' at the expense of 'concessions to beauty' that were 'not acceptable to simple Australians'. But if Australia's prosperity in this time had shallow foundations, artists were not complaining. Works at a 1926 group exhibition at the Athenaeum were reported by *The Bulletin* as being 'priced as much per foot of canvas as a frontage on Collins Street'; a three-week show at the same gallery the following year by Harold Septimus Power earned him £3000, including a watercolour sold to Melba. After three shows of his own, Colahan could afford a Victorian six-roomer at

14 Yarra Grove, Hawthorn, on a third of a hectare stepping down to the riverbank. He dubbed it 'Pangloss', for Voltaire's incurably optimistic philosopher who teaches in *Candide* that 'troubles are just the shadows in a beautiful picture'. It might have been a personal motto.

With Meldrum himself pursuing opportunities as a lecturer in Europe and the USA, there had been changings of Melbourne's cultural guard. By the late 1920s, the self-styled 'seventh city of Empire' could consider itself as nurturing a genuine intelligentsia, constituted by several overlapping circles. The location of the Albert Street Conservatorium in the Victorian Artists' Society building had always drawn musicians into communion with painters. Fritz Hart, the composer Oscar Mendelsohn and the violinist Stanislaw de Tarczynski were old chums of Meldrum; Justus and Lil Jorgensen were friends of the soprano Florence Austral and flautist John Amadio; the Colahans socialised with the Bradleys, a family of instrumentalists and singers. Another circle orbited the novelist Vance Palmer and his critic wife Nettie, who settled in Hawthorn in April 1929, and dramatist Louis Esson and his doctor wife Hilda, who moved in across the road from them, not to mention her boss and platonic admirer Dr John Dale, the government medical officer. They intersected at points with writers fostering a Society of Australian Authors, including the editors Serle and Lavater, the novelist Bernard Cronin, the balladist Myra Morris, Frank Wilmot who wrote as Furnley Maurice, and Marjorie Clark who wrote as Georgia Rivers. Other notables of the city's various salons included the anthropologist Donald Thomson, the philosopher Norman Porter, the political scientist William Macmahon Ball and the psychiatrist Reg Ellery. Garry Kinnane would call it a 'virtual Melbourne Bloomsbury', and if it was not perhaps so multivalent, the Meldrumites at its core provided a creative and personal colour that belied the subtle and restrained tones of their canvases.

In some respects, in fact, they fulfilled a need. 'The artist' in Australia, like so much, was a constructed identity. Melbourne could claim lineal descent from the Paris of Montmartre, the Left Bank and the Latin Quarter classically immortalised in *Scènes de la vie de bohème*: Murger's flamboyant character Marcel had been inspired by Antoine Fauchery, who, drawn to the colonies by gold in 1852, stayed to establish the Café-Estaminet Français in Little Bourke Street, the first such establishment of its kind. Before World War I, bohemianism had thrown up impresarios like Marcus Clark, George Gordon McCrae and Charles Conder, along with institutions like Politzer's Cafe Boulevard in Collins Street, the Old Mitre Tavern in Bank Place and the Fasoli family's Pension Suisse in Lonsdale then King Street, with its slogan above the entry of 'Light Hearts and Empty Pockets' and enticing promise of 'free wine with every meal'. 'This is the age of unrest, as electricity and steam have turned us all into Bohemians,' proclaimed Fergus Hume in *The Mystery of a Hansom Cab*, his sensational novel of 1886. The Melbourne craze for George du Maurier's *Trilby* ten years later caused an exodus of artists to Paris, and an appetite for Trilby shirts, pies, chewing gum, toothpaste and even trifle.

The clichés, however, gradually grew shopworn. In an influential 1907 essay, 'Australia and the Bohemian Ideal', Vance Palmer rejected imported pretentions. 'Murger and others have written of it once and for all, and after they have reaped there can only be a sorry gleaning,' he wrote. 'The real Australia is not to be seen from the windows of bohemia.' 'Boheeming' was rejuvenated in Sydney after the war; it took in Melbourne a lower, more recreational key, knighthoods for John Longstaff and Arthur Streeton affirming their induction into the establishment. Nobody to the south was crowned 'Queen of Bohemia' like Dulcie Deamer to the north; artists' balls in St Kilda were not nearly so notorious as the annual 'jazz fantasies' of the artists' balls at the Sydney Town Hall. 'Do you call this Bohemia, laddie?' complained a Sydney critic from *The Triad* visiting Melbourne in May 1926. 'This is a parody, a pasteboard imitation . . . Yes, everything passes. Only the spaghetti remains.' Three years later, a correspondent of *The Argus* sent round artists' studios in search of Melbourne's modern Murgers experienced a 'day of disillusionment': he found Longstaff dressed 'like a prosaic businessman', Harold Herbert ensconced in space that looked 'more like an office than a studio'. Thank goodness, then, for the Meldrumites, with their aesthetic contrarianism, signature beards and taste for osso buco and cheap red at the Latin at 206 Exhibition Street and the Italian Club in Little Bourke Street. In the absence of their prophet, often pessimistic, sometimes melancholy, their railleries were also rather more fun.

The sect's ranks had by now been swelled by a figure of great popularity: Percy Leason of *Table Talk* and *The Bulletin*, converted to tonalism in his painting by reading *Max Meldrum: His Art and Ideas*. He had lived the bohemian life with a joyous flourish. 'You go up X street until you come to Y lane,' he would explain to the visitors to his first studio. 'Go up there right to the end and you'll find yourself at the back gate of a factory. You'll find the gate closed; but if you reach over the gate you'll feel a cord with a brick on it. Give that a good pull and in my studio a hanging beer bottle will hit a frying pan. Then, if I'm in, I'll come down.' If those raffish days were behind him now that he was Australia's best-paid cartoonist, he felt nostalgic for them. Leason was an improbable recruit to Meldrumism, because his black-and-white art was characterised by superb draughtsmanship and an elevated vantage. But his admiration was entirely sincere and enhanced his peers' prestige: seemingly the whole country followed his cartoons set in 'Wiregrass', a rural hamlet full of folksy doings. Chez

Leason in Eltham, a two-storey, triple-brick bungalow at the top of a slope, became a Meldrumite fastness, as well as a wonderland for his five children with wife Belle.

The movement obtained a fervent advocate when Leason lured his *Bulletin* colleague Mervyn Skipper to an exhibition by Justus Jorgensen, not long returned from Europe. Jorgensen had at first been regarded as a lugubrious contrast to his confederate Colahan, ponderous in his pronouncements, awkward around women. He had pursued a nurse at St Vincent's without success – to console himself he would go forlornly night after night to the movie *The Woman of Bronze*, in which the actress Clara Kimball Young, playing an artists' model, disrobed. He then grew infatuated with a pretty medical student, Lil Smith, who rejected him until the instant he decided to go abroad. For Jorgensen it proved an advantageous marriage, for Lil's work as an anaesthetist subsidised his art, and his confidence blossomed. He began regarding himself as not just a painter but a philosopher, and when he had an affair in London with a voluptuous model named Lynette justified it by reference to a 'theory of consideration': that because *not* having the affair would have made him resentful of his wife, it was best for all that he had it. When Lil was shortly prostrated by what seemed to be multiple sclerosis, Jorgensen dismissed it as psychosomatic.

Returning to Melbourne and settling in Brighton, Jorgensen set up as a teacher, while his wife recovered sufficiently to resume work at St Vincent's. His first solo exhibition, opened by Fritz Hart in March 1929, proved controversial: Bernard Hall, who dismissed Jorgensen as a Meldrum *manqué*, sent gallery students with advice that they would learn from it how not to paint. But no sooner had they been introduced than Skipper fell under Jorgensen's spell: 'He did not seem to be aware that I was one of the most eminent critics in the metropolis and that behind me was the power of the press; on the contrary, in a soft voice and hesitating for the right word, he talked to me as if he were teaching me my ABC, though without the slightest trace of arrogance.' To 'The Palette', *The Bulletin*'s art column, Skipper contributed an effusive review: 'Here you are in a world that is sometimes harsh and ugly, sometimes meaningless and often merely dull, but it is also extraordinarily stimulating, subtle and various.' Painters began to excite Skipper as actors and actresses had palled, and the Meldrumites had special appeal as unacclaimed but unbowed – much as he felt himself:

> In my articles began to appear the names of the great masters of the past, names which had hitherto only been names to me, which I had reverenced unthinkingly. Now they began to live for me. It was pleasant to know that they had been vilified and misunderstood, like my friends; that they had starved in garrets without losing their serenity. I eagerly read their biographies and waxed indignant because my friends were rewarded with the same obscurity, and at the same time I took a melancholy delight in pointing out that this obscurity was inevitable. But besides this I began to demand the right of the artist to be heated in his own defence, or rather, I maintained that it was not he who was on his defence but the public which misunderstood him and the critic who presumed to judge him; he was his own judge, I said, and the only competent one.

Skipper's *Bulletin* pulpit provided the Meldrumites with a promotional capability. He could publicise and praise their exhibitions; he could scourge their rivals, whether it was a formalist like Hall ('Artistically, his work is as dead as last year's mutton'), or a deviationist like Arnold Shore (whose experiments in modernism, Skipper thought, 'should be viewed sideways' and belonged 'with the carpet maker and the chintz manufacturer'). Jorgensen, Colahan and the rest would make fine subjects for Skipper's facile pen in *A Pressman's Soul*. A spinster 'whom all the others treated with grave respect' was clearly patterned on remote, seemingly untouchable Clarice Beckett:

> She had finely modelled features, a straight nose, a firm mouth and a weak voice which was seldom heard and when it was said nothing important. She was sedate and silent and as if drawn in but her eyes arrested one. You were astonished to observe that they were not the eyes of an old maid turned inwards on herself . . . Rather they were eyes with a keen edge, like an instrument the owner knew how to use.

Tied ever more tightly to her ailing parents, however, Beckett seldom socialised. When the Skippers hosted their new friends at Eaglemont, or joined them at the Leasons' in Eltham or the Tarczynskis' in Mont Albert, the festivities were boisterous and masculine. Lena had begun to paint using 'the Meldrum palette', deferring to him as 'the greatest art teacher who has come to our shores'. But from the intellectual whirl, she felt at a remove, not much more than a caterer. 'It was only men so I hardly heard any talk,' she grumbled after a soiree that Mervyn hosted with Percy Leason in August 1929. 'I get a little tired of their continual art talk and would sometimes like to hear other opinions from a girl.'

Perhaps for that reason the Skippers welcomed to the circle vivacious Betty Davies. Davies had been wife since 1923 to a wealthy mining engineer almost twice her age who was seldom at home, and mother since 1924 to a son ravaged by cerebromeningitis who was taking a harrowing time to die in care. But, inspired by an affair with journalist Frank Russell from *The Herald*, she had written a play about

'Seldom heard': Clarice Beckett

a French woman, Jeanne, living with her ex-digger husband, Jim, in a flyspeck town ten years after the armistice. Deprived of culture and comfort, Jeanne is seduced by the local spiv into squandering the family savings on silk lingerie ('Oh the touch of silk against my skin.'Ow often I have thought of it . . . Monsieur, I think you are right. I need these things . . . to make up for other things'); in a fury, jealous Jim fells the spiv with a mortal blow. *The Touch of Silk* premiered in November 1928 before rows of empty seats, but earned from Skipper a rare rave: 'Last Saturday, at the Melbourne Playhouse, the birth of good old Australian drama, announced so many times in the past, finally took place.'

Not yet thirty, with a dull dog of a husband who could nonetheless be persuaded to buy tonalist paintings, Betty was a decorative and valuable addition to the community, and an astute, if not always factually reliable, observer of it. Coming to Eaglemont for the first time, invited in by Lena, she quickly discerned the straightforward acolytes, the likes of Jim Minogue, John Farmer and Skipper himself, 'sunk down in his chair, smoking, saying very little but absorbing everything that anybody said or did'. The stars of the gathering were Colahan, 'a puckish man looking on with merry eyes, a moist red mouth and bulbous nose who got up from his seat and shook my hand with every sign of friendliness', and Jorgensen, who established himself as 'the dominant personality of the two by the use of a simple clearly stated comment spoken in his soft persuasive voice'. Here, Davies felt, were true bohemians: she was unable to sleep afterwards for her sense of having felt 'inadequate and commonplace and middle-class' in the presence of a group 'the most remarkable, intelligent and stimulating it had ever been my luck to meet'.

On 25 October 1929, Colahan reciprocated the Skippers' hospitality by inviting them to a gathering of a score of artists and musicians at Pangloss. It was three weeks since Vi Colahan's appearance in Fritz Hart's *The Woman who Laughed at Faery*, and she had laid three festive tables with meats and beetroot, a large vegetable pie, two dishes of soused fish and two huge trifles. Vi's husband set the intellectual tone with a seminar's worth of theory and digression about painting, writing and music making. 'It is all ideas until one's brain could burst,' diarised Lena. The walls were covered in tonalist art. Chamber music was played by David Sisserman, Pavlova's cellist. Then, as the conversation dissolved into camps, Lena talked imperialism with Jorgensen and Buddhism with Hubert Clifford; she also caught sight for the first time of a young woman, probably chaperoned by Clifford, who seemed to be following Colahan's words 'as if he was Jesus'. In all the intellectual froth and bubble, Lena thought, Mollie Dean seemed out of place: 'She is young and teaches the mentally unfit and is at a most impressionable age. What will her future be?'

6

A GIRL IN A MILLION

'I'm a model, you know . . . I'm posing for Durien the sculptor,
on the next floor. I pose to him for the altogether.'
'The altogether?" asked Little Billee.

                   – George du Maurier, *Trilby* (1894)

Colin Colahan had made the best of his reluctant repatriation, reconciling himself to Melbourne by painting its city scenes and streets. Out from under Meldrum's direct oversight, he was more expansive, more colourful, even experimental: *Service Station, Olinda, Elizabeth Street* and *Melbourne, 1929*, three of his most successful works, date from this period. The glint of cars, trams, buildings and urban clutter partly reflected a new *plein air* method, employing a Chevrolet van customised as a mobile studio with a large skylight and a sheave system for his easel. 'When the artist sees a suitable streetscape framed in his windscreen, he parks his vehicle and sets to work with his brush,' explained *The Bulletin* in fascination. 'The picture is painted through the extreme back of the van looking through the windscreen. To obviate undue exertion the canvas is mounted on rails with a rope and pulley attachment. Instead of retreating in order to observe the effect of a brush stroke, Colahan pulls the cord

and the easel careers to the front end of the studio.' In further tribute to Voltaire, he christened the van 'Cunégonde' after *Candide*'s
beauteous heroine.

Working at speed and in startling quantities of paint, Colahan's
portraits also developed a heady spontaneity: a 1929 profile of
Stanislaw de Tarczynski in the act of playing his violin against a green
curtain was widely praised. His growing reputation as a portrait artist drew other commissions, including from Lance Wilkinson, a gifted
economist who had helped establish the Gold Producers' Association
of Australia and who now wanted a memento of his exquisite French
wife. Wilkinson had married 24-year-old Mireille Larreguy de
Civrieux, twenty years his junior and descended from forebears in the
Basque aristocracy and Grande Armée, in Paris in December 1924.
They lived in splendour on Brighton's Esplanade, but she was as bored
in Australia as Betty Davies' Jeanne, perhaps not least when her husband decided in May 1928 to run for the Legislative Council seat of
South Eastern Province. With cool blue eyes, startling cheekbones
and blonde hair combed off a high forehead, Mireille already looked
like a work of art, and Colahan painted her several times. As would
regularly be the case with him, this also meant sharing his bed. It was
not long before she was pregnant.

Colahan might conceivably have abandoned his wife; Mireille was
not about to sacrifice her wealthy and generally benevolent husband
for the uncertain prospects of a painter. By some contrivance, she
persuaded Lance Wilkinson that the child was his, and after he failed
at the polls that they should return to Europe. The Wilkinsons left
via French Indochina and Java in January 1929. Six months later in
Paris, Mireille gave birth to Marc, named for her poet brother, killed
at Verdun. Colahan had to settle for a successful exhibition at the
Athenaeum, loyally bolstered by fellow travellers. 'These pictures

are their own best agent,' stated Leason in *Table Talk*. 'The score of beautiful arguments that the critic might readily work out seem unnecessary.' But it was Colahan's artistic rather than his personal life that deserved Leason's description of 'so richly harmonious as to be a sheer delight'.

Skipper praised the exhibition in the terms of an arch-Meldrumite: 'Imagination and sentiment have their throats cut without so much as a by-your-leave. Every impression is set down as it impinges on the optic nerve and in its correct relationship; and when he is satisfied that he has registered all his eye can honestly see the artist drives on.' A couple of months later, Skipper judged a Colahan nude the most distinguished work at the annual Victorian Artists' Society exhibition, amid another paean for the Meldrumites: 'Their steady questioning after the plain truths of nature gives their work a solidity, which makes both the incompetent realists and the sentimentalists look pallid.' Yet a point of distinction between mentor and protégé had been their attitudes to the nude, and its potential enticements: Meldrum liked nothing to impair his disinterestedness; Colahan did not share that aversion, and commonly painted a fleshy Irish model, Biddy Moloney, with whom he may also have had a casual affair. This becomes relevant in considering how relations may first have blossomed between Colahan and Mollie. Lena Skipper's glimpse of Mollie Dean at Pangloss engrossed by Colahan's quick-silver mind suggests a seduction of the intellect; Colahan's taste for painting as foreplay, honed on Mireille, hints at consummation by art.

In Fritz Hart's private retelling of the Mollie Dean story, *James Goes Home to Dinner*, that's pretty much how it does happen, with painter James Montague half-jokingly mooting that teacher Eileen Coote act as his model, and Eileen calling his bluff with a coquettish note.

Dear Mr Montague,

If you really want to see me, as you said you did, I'll be at Flinders Street station – under the clocks – at 8 o'clock tonight. I'm a fool to come, because I know you are a married man; but I'm fed up with things all round – and, after all, what does anything matter? If you are not there by five minutes past eight I'll go straight home like a good little girl – which, by the way, I still am – though for how long heaven only knows – or perhaps you do!

Colahan's skills of seduction were later sketched by Patricia Cole, a 25-year-old with a temporary job at Australia House when they met in London in 1937. 'When he saw a good-looking young woman,' she remembered, 'he immediately saw her as a subject for his painting.' Playful badinage at a party and an invitation to his Notting Hill digs preluded relations in which picture-making and lovemaking were inseparable. 'It was his idea of an enjoyable evening, me perched up on the model stand, him industriously painting, until I got tired and his arm ached, and we went to bed,' Patricia recalled. 'I enjoyed these painting sessions because we talked all the time . . . Colin talked. My God, how he talked. I listened spellbound. I had never met anyone at all like him.' Certainly it was an era with fewer Colin Colahans than Lance Wilkinsons.

There were practical reasons for Colahan to evaluate Mollie's aesthetics. Australian art was proverbially held back by the dearth of adequate models. In August 1917, Colahan had even contributed a cartoon to *The Bulletin* about it: 'When the model doesn't turn up' showed an artist trying to work up a female portrait by dressing in drag to pose for himself. 'The difficulty of obtaining the right kind of model in Australia is only to be overcome by those who are fortunate enough to possess friends, who, in their goodness and unselfishness wish to materially assist in this work,' complained Frederick Reynolds in the journal of the Victorian Artists' Society, with the caveat: 'Care must be exercised by those devoted to the study of the nude for its own sake, lest their good intentions be misconstrued and turned to evil.' But not every painter could be as sternly objective as George Bell, who exhorted his students to think of a nude model as 'lumps of sausages'. Some artists, such as Norman Lindsay, were notoriously possessive of their models; others, like Jock Frater, went so far as marrying theirs.

A particular appeal must have lain in Mollie Dean's origins. The Australian intelligentsia were already rehearsing themes set to endure, of suburbia's stifling materialism and homogeneity – such a contrast to the frontier legend of sturdy settlers and explorers subduing the hostile landscape. 'The suburban home must be destroyed,' Louis Esson had argued in a reverberating essay, 'Our Institutions', published with 1912's *The Time is Not Yet Ripe*. 'It stands for all that is dull and depressing in modern life. It endeavours to eliminate the element of danger in human affairs. But without dangers there can be no joy, no ecstasy, no spiritual adventures.' Esson execrated bourgeois settlement as 'a blasphemy' and a 'moral morgue', inferior even to 'more vivid and picturesque slums'. To Vance Palmer, the suburbs of the 1920s embodied 'the dominance of villadom' over the soulfulness of 'the Bush'; to the historian Keith Hancock, they represented 'comfort without taste', their 'stolid mass' an 'abuse of space'; in the memoirist Graham McInnes, they induced 'a sense of overpowering dullness, a stupefying sameness'. Even when Walter Burley Griffin strove to break that mould in Castlecrag, visitors saw it as encroached on by a rising 'tide of red-roofed ugliness'. Colahan's painting *Suburbia*, hung in the Victorian Artists' Society's 1928 exhibition, required no elaboration of its title.

Now, from this improbable backdrop, like a rare orchid bursting from a privet hedge, a 24-year-old provocateur who lauded Swinburne, quoted Shakespeare, lived and spoke for herself. At one of her first social gatherings with the Meldrumites, Mollie rolled out a test in use with her students. 'There was a puzzle you had to do to establish mental efficiency,' John Farmer recalled. 'She set it for the people at the party. None of us could do it, so we were all mental deficients! None of us could work it out, even Colin and he was pretty clever.' To Francophile Colahan, Mollie would have appealed as the classic *grisette* – that stock figure of the young working woman of Belle Époque bohemia, flirtatious, ambitious, often with her own intellectual pretensions, somewhere in the demimonde between prostitute and courtesan, and incarnate in Mimi in Puccini's *La bohème*, with her 'cold little hand', and the eponymous heroine of *Trilby*, so blasé about posing in the 'altogether'. Colahan must also have felt confident of his ability to contain any dalliance. From his wife and friends he had just managed to conceal an *amour fou* and an *enfant naturel*; a *grisette* must have seemed a bagatelle by comparison.

Forty years after his encountering Mollie Dean towards the end of 1929, Colin Colahan, recently married to his third wife and settled in France, sat down with Eric Westbrook, director of the National Gallery of Victoria, to record some autobiographical impressions on a reel-to-reel tape recorder. Westbrook, studiously courteous, largely let Colahan speak for himself, with minimal direction – an arrangement with which the artist was entirely comfortable. His recollections flowed freely, albeit in words carefully chosen. They became especially well chosen when, at about the 53-minute mark, Westbrook tentatively approached the events of 1929 and 1930.

" WISTFUL AND SWEET "

Bohemian: Du Maurier's Trilby

Westbrook: So, Colin, how long did this good period of some success last?

Colahan: Oh, that lasted quite reasonably well. Then I bought a house in Hawthorn, on the river, lovely place. And there we lived quite comfortably.

Westbrook: Did you have a child by then?

Colahan: Yes, the child was born in Paris.

Colahan, of course, had by then *two* sons, both born in Paris, to different women, although Marc remained an intimate secret.

Westbrook: How did this good period end?

Colahan: It ended rather catastrophically. It ended . . . my wife and I quite definitely started drifting apart. Very much so.

And then . . . I . . . got entangled with a young woman. Very, very attractive, very beautiful . . . *very intelligent.* This became an embroilment which lasted for . . . I think it must have lasted for close on a year.

By September 1969, Colahan had spoken of Mollie Dean to a number of friends: George Johnston's fictionalised version of their relationship had been in print for five years. Yet his answers to Westbrook are the only remarks that survive in his own words. These grow more guarded. 'Could you give a very brief sketch, Colin, of her, of her character?' asks Westbrook at one point. There is a long, uncharacteristic pause. At last he says, almost with a sigh: 'One could say so much.' He doesn't. Rather does he repeat himself, adding only a couple of literary allusions:

> She was a very, very brilliant girl. Very beautiful, and challenging, a challenging beauty. She knew her power with men. And unfortunately she'd fallen in love with me, more than I with her. Although I liked her enormously, and so forth. But she was a girl of . . . she had this challenging beauty. Very intelligent. Almost a Shavian new woman. Very much in those days in the Aldous Huxley line of thought.

Even when Westbrook asks Colahan to identify Mollie specifically ('First of all, let's get her name right'), he shrinks from doing so. Eventually her Christian name rather falls from his mouth, but never her surname. After forty years, the challenge of a story is usually memory – this reticence borders on superstition. For into 1930, Vi Colahan remained unaware of any other woman in her husband's life. In the first week of the year, the Colahans joined a painting and camping holiday at Anglesea with the Leasons, the Skippers, the Tarczynskis, John Farmer and Clarice Beckett. One night Vi sang to the accompaniment of Stanislaw Tarczynski's violin; another, Tarczynski's wife, Jadwiga, read a paper on their Polish countryman Vladislav Reymont, the 1924 Nobel Prize laureate for literature. And for several more months, Vi seems to have abided her husband's frequent trips away in his customised painting van. They were, after all, public: *The Herald*'s 'In Town and Out' column profiled him as the 'caravanning artist', a familiar sight to those who 'have probably envied the young man who apparently had nothing to do but drive about the country and register its scenes on canvas'. The likelihood is that these journeys were not only about painting.

In this period, according to Lena Skipper in her diary, Colahan *did* paint a nude of Mollie, then painted it out when Vi objected to its frankness. Yet there is also a case that something at least similar survives. When Colahan exhibited in April, George Bell in *The Herald* praised a nude for its colour and composition, adding that it was 'suited by its old Italian frame'. The reference can only be to an oil on a board painted to fit an ornate Florentine tabernacle mounting, featuring in full-frontal form a slim, small-breasted, *contrapposto* figure with indistinct features holding a drape or wrap behind her that she appears about to drop. In what is sometimes referred to as *Standing Nude*, the model's hair is parted on the opposite side to Mollie's in that ubiquitous photograph, but this might itself have been intentional, to obscure her identity from inquisitive employers – as we shall see, a consideration. Mirrors were standard in any studio – Colahan showed the artist using a full-length glass in his *Bulletin* cartoon described on page 97.

Whatever the case, the subject's anonymity has remained impenetrable. It might have been the aforementioned Biddy Moloney;

it might have been Mollie, having escaped Vi's disapproving eye. And if the latter, what a heady release, the young woman who hankered for the life of art having been turned into it.

Mollie's infatuation with Colahan was of a pattern: she had always been drawn to men of experience and accomplishment, preferring the likes of Fritz Hart and George Browne to Teddy Sell or Hubert Clifford. The role of *grisette* also came easily. Mollie was partial to the works of the Irish novelist George Moore, whose *A Modern Lover* hinges on the self-sacrifice of shopgirl Gwynnie Lloyd in posing chastely as Venus for her impecunious artist boyfriend, Lewis Seymour: 'I will sit for you, Lewis, since it is necessary; but I am not a bad girl, nor do I wish to be, but it cannot be right to see you starve or drown yourself, when I can save you.' Not that she would have seen herself saving Colahan. It was from the mundanity of her own everyday life she sought deliverance – and with good reason.

Mollie had continued receiving glowing testimonials from her inspectors – 'Keen and interested, makes good preparation and teaches diligently. Doing good to very good work'; 'Very well qualified for her particular work and possessing thoroughly good organising and teaching ability'. Her school life, however, must have been an ordeal. Understaffed, dilapidated and in an area stricken with poverty, Queensberry Street was a veritable display case of worsening education austerities. In April 1926, a capable young female teacher had been badly injured in falling through rotten floorboards into a pit 1.5 metres deep. It caused a flurry when the crumbling buildings, ancient equipment and staff ratio of one male head and eleven female teachers to more than 400 pupils was then reported in *The Herald* and *The Sun* – the latter's headline was simply 'EDUCATION?' Yet as public-sector budget cuts bit, there was not even money to repair glass broken by vandals. Correspondence with the Education Department was a litany of woe: the school's window frames were rotted shut; its stormwater drains backed up constantly because of faulty spouting; its floorboard holes had to be covered by rugs; earthworks for sewerage lines remained unfilled; the school bell was muted by dead pigeons in the tower; a burst pipe had left the head teacher's office uninhabitable and the atmosphere clammy and rank. A report from April 1930 went into Dickensian detail, finding the precincts emanating 'an unpleasant and musty smell', the pine floor 'thin to breaking point', the walls 'smeared with the dirt of years of occupation', and the students near destitution: 'Poverty is apparent, individuals in this poor suburb being ill-nourished, poorly clad and prone to every ailment of childhood. Soup is given to them and on cold days teachers are obliged to bring out the coldest sufferers to get warm at the fire while it lasts and while those at a distance shiver.' Mollie's 'opportunity class' was one of the worst affected, occupying one half of a long room, incompletely partitioned, and farthest from a fireplace. Indeed, it is a measure of the school's abject state that a 1931 Board of Inquiry into education would simply recommend its closure, which duly took place four years later. Little wonder that the purlieus of art and culture looked so tantalising.

Something less material also bound Colin Colahan and Mollie Dean – the elation of secrecy. Colahan was not only a well-known painter about town, but a husband married in the eyes of the Catholic Church. Mollie was not only indentured to the Education Department, but bound to a jealous household of fatiguingly obvious minds. Now they shared something private, heady, volatile, dangerous to them both. Ethel Dean seems never to have been aware of Colin Colahan – the only names with which she was able to provide police were Fritz Hart, as we have seen, and Percy Leason and Mervyn Skipper, whose homes Mollie must have mentioned as social destinations. Ethel was aware of Mollie moving with a 'bohemian' crowd, and that they influenced her thinking: one day, for example, she recalled Mollie complaining that 'it was stupid to have a lot of furniture in a house', preferring 'the scantily furnished rooms and studios in which her artist friends lived'. But whose interior design Mollie had in mind was never specific – a creditable effort on her part when it seems that Ethel's postal surveillances continued unabated. The source of the eventual 'leak', as it were, was not Milton Street but Yarra Grove.

In her subsequent divorce filings, Vi Colahan dated the cooling in relations with her husband as beginning around mid-1927, ascribing it to 'the difference in our temperament and ideas'. Colin's painting pilgrimages took on a different complexion around March 1930 when Vi found 'a magazine with writing in a woman's handwriting in it' in Cunégonde. Vi challenged him; Colin 'laughed it off'; she 'brooded over this'; he consented to a separation, providing maintenance of £3 a week for her and their son, David Michel. Mollie was suddenly anxious – 'tearful and pale' about the 'wretched mess', said Lena Skipper, out of fear for her job should she be identified. But her name did not emerge – except, in a classic instance of hiding in plain sight, on a gallery wall.

Even as Colahan's marriage was disintegrating, his career was coming together. His new exhibition was opened on 1 April in glamorous fashion by the American actor Leo Carrillo, later to endear himself to television audiences in *The Cisco Kid*, but then just finishing a successful season as the guest star in the J. C. Williamson production of *Lombardi Ltd* at the Comedy Theatre. That Colahan's show was bookended by exhibitions of Archie Colquhoun and Justus Jorgensen showed the artistic heights that the Meldrumites now commanded, although the critical welcome was as much about his backing away from doctrinaire tonalism to dabble in impressionism. In the *Herald* review in which he praised the tabernacle nude, George Bell perceived Colahan breaking with 'the rigid precepts of that cult' and exhibiting a 'capacity for design which declines to be submerged'; Colahan himself indulged in a self-conscious joke with a colourful landscape entitled *Meldrum Gloom*. There was another less obvious joke in the 'Chinese proverb' that adorned the catalogue: 'If you have two loaves of bread, sell one and buy a lily.' For on display were three portraits: not only *Vi Colahan*, shortly to move into an apartment in Hawksburn, and *Molly Dean*, the 'other woman', but *Sylvia Vanderkelen*, the other 'other woman'.

Just as Mary Dean was almost invariably Mollie, Sylvia Vanderkelen was usually Sue – perhaps it made her classic beauty and exotic origins more accessible. She was the daughter of François Vanderkelen, a diamond importer from Antwerp who had been Belgium's honorary consul, and his wife, Alice, whose wealthy family had founded that temperance landmark the Victoria Coffee Palace. On Alice's death from appendicitis, François had remarried: blessedly, Sue and her siblings adored their stepmother, Jeanne.

Sue cultivated interests suitable to her social position, and as an arts undergraduate at Melbourne University had encountered medicine undergraduate Colin Colahan, both wandering about in a happy daze for a time, until Colahan peeled off to follow his muse, and Sue left to join François and Jeanne, then travelling in Europe. 'She is a beautiful girl, with a distinctive air of personality and chic,' reported *Table Talk* on her departure. Sue was still that when she returned to Melbourne, but by then Colahan had left, and circumstances conspired to separate them for much of the ensuing decade. It was probably not until after Sue returned from another six-month sojourn in Europe in November 1929 that their paths crossed again, with the complication that Colahan now had both wife *and* mistress. The portrait of her, which Bell praised as 'well composed' and 'convincingly constructed', was at this stage the extent of Colahan's gift.

Sue gazes out from a photograph on the 'When Beauty and Beauty Meet' page of the 1 February 1930 edition of *Home*, as pale and slender as a romantic heroine. 'Miss Vanderkelen is on a visit to Australia' reads the caption. In fact, she never left. On 8 August 1956, the landlord of Little Collins Street's St James Building, worried by her silence, broke down the door of Sue's one-room flat to find her dead in bed of a heart attack aged fifty-seven, with little more than a few sticks of furniture, and a handwritten manuscript in three exercise books inspired by her minglings with the Meldrumites, subsequently lodged with the State Library of Victoria by her devoted niece Margaret Ringersma. The most substantial, 'Sue's Story', pertains to her relationship with Colahan, barely obscured by aliases. Sue is Paula; Colin and Vi Colahan are Simon and Ina Orr; Justus and Lil Jorgensen are Sven and Ann Janssen; Percy and Belle Leason are Cedric and Jenny Dobsen; Merv, Lena, Helen and Sonia Skipper are Garnham, Stella, Diana and Tania Stark; Mireille and Harold Wilkinson are Miranda and Leonard Martin; Mollie Dean, referred to only in retrospect, is Milly Bond. Sue would spare nobody, least of all herself.

At the time of his exhibition, Colahan was wholly in the throes of his relationship with Mollie, captivated by her sexual precocity and intellectual receptivity – he left with her in Cunégonde while the show was underway. 'Poor Colin,' said his friend John Farmer. 'He *did* fall for her.' Mollie was a guest when the Leasons held an Easter party to christen Percy's new Eltham studio. Officially, Mollie was accompanied by Alma Figuerola, another dedicated Meldrumite, and housed in the summer house on a camp bed, sharing the Leason kitchen with Farmer and Norman Lewis, a 28-year-old Agriculture Department analyst with artistic pretensions. But Colahan arrived, and Mollie's presence grew more conspicuous. Her contributions to the camp's 'long talks' irked Lena Skipper: 'One night they talked Shelley and poets until midnight. Molly talked a good deal.' The whole Meldrumite circle seems to have been aware that Sue also loved Colahan, and perhaps out of misgivings about Mollie's irruption looked on sympathetically: in addition to her aura of high birth, Sue had a personal kindness and delicacy that engendered feelings of protectiveness.

On 30 May 1930, Colahan acquiesced in the choreographed infidelity that would permit his divorce to proceed by allowing Vi to report to the court that 'I was present when respondent was found in bed with a woman in the conjugal residence at Yarra Grove'. The woman was not Mollie, to protect her from any employment consequences. As it was for Tony Last in Evelyn Waugh's *A Handful of Dust*, she might even have been a prostitute. There seems to have followed a gathering at the Skippers' where Colahan, as Betty Davies looked on, sat flanked by Sue and Mollie, for Betty recalled the painter giving 'quite a hilarious account of his recent divorce' – Betty recalled her shock, coming as she did 'from a world where the word mistress was never employed and where divorce if it occurred was looked upon as a disgrace'. It may not have been *quite* like that – Betty had a flair for confusing and conflating. Yet her image of Colahan between the rivals for his love faithfully reflects his ménage. Sue 'was very beautiful but seemed subdued and sat with downcast eyes while Colin proceeded to enlarge on one of his wildly improbable ideas'; Mollie, 'dark-complexioned, sultry-looking', sat with a 'petulant expression on her face and kept on interrupting' until Colahan 'rather sharply told her to be quiet'. Betty believed that Sue 'inwardly . . . felt she was no match for Molly and was playing a losing game'. Indeed, in 'Sue's Story', Paula recalls Simon as at this stage 'quite crazy' about Milly, confiding that this 'wonderful creature' is 'a girl of almost masculine pride and independence – a girl in a million!'

Yet nor could Mollie have felt relaxed. No sooner had she cajoled Colahan into moving on from his moribund marriage than another woman had hove into view. Was this how it was to be? The dynamic expressed itself soon afterwards when Mervyn Skipper invited Mollie to the theatre. Mollie declined, suggesting he 'ask Sue' instead. Mervyn put this down to Mollie's faithfulness to Colahan; Lena was less impressed, and suspicious of Mollie's other efforts to be friendly. 'She is a capricious lady, likes to put down and take up as she pleases,' wrote Lena. 'She is giving her time to the women now as she is probably Colin's mistress, and is very conscious of the fact, or if we know.' Betty Davies observed that in response to Colahan's rebuke Mollie left her chair to join 'the other women seated round the fire'. It was unusual for Mollie to accept such a demotion. The reproof must have smarted. To this gifted man she had become a mistress. But what did that really mean?

7

THE VISIBLE WOMAN

'Youth, youth – nothing but youth!'

– Dulcie Deamer, 1923

The 1920s were a decade of unexampled female visibility. War, commerce, suffrage and popular culture had dissolved the Victorian construct of the 'New Woman' into a range of tantalising typologies: the Modern Woman, the City Girl, the Business Girl, the Vamp, the Flapper. Brute statistics played a part: five years of male mass casualty had left an excess of marriageable women in much of the western world. More subtly, urban and industrial growth were intensifying women's occupational and social proximity to men. Australians took note. To the actor Oscar Asche, 'the Australian girl' was a source of patriotic satisfaction. 'It is a fact that I am prouder than ever of being an Australian every time I see an Australian girl,' he informed *The Triad* in December 1923. 'There are beautiful girls and happy girls and friendly girls in other parts of the world, but the Australian girl has a quality altogether her own. She is independent, she is courageous, she is natural, she is vital, and, above all, she is sincere.' To the wife

of Prime Minister Bruce, Australian women exuded emergent promise as citizens. 'What strikes one as the result of observations in other
countries is the high intellectual capacity of Australian women, their
courage, and their self-reliance,' she told readers of *Woman's World*
in January 1925. 'In a comparatively new country such as Australia,
women play a far more important part than in most of the older countries. It therefore behoves them to take a greater interest in public
affairs, for in this sphere there is much that concerns them, and much
that can be accomplished.'

The young, in particular, looked startlingly different. A tubu-
lar, almost androgynous look was in vogue. Hair was being bobbed.
Hemlines were rising to reveal stockinged calves. Introducing beauty
contests to Australia in 1922, Melbourne's afternoon daily, *The Herald*,
knew exactly what it was looking for: 'The beauty of today is beauty
unschooled and unrestrained. The perfect oval face is today considered formal and lifeless; it is as far from favour as the demure bearing
and the downcast eyes of 50 years ago.' More contentiously, women's
right to libidinal pleasure was asserted by the likes of Marie Stopes
and Havelock Ellis, even if it was not widely assented in. For male
prerogatives were not to be lightly surrendered, and female objections
were embedded also: many altogether serious women regarded sexual
freedom as degrading, even as an obstacle to emancipation. In the end,
as so often, stereotypes spoke loudest: a stock character of cartoonists
was the slimlined party girl, mercenary and materialistic; her *épater le
bourgeois* conversation was a subject for merry verse:

> She formerly talked of the weather,
> The popular book, or the play;
> Her old line of chat
> Was of this thing and that

In the fashions and fads of the day.
But now she discusses eugenics,
And things that a pundit perplex.
She knocks you quite flat
With her new line of chat,
And her 'What do you think about sex?'

Such clichés have stood the test. From the vantage of nearly a century later, 1920s Australia presents as a nostalgic feminist montage: Dulcie Deamer's leopard-skin and dog-tooth ensemble; Margaret Preston's jaunty *Flapper* with her bare knees and plumed hat; intrepid aviatrix Amy Johnson beside her Gypsy Moth in flying helmet and jodhpurs. But for Mollie Dean, being a woman of her time contained more complex entailments.

From the Dean crime scene, police gathered and inventoried a variety of objects. Mainly these were items of Mollie's clothing and jewellery scattered on the footpath: her black coat, her red beret and scarf, her wristlet watch, its band broken. There were also contents that had spilled from her black patent-leather handbag with its red facings, consisting of a purse, some letters, newspaper cuttings and school papers, and various publications. All the foregoing were dutifully reported, some news outlets troubling to identify the literature in question as an illustrated French magazine, an English–French dictionary and *Main Street* by Sinclair Lewis, who had just become the first American awarded the Nobel Prize in Literature. The only item logged that newspapers shrank from noting was a 'rubber pessary', found half a metre from the bloodstained gate of 5 Addison Street, where Mollie was felled. Yet here was a telling signifier, of the need for a young, unmarried, sexually active woman of 1930 to take responsibility for her fertility. After all, someone had to.

The pessary was a contraceptive device, comparable to a diaphragm, usually either a metal cap or an indiarubber ring. The former required insertion by a doctor. Indeed, the pessary would surge to fame in the first line of Chapter 3 of Mary McCarthy's scandalous 1963 novel *The Group*, when Dick Brown, having deflowered Dottie, gives her brisk instructions. 'Get a pessary,' he says, only for her to hear it as 'peccary', so that 'a vision of a coarse piglike mammal they had studied in zoology' crosses her drowsy mind. When she looks puzzled, Dick elaborates minimally: 'You get it from a lady doctor.' Victoria's chief secretary, Arthur Rylah, regarded the ensuing medical passages as so obscene that he excluded them from a denunciation of *The Group* in parliament in March 1964 to justify its seizure by the vice squad under the *Police Offences Act*. 'Needless to say, I will omit some portions,' he explained, before citing others to demonstrate that there was 'a pretty thin line between what is plain pornography – good clean dirt, as one of my friends refers to it – and this pornography which is supposed to be submerged by some literary merit but which to my mind is usually fairly hard to find'. With a quiver of rectitude, Rylah concluded: 'Do we want the youth of our community to be depraved and corrupted by this filth? I say firmly: we do not.'

Thirty-three years earlier, contraceptive methods were more or less publicly unutterable. It was forbidden to advertise condoms, daring to stock them, dicey to possess them: 1930 was the year in which William Empson was famously sent down from Cambridge after a servant found prophylactics in his college room. The pill was not even an ambition. In her pioneering pamphlet *Family Limitation*, Margaret Sanger enjoined women to overlook niceties. 'It seems inartistic and sordid to insert a pessary . . . in anticipation of the sexual act,' she agreed.

'But it is far more sordid to find yourself several years later burdened down with half a dozen unwanted children, helpless, starved, shoddily clothed, dragging at your skirt, yourself a dragged-out shadow of the woman you once were.' The indiarubber version, after all, required little or no medical assistance: in his 1924 guide *Birth Control*, Austrian campaigner Johann Ferch noted that 'a skilful, intelligent woman can introduce it herself after the doctor has done it several times'. Yet contraception remained a fiercely contested concept. The Christian position, at the time more or less monolithic, was summed up by the British medico Halliday Sutherland: measures to prevent conception were 'contrary to the laws of nature and the process of physiology', and 'incompatible with the progress of civilisation'. As for pulpits so for parliaments. When a health minister in New South Wales tentatively suggested in September 1928 that persons suffering serious diseases be instructed in birth control, he was assailed for preaching an 'unchristian and immoral doctrine' and 'desecrating the marriage tie'; Sydney's Catholic archbishop argued further that contraception 'should not even be mentioned in conversation', and was certainly 'too delicate for newspaper controversy'.

How Mollie came by her knowledge, in fact, must remain a mystery. It is especially hard to imagine its passing down by Ethel. Mothers were nurturers but not educators. 'Never let a man touch you' was the only advice that Mollie's friend Clara Behrend recalled from her mother, and her sister Elsa laboured into her twenties under the belief that kissing could cause pregnancy. Yet the stark warnings also had an underlying logic. The wages of unprotected sex could be severe. Venereal disease pullulated freely: gonorrhoea killed 34-year-old Katherine Mansfield in 1923, and so ravaged 28-year-old Sunday Quinn in 1929 as to preclude her from children with second husband John Reed. When Betty Davies found that her husband, Ellis, had contracted gonorrhoea in Kalgoorlie, she withheld conjugal relations, to his mounting fury.

Termination, meanwhile, had all the hazards of illegality: in the 1920s, Victoria's coroner investigated 172 deaths explicitly related to abortion, and numberless others implicitly related. The detective who would look into Mollie's death, for instance, had just been commended for his investigation of a body wrapped in a Gibson blanket in a field in Langwarrin. So decayed were the remains that it was necessary to interview 250 dentists before identifying teenage farm girl Irene Argent from a recently filled incisor – said tooth is still part of her inquest file at the Public Record Office. Irene, working as a domestic in Hawthorn, had disappeared after wiring to break a date with a friend in May 1929: 'Going under an operation . . . Will write as soon as possible'. It transpired that she had fallen pregnant by a young railway porter who had organised with another railway porter who 'knew of a place', a sympathetic baker providing £30. Yet somehow the coroner felt unable to make a finding 'on the evidence adduced', and police looked no further – Irene, deemed just another girl who had paid the price of her foolishness, was not even dignified as a statistic. One of the first facts police wished to establish about Mollie Dean from her post-mortem examination was whether she was pregnant – it would have made for an excellent motive. They were disappointed when the pathologist reported that 'the uterus was normal'.

If Mollie sensed the potential consequences of ill-omened pregnancy among the Meldrumites, she was probably right. Whether it is based on her own experience or an imagining of the likely reaction, Sue Vanderkelen's 'Sue's Story' includes a sequence where Paula believes herself pregnant and turns to a briskly pitiless Simon Orr:

'Seen a doctor?'

'No.'

'Then go and see a medico at once, you idiot; go today and if he confirms it, well, you know what to do. No need to worry these enlightened days.'

Paula sat down, feeling a sudden rush of nausea.

'Of course, you could have the child,' Simon went on, 'and if your respectable old dad kicked you out, penniless, there's always the dole.' He was still touching up his portrait, his back to her.

She stared at him incredulously. Surely he was only acting and in a minute he would bow mockingly and they would both laugh . . . but no, it was no subject for burlesque and mirth and she stared at him in terrified disbelief . . .

It was a bad dream, then, from which she would wake, in a minute, thankful that it was but a nightmare? But it was no nightmare to end in relieved wakefulness. It was real enough. She had seen that ruthless, brutal quality in Simon before, in relation to Ina [Vi] and Milly [Mollie], but she never imagined that it would come her way, this unpitying denial of all concern, responsibility and affection.

A few years later, after the remaining Meldrumites had followed Jorgensen to their new redoubt at Montsalvat, the Skippers faced a double dose of unwed motherhood, both their teenage daughters falling pregnant: Sonia to new disciple Arthur Munday, then Helen to Jorgensen himself. Sonia recalled the hastily improvised response, beginning with Munday's comment: 'Oh, you will have to get rid of it.' She was shocked: 'Did he mean I should have an abortion? Well, I wasn't going to be in that.'

Yet even the master, concerned about his reputation, was prepared to disown her: 'He [Jorgensen] talked away for ages, and as far as I could make of it, it had nothing to do with my problem, nobody bothered to ask me what I thought or felt, apparently that didn't count.' But then, with one bound, Sonia was free: Helen was pregnant. 'Now it would appear as a calculated idea,' Sonia recalled. 'Society would see how, with responsibility and forethought, a man in his situation with an invalid wife and a mistress, with their children, could live in a reasonable way, devoting their energies to the furthering of his work yet living a fulfilling life themselves.' That disregarded pessary, then, was what stood between Mollie and the contingent masculine moralities of her age.

Mollie's birth control was not mere prudence. It extended to philosophy, which the circle she had joined rejoiced in discussing. The group shared a provincial sense that ideas happened somewhere else, that travel was a necessary formative experience. But the freight on 'progressive' notions was surprisingly cheap. Mervyn Skipper's eclectic reviewing and Lena Skipper's chatty diary offer guides to the books circulating among them. Enthusiasm for a handful of works aside, their embrace of local literature was at best half-hearted, but excitement attended the bold new works of Evelyn Waugh, Wyndham Lewis, Evadne Price and Aldous Huxley. When Colahan described Mollie as 'very much in those days in the Aldous Huxley line of thought', in fact, he probably had in mind Lucy Tantamount, the slim, dark-haired sexual cyclone who whirls through *Point Counter Point*, sweeping up helpless men like so many dry leaves: 'What he wanted was Lucy Tantamount. And he wanted her against reason, against all his principles, madly, against his own wishes, even against his own feelings.'

One book both Skippers read and that Mollie perhaps borrowed from them was *Marriage and Morals* by the British polymath Bertrand Russell. Lena recorded a conversation with Mollie verging on the ecstatic: 'She [Mollie] said she only enjoyed Colin because of his mind and she said if she met someone with a greater mind she would leave him for them. She hoped to meet Bertrand Russell the old and wonderful writer in England. She said she would unite herself with him physically and mentally.' *Marriage and Morals* arrived in Australia around the time Mollie met Colahan, was widely debated and freely denounced. The well-scuffed copy in the State Library of Victoria, dated December 1929, has been scrawled in by multiple hands: 'Of course!!' and '??pure shit!!' cry from the margins. And it would have exhilarated a 24-year-old woman determined to live her own life.

'She should unite with him': Bertrand Russell

Time has dealt unkindly with a number of Russell's pronouncements in *Marriage and Morals*. He looked tolerantly on communism, and on eugenics. In succeeding editions, he walked back a little on 'negroes on the average are inferior to white men', although he stuck by 'women are on average stupider than men', which he defended to his publisher with the comment that 'the habit of flattering women does a lot of harm'. Yet it was not these views that contemporary critics discountenanced. Rather was it Russell's opinions of marriage, which in some respects are relatively conservative, for he was concerned chiefly to preserve it from the march of science and reason. The insistence on absolute fidelity in the marriage bond, Russell claimed, was a 'mutual prison'. But the purpose of marriage as 'the best and most important relation that can exist between two human beings' remained the vital one of providing children with a secure and nurturing environment: 'I think that where a marriage is fruitful and both parties to it are reasonable and decent, the expectation ought to be that it will be lifelong, but not that it will exclude other sex relations.'

Marriage and Morals is an exceedingly quotable book, from Russell's express desire to 'cleanse sex from the filth with which it has been covered by Christian moralists' to his almost poetic conclusion: 'To fear love is to fear life, and those who fear life are already three parts dead.' One can imagine Mollie nodding her head at Russell's approval of prenuptial sex and deprecation of existing balance of gender power: 'Modern feminists are no longer so anxious as the feminists of thirty years ago to curtail the "vices" of men; they ask rather that what is permitted to men shall be permitted also to them.' Russell can also be a decidedly funny writer, as when he envisions two possible futures, one in which taboos relax further, one in which they are suddenly retightened. His *reductio ad insanitatem* of the latter involves requiring not only 'very severe censorship upon all books giving information on sex subjects' but the eradication of contraception, the imprisonment of all unmarried women found not to be virgins, the removal from young women of 'all opportunity of being alone with men', and the 'castration of all policemen and all medical men'; for absolute safety he concludes: 'I am inclined to think that moralists would be well advised to advocate that all men should be castrated, with the exception of ministers of religion.' The kicker is a droll footnote: that since reading *Elmer Gantry*, Sinclair Lewis's satire of evangelical hucksterism, Russell has 'begun to feel that even this exception is perhaps not quite wise'.

Despite this, there was no doubting Russell's serious intent. As *Marriage and Morals* was being publicised and pilloried, he was coming to terms with his activist wife Dora being pregnant to a journalist, Griffin Barry, while he was shortly to embark on a relationship with his family's nanny, Peter (Patricia) Spence, who would bear him another child. Dora was to have a second child with Barry before bitterly and protractedly divorcing Russell. So where the Skippers merely noted reading *Marriage and Morals* and continued their conventional bourgeois marriage, there was something perceptive about Mollie's intuitive response to the book – *Marriage and Morals* was, as one Russell biographer has put it, a 'personal testament through and through'.

It may also have been reading Russell that prompted Mollie to try her own hand at philosophy in May 1930, when *Verse* published an essay by a Brisbane poet, Llewellyn Lucas, criticising Australian poetry for its philosophical shortcomings: 'Among the old masters, philosophy is the element in their poetry which keeps them alive . . . Where is our philosophy of south, and of the sun, to be sung to the world?' Mollie's studiously handwritten response forms part of the papers of her old editor, and one-time visitor, Louis Lavater.

'A work of art is distinguished from mediocrity not by its subject but by its content,' Mollie challenged. 'Thus of fifty pictures of the crucifixion, only one might be a work of art; of a hundred fugues on a given theme, none but Bach's; and of a thousand poems on spring not one! Yet the subject in each case has been the same.' It elaborates the view she shared with A. E. H. Nickson about the matter mattering, elucidated by quotations from *The Tempest*, *Love's Labour's Lost* and *The Song of Songs*, invocations of Plato, Kant and her perennial favourite, Swinburne, with the occasional Russellesque jest: 'As well say poetry survives because of the mathematics or cookery contained in it.'

Lucas was an ironic target – she had written Lavater in praise of the 'fine unity and atmosphere' of Mollie's 'Merlin'. But the aspiring essayist, not to know that, carried through her argument. 'Our selection of a subject is a human selection, motivated by sex, curiosity, melancholy due to indigestion, or what not,' wrote Mollie. 'But the instant the poet commences to write, he is no longer interested in his subject per se, only the definition and presentation of it. As long as the subject remains interesting to him, so long he is a philosopher, or a field naturalist, or a lover, or a psychologist – and not a poet.' How Mollie would have enjoyed kicking 'Subject and Content' around with Bertrand Russell. She was never to see it in print.

It was not only convention that Mollie found herself pitted against; it was unconvention too. To the ranks of the Meldrumites, she was a unique addition: young, bold and a bit barefaced, a misfit by gender, class and youth in being a woman who worked outside the home at a time it still in some circles engendered pity and contempt. Her manners were modern. It was said of her that she could not pass a telephone without thinking of someone to call, regardless of the time. It was thought of her that she had rather much to say for one so young, irrespective of her addressee. And for all their self-conscious *épatage*, the Meldrumites observed social conventions reflecting their leeriness of modernism. Women were fetchers, carriers and cleaners, and certainly not co-creators. Meldrum himself believed that there 'would never be a great woman artist' for women lacked 'the capacity to be alone'; he was once heard to praise Hitler for having 'given women the freedom to be women'. Colahan was barely less dismissive. 'Colin's opinion of female intelligence was not, on the whole, very high,' noted his later lover Patricia Cole. To be fair, the generalisations of both men always excepted fellow tonalist Clarice Beckett, with whom Colahan once contrasted Mollie in terms favourable to both, likening the former to Jane Austen, the latter to George Sand. But other men found Mollie disconcerting. She asked Mervyn Skipper about a job at *The Bulletin*. Nothing came of it. She asked Justus Jorgensen about painting lessons. He refused. Colahan's other friend John Farmer, rather chastely married to Polly Hurry, fifteen years his senior, thought Mollie 'a very queer girl', albeit 'very good looking' and 'with that charisma, they call it now'. Her embrace, he told a later interviewer, felt like a come-hither: 'Molly Dean came up and put her arms round my neck, and I said "Molly, you can't put it over with me." She was that type, you see. I said: "It won't work with me, Molly." Because she was mixed up with quite a number [of men] . . . But I was married and I was quite happy thank you.'

About this, funnily enough, not everyone agreed, Farmer being a handsome young man, and Hurry, tied to their home in Olinda, often appearing something of an old maid. Some years earlier in Paris, Farmer had had a brief and panicky fling with a model. It had not ended well. Betty Davies would recall being invited to dine at Pangloss sometime in 1930 with what emerged as the express intention of pairing her and Farmer off. After Colahan and Mollie retired, that did not end well either:

> We sat rather awkwardly before the fire. I was disappointed, John was nervous, and the prospect was not promising. That the whole thing had been planned did not occur to me till Molly opened the door and threw the eiderdown, quilt and two pillows. 'There you are,' she said. 'I hope they'll be enough to keep you warm all night.' Whatever chances poor John might have had were ruined by this ill-chosen remark, so I went, leaving him alone to wrap himself in the eiderdown and spend the night alone.

Yet the discontents were probably greater on the distaff side of the Meldrumites. The circle had always incorporated young women – Chica Boileau, Maude Rowe, Alma and Silvia Figuerola, Archie Colquhoun's sister Elizabeth and future wife, Amalie Feild. But about Mollie – a little too pert and too partial to male company – there developed abiding misgivings. Kindly Belle Leason, whose husband, Percy, consented to teaching Mollie to paint in his Eltham studio, was sympathetic to her stories of a harsh home life. But Betty Davies' views fluctuated, partly because of her affection for Sue Vanderkelen, partly because she was wrestling with her own promiscuity. Lena Skipper, meanwhile, could hardly mention Mollie in her diary without disparagement, defending this when her husband accused her of jealousy: 'I was only protecting myself in my own way.'

Mervyn's wife was a peculiar mix of altruism and aloofness. 'She takes the smallest cake and the toughest chop on the dish,' noted Mervyn. 'The soul-searchings, the self-analysis, the struggles to rise above themselves of the poets, the artists and the writers are utterly incomprehensible to her, though she does not blame them. She feels towards them as she would feel towards a bewildered and unhappy child.' Actually, children rather perplexed Lena too. She was a brusque and irritable mother, viewed the Leasons' growing brood with distaste, and thought the institutions of maternity ripe for reform: 'The future will see children all in homes and only those who can afford it will be allowed to keep them at home, especially among the lower orders. This, I think, will work out quite well under understanding matrons.' Nonetheless, Lena possessed a surface equanimity that seemed to invite confidences. She listened calmly; she enjoyed knowing. But the more she knew of Mollie, the less she liked.

Initially, Lena found Mollie 'most candid and frank', and 'very clever and interesting to listen to as she expresses herself so well and weighs all she says', while noting she also devoted 'most of her attention to men' and that the fascination was mutual. 'She [Mollie] told me frankly all the men in the end are only interested in sex and her sex-life, which she freely says has not been virginal,' Lena recorded in her diary. To unravel this 'feminine conundrum', she had growing recourse to cod psychoanalysis:

> Molly, to my mind is afraid of many things. She is afraid of her mother, she is afraid of love (legitimate), she is afraid of public opinion, she is afraid of rich people, she is afraid to break away and travel alone . . . Is she to go on from one flirtation to another, she asks desperately? She knows that sex is a gradual development; the unfolding of a rose, and she must bask in some man's love for years in order to develop mentally and physically and get sex and all her other world[s] into their right relations. She told me she had only met two men she ever cared for, presumably Colin and, we hear, Fritz Hart. But he already has an established mistress.

Why isn't it Molly? Somewhere she fails. She certainly isn't a mascot.

Mollie attempted to form a friendship with Lena, telephoning her, inviting her shopping and to the cinema. Lena found the gestures cloying, attempts to 'wheedle' into her good graces by a young woman who did not know her place. 'She used to stay up all night and talk to the men when the other women, who were wives, wanted to go to bed with them,' Lena complained, with a none-too-subtle assertion of her wifely rank. 'As a matter of fact, Molly was only tolerated for Colin's sake. All we women hated her habit of squeezing into other people's lives.'

By the middle of 1930, relations had quietly soured. One night, when Mervyn brought Mollie to Eaglemont en route to the Leasons, Lena realised that cordiality dictated they have their visitor stay for dinner. She rebelled, insisting that Mervyn drive Mollie the rest of the way. 'I could not bear even being polite to her,' Lena wrote. 'In spite of the fact she asked me to lunch and rang me up and invited me to go shopping I never gave her an inch.' Lena was usually a reticent diarist. 'Every woman is a Mona Lisa,' she would say. But where Mollie was concerned, she made an exception, conscientiously recording any unkind comment, such as Leason calling her 'a bit thin and no cutey', Norman Lewis deeming her 'cold and not maternal', and the view of 'some women' that she 'repulsed them' by being 'so selfish'. Her own descriptions of Mollie were likewise edged with hostility: 'She looked a virgin; she looked a barren woman; she did not want children, she hoped she would never have one'; 'Her feet were broad and her hands large and capable and ill-bred.'

When the diaries were recovered from a rubbish pile at Montsalvat forty years later, the depth of Lena's animus surprised her old friend Betty. She struggled to reconcile Lena's habitude of 'serene benevolence' with 'the venom displayed in her account of Molly'. It is curious, too, that Lena should have quibbled about Mollie's maternal instincts when her own were so muted, and for Mollie joining conversations she had also felt excluded from ('I get a little tired of their continual art talk and would sometimes like to hear other opinions from a girl'; 'Personally I am rather tired of it all as I play no part but sympathise and listen'). But perhaps there was the rub: that Mollie aired the discontents Lena was disposed to suffer. 'She has a strong character and wants what she wants badly,' Lena diarised. It was a criticism. Women were not meant to want but to nurture and provide – however, in Lena's case, grudgingly.

For her part, Betty Davies rather approved Mollie's pushiness amid women otherwise 'content to sit silent in the background, cook and serve food and do the cleaning-up while the men sat around and drank and argued noisily'. Mollie *never* cleaned up and *always* sat with the men, noted Betty: 'Her rival for Colin's affections, Sue, was very beautiful and that was something I admired, but Molly held my interest. She was ruthless and, I felt, might be dangerous, but she was never dull.' Yet she also felt Mollie 'a predator, a mischief-maker, flitting restlessly from love affair to love affair', even if that description would in a few years affix readily to her. Again the rub, that unwed Mollie coveted openly what married Betty for so long could pursue but furtively.

Perhaps, though, Betty also had a nose for danger. Just then, another impatient young schoolteacher was undergoing the experiences that she drew on for her 'portrait of a liberated young woman'. In Dymphna Cusack's *Jungfrau*, Thea MacKinley would be destroyed by the consequences of an affair as doomed as it is passionate, despite the risks, despite the warnings:

'I can't give it up, Eve. I've got as much right as anyone to get something out of life. I'm 25 and I've got nothing. My life's empty . . . I thought it was just a lovely accident this affair. But now I know it's part of a new philosophy I've consciously worked out. I'm going to take life – use it – now, instead of letting it use me. It's taken me twenty-five years to work that out, which really means I've spent eight years getting over being educated.'

'You're really only paraphrasing Nietzsche, darling,' Eve said slowly, 'and I don't think it's going to work. These things are much safer in books.'

8

MONSTERS NOT MEN

'To ladies who would be writers, he says, "Marry a man with money, and then lay in a supply of typewriter paper and begin work on your masterpiece."'
– H. L. Mencken's 'Advice to Young Authors',
The Triad, 1 April 1925

In Australia, 1930 dawned dark and grew darker. Weak markets for primary products weakened further; slack conditions for employment continued slackening, forcing the jobless onto Melbourne's streets in April. In May, the annual loss to national income was put at £50 million; in June, the annual loss to share values was estimated at £100 million. It was not only the challenging nature of his art that restricted sales at Justus Jorgensen's July exhibition to £130. The Athenaeum was crowded for the opening, by Florence Austral and John Amadio. Mervyn Skipper provided a stentorian review of the works, Colahan a witty evening address about realism in art. But nobody was buying – there was no longer the money to be had.

When Colahan hosted his peers at Pangloss afterwards, Lena mourned: 'I thought what tragedy sat round that little table in intellect and talent, the best Australia can produce, but not a penny between them; living in a world of misunderstanding and lack of sympathy.' Not a penny was an exaggeration; their prospects, though, were clouded. Under the pall of his impending divorce, Colahan faced losing his home and custody of his son. Mollie, Lena noted, 'was there as usual, worried over sex and her position as his mistress'. But she had also taken a considerable step. Having been 'discontented' at Milton Street, as her mother would delicately put it, she had found a 'quiet place': a furnished room in a small private hotel in Collins Place.

Virginia Woolf's *A Room of One's Own* had reached Australia late the previous year. If Mollie read it, she would have identified with Woolf's statement that 'a woman must have money and a room of her own if she is to write fiction' – this was precisely her intent. She was devoting her evenings after work to writing a novel: sometimes, she told Lena Skipper, she fell asleep over its pages. Older friends reported losing touch with her in this period. Mollie had little spare time and certainly no spare money: to assuage her mother's misgivings, she was continuing to send 30s a week home in lieu of rent. But nor could she go on emulating Jane Austen, whom Woolf recalled as writing in her sitting room and covering her work with blotting paper in the event of interruption. 'There must be freedom and there must be peace,' insisted Woolf. 'Not a wheel must grate, not a light glimmer. The curtains must be close drawn.' Mollie would surely have agreed.

Of the novel, next to nothing is known. Colahan never read it. Fritz Hart recalled Mollie commencing at least two works of fiction, abandoning a first, which he thought showed 'very considerable promise' but 'was not working out too satisfactorily', in favour of a second, 'which she thought would find greater favour with publishers' but which she 'kept entirely to herself'. Betty Davies remembered

similarly that Mollie 'would let nobody see this thing', and that the
only person to read any was Lena Skipper, who cluelessly picked
up and perused the manuscript one day to the author's intense irri-
tation: 'Mollie could have killed her.' Confusingly, however, Lena
referred to 'someone . . . who read a little', who reported the characters as 'too hard and inhuman, in fact Monsters'. In that sense, at least,
the manuscript lived up to the title, which is all of it that survives:
Monsters Not Men.

In setting verse aside for fiction, Mollie was ahead of an emerging
curve. Between 1917 and 1927, twenty-seven novels and eighty-seven
volumes of verse were published in Australia; from 1928 to 1939, the
ratio was virtually reversed, 106 versus fifty-seven. Half of these were
by women, granting them a share of cultural life unmatched in any
other art form. Quite right too, thought Vance Palmer. In 'Women
and the Novel' in *The Bulletin* in July 1926, he had argued encour-
agingly that the novel was particularly suited to the female mind.
Women, he claimed, had a natural eye for detail, an affinity with
stories and a 'gift for loose, flowing narrative'; writing a novel seemed
'as easy to almost any literate woman as making a dress'.

What Palmer overlooked, of course, was that dressmaking was
the better-paid activity. The local literary market was minuscule, the
domestic economy stagnant. 'The best Australian writer,' lamented
Verse's Percival Serle, 'has not a dog's chance of making a living under
present conditions.' For a woman writer, the predicament was sharper
still. Woolf imagined the writer in her cosy nook ideally endowed by
£500 a year. Nettie Palmer, productive as she was, earned barely half
that; most a fraction of it. The vast majority depended largely on the
subsidy of either a marriage, such as Nettie's to Vance, Eleanor Dark's
to a general practitioner and Katharine Susannah Prichard's into a
successful mercantile family, or a job, Marjorie Clark and Doris Boake

Kerr subsisting on office work, Marjorie Barnard as a librarian at Sydney Technical College and Flora Eldershaw as a resident mistress at Presbyterian Ladies' College Pymble. Seeming to have exhausted the possibilities of the latter, Mollie began toying with the former.

Mollie had never appeared the marrying kind. The example of her parents had been no inducement. Cousin William, son of her uncle Peter, had contracted a turbulent marriage to Gladys, at one time duelling in court for custody of their daughter Lavinia. Cousin Jean, daughter of the Blyths in Addison Street, was widowed in July 1930, the death of her 36-year-old husband from a lung infection leaving her with an infant son to raise alone. Mollie had been an eyewitness to the estrangements of the Harts, and maybe also the Webers; she was privy to tensions between the Davies, the Jorgensens, the Farmers, the Lavaters; she had, of course, hurried the Colahan marriage to its ignominious conclusion. So what made her conceive of Colin as a potential husband? Perhaps it was the one way she could secure him from the allurements of Sue Vanderkelen, and ward off her mother's patronage of Adam Graham. It was also simplifying. There would then be no need for furnished rooms to write in, no need to obscure her features when she posed for Colahan, no need for dodging about in dark corners generally. The inspiration may have been *Marriage and Morals*, where Bertrand Russell had advocated 'companionate marriage', recently popularised by a Colorado jurist, Ben Lindsey: a kind of union devised to stabilise relations between the young who wished for sex but not, at least immediately, children. In the event the partners did not change their minds about children but did change their minds about each other, divorce would require no more than mutual consent. Russell had thought it 'a step in the right direction' that would 'do a great deal of good', and his wife had writ-ten the foreword to Lindsey's new book. *The Companionate Marriage* ran an inevitable gauntlet of disapproval, Lindsey being identified by an angry congregation in New York's Cathedral of John the Divine, beaten and ejected. But where gauntlets were concerned, Mollie was an instinctive runner.

It was easy afterwards to regard Mollie as a woman obsessed in her craving to be Colahan's bride, who loved too ardently and too desperately. Betty Davies would describe her as having 'decided he [Colahan] should marry her', and that 'no matter how firmly he repulsed her she came back, pleading and cajoling, playing on his vanity, not scrupling to make use of every feminine wile in her con-siderable range'. But there was a practicality to her ends that eluded Davies, whose writing was underwritten by her wealthy husband. Mollie loved Colin – as she once acknowledged to Lena Skipper, more than he her. Her urgency around marriage, however, was as much about shelter for her work as for herself. She was not like Vi, who would be assigned the family home in the property settlement with her ex-husband, or Sue, whose private income allowed her to paint, and sew, and act as treasurer for the local auxiliary of the Women's Hospital. Mollie dreamed of a literary career in a country where John Shaw Neilson, whose verses she had so admired, calcu-lated his annual pittance from poetry as 'six shillings and eightpence', and where not one woman lived by her pen alone.

Marriage, of course, was far from Colahan's thoughts. His decree absolute was still to be granted. Mollie was first and foremost a foil. Publicly, Colahan referred to her as his 'Sergeant-Major'. At a party at Eaglemont, Mollie's insistence that everyone keep quiet while her lover held forth on art led indirectly to his nearly trading blows with *Table Talk* artist Frederick Ward. Privately, Colahan was less available.

After all, there was Sue, gracile and sympathetic. One confused and confusing night in September, Mollie rang the Skippers to invite Mervyn to dinner. Mervyn said he already had plans to dine in town with his wife, but that Mollie was welcome to join them; Mollie, at last perhaps leery of Lena, declined. But when the Skippers arrived at the Italian Club, Mollie was in the company of what Lena called 'a young man with eyes like a bookie's clerk'. A somewhat uneasy four-some ensued. When Mervyn and Lena left, they ran into Colahan and Sue 'both looking like gay young fauns walking down the street'. The Skippers nudged them in the direction of another cafe lest they 'run into the Sergeant-Major with her man'.

Not long after, the open road beckoned. Colahan was destined to lose Pangloss but still owned Cunégonde, and it occurred to him that there might be a market for his works in Adelaide. Percy Leason decided to hitch a ride – Belle was pregnant, somewhat gloomily, with their sixth child. Packing provisions and paintings for an exhibition organised by Mervyn Skipper's brother, they held a farewell party. Pervaded by a sense that this might be the last big gathering chez Colahan, it went off. Mollie and Sue cooked – 'very nice eats', said Lena. But the alcohol drained fast as the atmosphere grew wilder and noisier, requiring Mervyn to drop Colahan, Leason and John Farmer at a notorious source of late-night alcohol, Stokes Hotel on Beaconsfield Parade. Since the death of his erstwhile partner, Squizzy Taylor, Henry Stokes had been Melbourne's kingpin of two-up and sly grog, and it happened that the artists arrived just ahead of a police raiding party. Leason and Farmer dashed into a toilet cubicle, clos-ing the door behind them; Colahan came up with the story that his friends were staying in the hotel and that he had followed them into the gents to finish an argument. In the event, the police ignored them, although the story made for a breathless retelling when the trio were reunited with Skipper after he had made his umpteenth circle of the block.

Colahan and Leason were away almost the whole of October, taking ten days over their leisurely outward leg through Ballarat, Beaufort and Hamilton with regular stops for relaxation and repair, stopping one radiator leak with paint rags. By night they feasted on Colahan's favourite curry, of garlic sausages, dates, bananas, bacon, onion and apples, and also spent an evening with the Heysens at their property in Ambleside. Results of the exhibition at the Society of Arts Gallery on North Terrace, however, were commensurate with neither Colahan's effort nor his reputation. Fifteen hundred visitors came; not one of the forty paintings was sold. He delivered a lecture on 'The Nature of Realism in Painting' with typical *éclat*, as 'Magpie' of *The Observer* reported: 'He took us through art with a breath-taking swoop like . . . well, I haven't tried the scenic railway, and the big dipper, but from descriptions I believe it must be something like that.' Yet the Art Gallery of South Australia ignored the show, despite Colahan significantly reducing his prices. The experience was costly and chastening. And in his absence, Mollie seems to have moved on in her thinking.

The hint comes in Colahan's 1969 interview with Westbrook. Colahan related that Mollie had, in his words, been 'trying to make our relation more closer tied' prior to the exhibition, even though he had 'no intention of doing so'. And although 'the liaison renewed itself more or less in the old way' on his return, Mollie appears to have thrown down a challenge: 'She made no effort to conceal, in fact, rather *affiched* [flaunted] that, during my absence, she had sought consolation.' Colahan, he claimed, was mainly intrigued as to who Mollie might 'go for', as a counter to his intelligence: 'And I said: "Now, who would she get hold of? I know, a muscle man." That was just a thing that flashed into my head.' The reference to Clarence Weber is unmistakable, for Colahan elsewhere describes the man as 'a very flashy socialite gymnastic teacher, very much in society, you know, champion swimmer and all this sort of thing'.

If Mollie did seek 'consolation' from Weber, in order to inflame Colahan's jealousy, it can only have been briefly: press reports indicate that Weber was also in Adelaide most of that month. So the conjecture about Weber must remain just that. Yet the broader inference is that in Colahan's absence, and around her twenty-fifth birthday on 14 October, Mollie had taken stock of her prospects, and was casting round for alternatives. By now she was back home. It was never going to work. She was ever short of money, time, respite. At this rate, *Monsters Not Men* would never get written. At the start of November, Mollie visited another old confidant, her former mentor George Browne. Mollie asked advice about 'lodging an application for three months' leave of absence in order to try her hand at journalistic work'. If all went well, Mollie said, she would take it up full time.

Mollie was thinking ahead, for she talked to others of heading to the United Kingdom – for writers a well-trodden route. Australia's outstanding female novelists, Miles Franklin, Henry Handel Richardson and Christina Stead, were all expatriates: Stead's *For Love Alone* would centre on the intellectual frustrations of a creative young woman bored by school teaching, who quits Australia for fear of being 'forgotten by the world and drying up in the chalk dust'. In April, Mollie as a member had probably attended the Society of Australian Authors' farewell of the zesty Myra Morris, shortly to ship for London: Morris, whose serial 'Enchantment' in the *Australian Woman's Mirror* had just been well received, enjoyed an affair with the captain of the *Jervis Bay* on the way. In May, Mollie had seen the last of her old admirer Hubert

Adventuress: Myra Morris

Clifford, who was leaving for London on the *Largs Bay* never to return: he was being followed by his intended, Marie Phelan, whom he had not long met. In slightly different circumstances, Mollie could have featured in either or even both of these adventures.

At other times, the future seemed almost close enough to touch. More exciting than Phar Lap winning the 1930 Melbourne Cup was joining Colahan that evening at the Essons' Victorian villa on Chrystobel Crescent, Hawthorn. This prestigious invitation had come through Hilda Esson's boss and Colahan's friend Dr John Dale, with the poet Bernard O'Dowd, his partner Marie Pitt, and Nettie Palmer in attendance. Nettie, in fact, warmed instantly to Mollie, thinking she looked 'eager and girlish in her tight red jumper that went so well with her slim athletic figure and olive face'.

Neuritis had cost Louis Esson, once the lion of Australian drama, his roar. He now wrote little, and spoke slowly in his high-pitched cockney twang. But the creator of *The Time is Not Yet Ripe* and *The Drovers* was perhaps the realest 'writer' that Mollie had yet met, his study musty with the smell of old books, including facsimile first editions of Elizabethan dramatists. The conversation ricocheted between art, literature and politics, Colahan free with his anecdotes and asperities, particularly about Betty Davies' former lover Frank Russell – now *The Herald*'s London correspondent, Russell had just followed unctuous profiles of Hoover, Hindenburg, the Pope and others with a fawning appraisal of Mussolini.

The world was so big. And London: somehow it seemed the centre of everything. The Colahans and the Essons had lived there; Vance Palmer, like Hubert Clifford and Myra Morris, was there now; Meldrum, despite being virtually penniless, was desperate not to return to Australia and 'be once more chained up in that convict settlement'. Yet Mollie also read her *Bulletin*, where Mervyn Skipper was praising Clarice Beckett's latest exhibition for its uniquely Australian vision, its scorn for 'conventions which earlier artists had brought from Europe', and where Nettie Palmer was lamenting the conga line of creators departing Australia, their losses a 'sort of national artistic and literary suicide'. So much to think on; so much to decide. Nettie watched Mollie appreciatively, noting her quiet eagerness to be part of things: 'Half worried about a paint stain on her flaring black silk shirt, half glad it was paint, not domestic grease. Listening to the talk about pictures with a still alertness as if she had escaped from a suburban background into an exciting new world. Now life begins! This is what I've been looking for!' Such youth, such optimism – perhaps a brilliant young writer in the making. But the permissibility of such feelings would seem shortly to drain away. A week later Melbourne was convulsed by a savage murder.

On Monday 10 November 1930, two unemployed youths, in search of some goldfinch hatchlings for which they had found a buyer, stopped at a derelict house on Wheatley Road, Ormond, to use the lavatory. Inside they stumbled on a female body, covered by a coat. The hands were folded across her breast. Her bloomers were heavily soiled. A gag made from her singlet was tied around the back of her head. They fled, returning with police.

Eleven-year-old Mena Griffiths, one of a family of twelve stretched thin by unemployment, had been strangled to death. On Saturday afternoon Mena had been approached by a short, middle-aged man in a blue suit while playing with her younger sisters by the joy wheel in Fawkner Park, a large common between Punt and St Kilda roads. He gave the other girls a penny each, and offered Mena ten shillings if she would run an errand for him. No concern was felt at home until Mena failed to return for the evening meal; a police search ensued. A widow told detectives she had seen a man and a girl on a bus on Commercial Road just before 5 p.m.: 'The child seemed very worried and agitated and made a remark that "she must be home by 8 o'clock". And the man replied, "That will be all right. You will have a good feed and return by car."' The widow thought she saw them get off then board a bus for Ormond. Investigators immediately intuited a suspect. All they had to do was find him.

Raw memories remained of the rape and strangulation of twelve-year-old Alma Tirtschke in the city's grim Gun Alley, for which Colin Ross had been hanged in April 1922. Police had taken careful note of similar offenders since, such as Robert James McMahon.

A year after Ross's execution, McMahon, working as a truck driver
and boarding in Essendon, was arrested for the 'carnal knowledge' of
a thirteen-year-old in Buckley Park. According to Detective Henry
Carey, McMahon smartly copped to the crime: 'I am relieved this
has happened. I was just on the verge of a nervous breakdown. I do
not know what came over me to do such a thing . . . It could have
been worse. Had the girl died I'd have been a second Colin Ross.'
McMahon denied the confession and pleaded not guilty. It was an era
in which such disputes tended to resolve only one way. In November
1923, McMahon was sentenced to seven years and to two twelve-
stroke lashings in the first four months of his incarceration.

Incarceration disagreed with McMahon. According to a Criminal
Investigation Branch file note: 'We were informed that when
McMahon was in gaol for a similar offence he had stated that when
he was released he would commit a similar offence that would be
"worse than the Colin Ross case".' It then happened that he had been
released from Geelong Prison on 17 October 1930 and had been seen
in the vicinity of Fawkner Park soon after, and also that Detective
Carey was among the pursuers of Mena Griffiths' killer. Mena's
sisters and others described the kidnapper as a dishevelled figure with
lank hair, greasy clothes and rotten teeth: it certainly sounded like
someone who had done time. In fact, McMahon was innocent, even
if his excuse strained credulity: on 22 October, he had started walking
to Sydney. The affidavit he later swore is a rugged artefact of life on
the road during the Depression: camping by roadsides, hitching rides
on trucks, picking up casual jobs, cadging baths in hotels to remove
the day's grime. On the weekend of Mena Griffiths' death, McMahon
obtained a lift into the country town of Leeton with an orchardist,
attended a salvage sale, tried selling a fan he had picked up on the
roadside, and conversed with some cubs playing cricket on a parade

ground ('I wished their little organisation the best of luck. They said "thank you" and they walked away again'). A week later, by now in Temora, he was recognised in the post office from a police bulletin, and arrested for vagrancy. Detectives Carey and James Bruce undertook a 1080 km round trip in a police Daimler – 'at speeds averaging 30 mph [about 50 km/h]', *Truth* reported excitedly – to fetch him.

Yet under rigorous questioning, McMahon's denials remained steadfast. More importantly, eyewitnesses failed to recognise him in a line-up. While unable to keep him, and forced to cover his train fare back to Temora so he could resume his broken journey, the police still harboured deep suspicions – indeed, they were far from done with their seedy suspect. But by the time McMahon had left the city the second time, the public were reeling from a murder still more violent, more mysterious and more shocking.

9

DAMNED IMPUDENT SLUT

'What's to become of me? What's to become of me?'
'How the devil do I know what's to become of you? What does it
matter what becomes of you?'
        – George Bernard Shaw, *Pygmalion* (1913)

It was Act 4 of the Gregan McMahon Players' evening mati-
nee of Bernard Shaw's *Pygmalion* at the Bijou Theatre on Thursday
20 November 1930. The audience had already laughed gustily at Henry
Higgins' spirited gamble ('I shall make a duchess of this draggletailed
guttersnipe') and Eliza Doolittle's lusty profanity ('Walk! Not bloody
likely. I am going in a taxi'), no less indecorous for it having been
seven years since the play's first Australian production, and seventeen
since its premiere. They had enjoyed the three-way interchange with
Higgins' foil, Colonel Pickering.

> Pickering: [*in good-humoured remonstrance*] Does it occur to you,
> Higgins, that the girl has some feelings?
> Higgins: [*looking critically at her*] Oh no, I don't think so.
> Not any feelings that we need bother about. [*Cheerily*] Have you,
> Eliza?

Eliza: I got my feelings same as anyone else.

Higgins: [*to Pickering, reflectively*] You see the difficulty?

Pickering: Eh? What difficulty?

Higgins: To get her to talk grammar. The mere pronunciation is easy enough.

Eliza: I don't want to talk grammar. I want to talk like a lady.

But now the play had come to that point where the co-conspirators return from the ball having accomplished their ruse of passing Eliza off as a duchess only for her to tackle them about the future. Where is she to go now, she asks, that her role in their game is over? 'You know I can't go back to the gutter, as you call it, and that I have no real friends in the world but you and the Colonel,' Eliza exclaims. 'You know well I couldn't bear to live with a low common man after you two; and it's wicked and cruel of you to insult me by pretending I could.' Higgins professes a cavalier indifference to everyone and everything, before softening: 'I have learnt something from your idiotic notions: I confess that humbly and gratefully. And I have grown accustomed to your voice and appearance. I like them, rather.' The sense of displacement and insecurity. The dismissive asperities, the stifled endearments. What a play for Mollie Dean and Colin Colahan to see after their tumultuous year.

It had not even been their idea. Betty Davies, a subscriber to the productions of McMahon's troupe, had posted Mollie the tickets: she had exchanged cross words with her husband about his dislike of her arty friends, then taken to her heels and retreated to the Gippsland Lakes. The Leasons were at the Bijou also, taking in the comic fury. Yet, to Mollie at least, it must have sounded like a version of her own dilemmas with Colahan.

Eliza: If I can't have kindness, I'll have independence.

Higgins: You damned impudent slut, you! But it's better than snivelling; better than fetching slippers and finding spectacles, isn't it? By George, Eliza, I said I'd make a woman of you; and I have. I like you like this.

Not enough for them to end the story together, of course. Higgins is not for changing. 'Women upset everything,' he complains. 'When you let them into your life, you find that the woman is driving at one thing and you're driving at another . . . One wants to go north and the other south; and the result is that both have to go east, though they both hate the east wind. So here I am, a confirmed old bachelor, and likely to remain so.' So would end the lovers' last night together: Colin Colahan going one way, Mollie Dean another, not to meet again.

The reasons for that are obscure. Perhaps they even were to the protagonists. Conversation had looped between them about Mollie leaving teaching behind to progress her writing. Colahan demurred. Perhaps he was conscious of his own financial vulnerability; perhaps he sensed the motive detected by Lena Skipper's gimlet eye: 'I was wondering if she was trying to compromise him by gradually making herself indispensable to him if she got leave from school, where she would write under his willows, of course. Her belongings were gradually left at his house.' The court had concluded Colahan's divorce during his absence in Adelaide, so the only remaining obstacles to marriage were emotional. But these were most formidable of all.

An expert if not disinterested perspective was that of Sue Vandekelen. In 'Sue's Story', where she narrated the end of her own subsequent affair with Colahan through the attenuating affections of

'Paula' and 'Simon', Vanderkelen clearly saw the history of his relationship with 'Milly Bond' as having repeated, a love object becoming a
liability: 'With the advent of Paula she [Milly] had begun to close in on
Simon, and Paula had seen his recoil and the subsequent brutality that
sent her slavishly following him like an imploring ghost.' She looked
back on the day that 'Simon' had 'made it very clear to her that his
feelings for Milly Bond were dead'; she recognised that her own relationship had now gone through the same cycle. 'Simon,' Paula observed,
'wanted to be charmed, not worried by a mistress's complaints.'

Paula's conclusion about Simon – implicitly Vanderkelen's conclusion about Colahan – was that he preferred forming rather than
maintaining relationships: 'His longing for the admiration and love of
women seemed to her like the avidity of a man who had known abject
poverty in the world of emotional love, now obsessed with the need to
compensate – a need that seemed insatiable, as if life itself was impossible without constant reassurance.' Simon lived by sucking the life
from his lovers: 'It was as if he could not feel quite sure of a woman
until she was half dead; and when she became a pale, tortured shadow
of her former self, he would turn his attention to another potential
corpse.' The inference is that Mollie's killer was more or less finishing
a job; the victim was 'half dead' already.

There are also indications that the urgency of Mollie's needs had
a further proximate cause, in a recent worsening of the atmosphere at
Milton Street. There was no sympathy at home for Mollie's thoughts
of writing full time. If Ethel remained unaware of Colahan, even
she could sense Mollie's agitation – and she had no interest in alleviating it. 'Molly . . . was an exceedingly brainy girl – too brainy, in
fact,' she would complain to a reporter later. 'She was always writing,
always saying she wanted to be a journalist. The company she kept
seemed to have turned her head, and for six months before her death

she was pale, listless and preoccupied, and seemed to be worried over something. The idea of a Bohemian existence was always in her mind.'

In Mollie's mind, too, was the continued presence of Adam Graham. Since buying a single-seater Amilcar in March 1929, his pervasion of the household had taken on a curious extra dimension. He would park each night in front of the Deans, remove the hood ornament, place it in a bedroom, or on the hall stand or wireless cabinet, have his 'cup of tea', and at evening's end walk home. His justification would be that illumination was poor outside his own house, and he had lost one hood ornament to souvenir hunters. It is one of those oddities of evidence decidedly difficult to interpret. It could have been an innocent idiosyncrasy; it might have been a staking-out of territory; Graham would concede that a new light had recently been installed nearby his family home, obviating the need for the practice; he was simply in the habit. Whatever the case, Mollie appears to have been contemplating moving away from Milton Street for a third time. In her handbag that night at the theatre were 'Rooms Vacant' columns clipped from newspapers.

In the last fortnight of her life, then, Mollie was teetering, both personally and professionally. On a visit to Queensberry Street, George Browne spoke to her head teacher, Harold Tate. Tate told him that Mollie's work had lately been 'very unsatisfactory', specifically in punctuality, and that 'he might have to report her to the department'. Mollie's old mentor took it up with her. 'What is the matter with you?' Browne asked. 'You are damaging yourself and you are spoiling this class.' Mollie burst into tears. 'I should like to tell you all about it,' she said. 'I shall come over to the college and see you there.' She never had the opportunity.

Yet, like dinner at the Essons', there remained soothing distractions from the diminuendo of Colahan's attentions. On 17 November,

Table Talk's prestigious Christmas edition included Colahan's still life *An Autumn Bunch* alongside W. B. McInnes's *Sweet Nell of Drury*: a pictorial extravaganza, the issue also featured photographic studies of Melbourne from Alexandra Avenue, basking beneath a summer sky, and lit up by night like a lantern. On the following afternoon at the Town Hall, Mollie watched Colahan deliver a lecture on Australian art with all his by-now-familiar fireworks: local painting was 'falling back to the primitive ideas', most artists were 'of a mediocrity', all works had to be the subject of 'international valuation', to which only Meldrum measured up. Mollie left Milton Street at 8 a.m. next day airily advising that she would not be home that night although not what her plans were – and there was to be one final, very striking collaboration.

Colahan's painting *Sleep* may have been inspired by a painting of the same title by the teacher on whom he had turned his back. Bernard Hall's *Sleep*, a lush exercise in British aestheticism, had been a *succès de scandale* in 1906. In a rerun of the brouhaha in Melbourne over Jules Lefebvre's *Chloe*, it caused the magazine *The Lone Hand* to be sued for indecency; the National Gallery then acquired the painting for an extraordinary 300 guineas. But where Hall's formality of design seems to preclude any hint of the lascivious, Colahan's *Sleep* exudes a truly post-coital stupor, Mollie curled almost foetally, skin aglow under a tight artificial light; and it was the fruit of Mollie's last stay at Pangloss that Wednesday night.

Perhaps it was also an attempt on Colahan's part to soothe matters between them. What with her lamplit literary toils, Mollie had found sleep hard to come by: Lena thought she looked 'tired around the eyes', George Browne that she appeared 'very tired and worn out'. An image of rest, of peace, of satiety, was something life might conceivably imitate. Meanwhile, Colahan told her, they were to be joined the following night at the theatre by the Leasons, the Skippers and also Norman Lewis. Was introducing more company another form of distraction, a gesture at easing their taut relations, or both?

On arriving at Pangloss from school late Thursday afternoon, Mollie set to preparing an evening meal of chops and Spanish rice. The guests arrived, dined, conversed cordially, then rose from the table to go. At this point, Lena, with her usual precision, observed a piquant interchange between the hosts – one at odds with her earlier observation of Mollie 'trying to compromise' Colahan. Colahan seems previously to have advised Mollie that it would not be convenient for her to stay that evening. But when Mollie gathered other of her belongings, including a red skirt and white blouse, and said she would take them home, Colahan reached under her arm and tossed them on the floor. 'No,' he insisted quietly. 'Leave them here.' All the pushing; now the pulling. Just like Henry Higgins.

After travelling into the city in the Skippers' car, the party split into three. Lena and Norman Lewis were deposited near Princes Bridge, heading for another Shaw revival, *Arms and the Man*, at the Playhouse on Flinders Street; Mervyn sought out *The Seekers*, a comedy by Aubrey Danvers-Walker, at the Kelvin Hall. Arrangements were made to reunite at the Leasons' car, which was parked near an Eastern Market grocery, W. Franz. First out of their evening's performance, Lena and Lewis sat gossiping and eating oranges for twenty minutes. The evening was mild, but it was after 11 p.m. by the time the group was returned to strength by Mervyn Skipper's arrival in his car, and the farewells were hasty: as she and her husband commenced the trek to Eaglemont, Lena saw Mollie place a parting kiss on Belle Leason.

With Colahan and Lewis, Mollie then strolled back down the hill to turn left into Swanston Street. As they approached the St Paul's corner, Mollie turned their conversation from the play to her perennial subject of writing for a living. During that last five minutes, Lewis recalled her saying, with an undertone of reproach towards Colahan: 'I wish to God I had not to go home. I want to spend all my time writing.' Then, with a start, Mollie realised that her train would shortly depart for St Kilda, and she broke with a hurried goodbye. Her trim figure in a green floral dress disappeared beneath the clocks of Flinders Street railway station. Colahan and Lewis adjourned to a tram stop to await the Number 48, which deposited Lewis at Hawthorn Bridge, then Colahan at St James' Park, from where Pangloss was a fifteen-minute walk.

Out of the station, the locomotive swung left to South Melbourne, threading through Albert Park then Middle Park. Behind Mollie burned the city lights, laid out like the tableau in *Table Talk*. Ahead lay a house in a humdrum street that Mollie could hardly call a home. Perhaps she huddled in her woolly black coat with its astrakhan borderings. Perhaps she dipped into *Main Street*, the tale of plucky college-girl-turned-doctor's-wife Carol Kennicott, who 'in the tense stalking of a thing called General Culture' sets out to beautify and enrich their kitschy hick town of Gopher Prairie. It is a novel of yearning, mainly unrequited, but also undismayed. 'Oh, is all life always an unresolved but?' Carol wonders, before sweeping her son off to Washington: 'We're going to find elephants with golden howdahs from which peep young maharanees with necklaces of rubies, and a dawn sea colored like the breast of a dove . . .' Freedom and empowerment beckon, although at the end there is also solace in security. First Eliza Doolittle, then Carol Kennicott: potential augurs were everywhere that night. Which may be why when

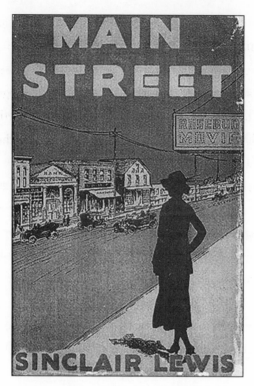

'An unresolved but': Lewis's *Main Street*

the train terminated around 11.45 p.m., Mollie did not immediately seek the tram that ran along Grey, Barkly and Mitford streets, and would in fifteen minutes have deposited her round the corner from 86 Milton Street. Instead, later identified from her red beret by a boarding-house manager, she paused on a bench next to a middle-aged woman, probably to give time for Colahan to make his way home. Then, around midnight, having composed herself, she adjourned to the station telephone box.

The act of the call itself seems to have been more significant than the content. Mollie had felt inhibited by Lewis's presence in her last conversation with Colahan; indeed by all Colahan's hemming and hawing around her future. She craved something resembling

a commitment from him. Approval for her plan of pursuing a writing career would at least be an acknowledgement; it might even put
them on something resembling par. Lifting the handset connected
her to a night-shift telephonist in the Windsor Exchange in Prahran.
'Hawthorn 5176 please,' she said. Edward Rider repeated the number
aloud for a colleague to log in a night book, then made the connection
while Mollie stood by with her 2d.

By Colahan's account he heard his telephone ring even as midnight's chimes were striking, and was delayed by his key jamming in
the door. He may also have hung subtly back, for he'd have known
at once whom the call was from – Mollie was no respecter of hours.
Of course, only his version survives of their first, brief conversation
recorded by the exchange as commencing at 12.04 a.m. 'It would be
difficult to remember it word for word, but I can give you the gist of it,'
he told counsel at the inquest:

> She said she was ringing from St Kilda, but did not say what
> place. She said she wanted to discuss the matter of obtaining
> leave from school. She asked if I did not consider it advisable
> to apply for six months' leave as she intended taking up journal-
> ism. In my opinion journalism at the present time is a precarious
> existence, and I tried to dissuade her. I said it was not a good idea.
> She tried to convince me it was a good idea. I pointed out it was
> impetuous and foolish to make an application at the present time
> with the holidays coming on.

At that point, Colahan recalled, Mollie 'rang off'. His recitation
packs a good deal of detail into a dialogue that can have lasted
little longer than ninety seconds. This being an emotional as well
as an intellectual dispute, the temper of the conversation sounds

understated, especially given its abrupt conclusion – and though Colahan suggested Mollie ended it, this seems doubtful. In fact, in Rider's statement, Mollie remained on the line:

> At 12.06 a.m. I said to caller 'did you get them?'
> Caller answered 'I want them again.'
> I then connected caller to Hawthorn. The caller in each instance was a female. As far as I can say the caller *did not hang up* between the calls [my italics]. When caller asked to be connected again I assumed she had been disconnected.

Whatever the case, Mollie was put through once more, and in Colahan's words 'tried to reopen the discussion'. He continued: 'I again calmed her with the same point of view. She then suggested she should go to my house the following evening to discuss it, but I told her it would be impossible as I had made other arrangements. She seemed particularly disappointed.' As well Mollie might have. Colahan was neither asked about nor volunteered these 'other arrangements'. But it's hardly unlikely he was trysting with Sue Vanderkelen, and that Mollie suspected same. The inquest would hear Colahan detailing his last conversations with Mollie as the sensible male dealing with an impractical, even hysterical woman: he called her, in fact, 'a very impulsive girl' who 'used to ring me at all hours and discuss all sorts of problems'. It ignored other possibilities, including that he was a practised philanderer sequencing his assignations, coolly succeeding one lover with another. Colahan put the conversation at between five and eight minutes, concluding with his advice that Mollie should 'sleep on it', although he would have known she had before, and that his unmindfulness would sting – a rejection of Mollie's writing was implicitly a rejection of her.

For this she had wished. For this she had waited. For this she had now missed the tram, which had left on time at 12.11 a.m. With only threepence in her purse, a taxi was out of the question. Her only choice was to walk – an ignominious conclusion to an evening that had begun with such promise. Mollie began on a familiar route down Grey Street, bearing south into Barkly Street, where at about 12.25 a.m. three young labourers noticed her 'walking smartly' on the western side, but with a handkerchief to her eyes, 'as if she had been crying'. She passed the Victory Theatre on her right, and the Village Belle Hotel on her left, at both of which her mother had come to spy on her – reminders that this was a decidedly involuntary homegoing.

The police originally supposed that Mollie had caught the tram, a conductor having thought he recognised her, and that her telephone call to Colahan had been from South St Kilda Post Office. This opened the possibility she had loitered in the vicinity of her home for a rendezvous. Their minds were changed by others who reported seeing Mollie. But those accounts were also confusing. The labourers described 'a man in a blue suit' who might have been following Mollie just over ten metres behind her; the boarding-house keeper had already referred to 'a man in a grey suit, no hat' lurking by the St Kilda railway station; a third witness, a bookmaker, saw 'a young lady' striding along Mitford Street between 12.25 a.m. and 12.35 a.m. wearing 'a green frock' but 'no coat' with apparently nobody following her. There was a new moon overhead. As Mollie approached home, the streets grew leafier, the pavements emptier, the illumination paler. People were looking; not necessarily seeing. Nothing about the night distinguished it from any other.

As Mollie passed out of Mitford Street, she was in the heart of Elwood's Poets' Corner, making for Milton Street by striding along

Dickens Street, past the mouth of Ruskin Street into Addison Street – all those names, savouring of a culture of centuries, on which one day she might make her own tiny mark, if only she could find the time, the succour, the serenity. Had she made it to the end of *Main Street*, Mollie would have been among the millions moved by Carol Kennicott's last blast, as she returned to her marital home after the 'inevitable tragedy of struggle against inertia' but unregretful and defiant: 'I've never excused my failures by sneering at my aspirations, by pretending to have gone beyond them! I do not admit that Main Street is as beautiful as it should be! I do not admit that Gopher Prairie is greater or more generous than Europe! I do not admit that dishwashing is enough to satisfy all women! I may not have fought the good fight, but I have kept the faith.' It might have momentarily uplifted the writer of an incomplete novel, lover of an unavailable man, the liver of an unfinished life. Her route took her past Knights Court, an apartment block; just then, law clerk James Nankivell switched on a lamp in the uppermost flat and opened a window. As Mollie looked up, light fell on her fresh, young face; as she receded into the dark, light caught the figure of a man in fawn trousers following on the otherwise empty roadway at a distance of about 20 metres. Both seemed to be heading for Addison Street. But Nankivell flicked the switch, returned to bed, and like the overwhelming majority of his fellow citizens quickly fell asleep.

Nothing but the *Truth*: *Truth* poses the questions about the murder of Mollie Dean that police were never able to answer. The mythmaking had already begun.

Age of innocence: second from right in the back row (top), alongside her friend Joyce Pyke, Mollie Dean poses with the editorial committee of University High School's *The Record* in 1920. Soon she would follow her father into teaching, with Sidney Nolan among her school's pupils. Might the bust in Nolan's *Brighton Road State School* (below) be his posthumous tribute?

The female figure I: the model for Colin Colahan's *Standing Nude* is unidentified, but thought to be Mollie Dean.

The female figure II: Colin Colahan used Mollie as a model for his painting *Sleep* the night before her death. He hurriedly disposed of the painting.

The Bulletin

Vol. 51.—No. 2650.

November 26, 1930.

FEAR.

"If they don't mean any harm, why do they say such dreadful things!"

Consequences: Percy Leason's political cartoon 'Fear' took on different connotations when it was published in the week of Mollie Dean's murder.

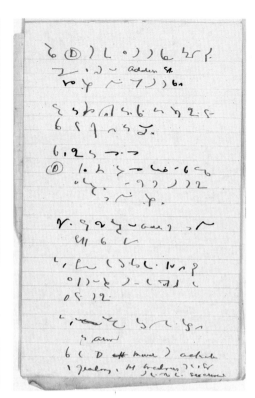

First on the scene: the shorthand notebook of Hugh Buggy, reporter extraordinaire, who covered the case for Sydney's *Sun*.

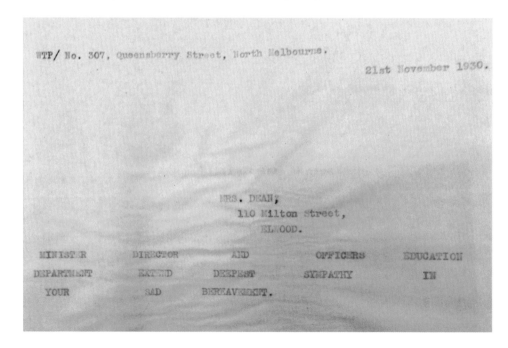

'Your sad bereavement': the Education Department offers condolences to Ethel Dean. She exhibited little sign of needing them.

'Many rows about men': the titillating details of the inquest filled the front page of Buggy's *Sun*.

Scenes from an inquest: Sadie Fields (left) and Ralph Dean (right) arriving at the inquest.

Accused and witness: mechanic Adam Graham (left) and his client Gladys Healey (right). They married seventeen years later.

Mollie on the screen: in George Johnston's *My Brother Jack*, Mollie Dean
and Colin Colahan became Jessica Wray and Sam Burlington. In the
1965 television adaptation by Johnston's wife Charmian Clift, Jess
(Tessa Mallos) palled around with Jack (Ed Devereux) (above) plus
Johnston's alter ego David Meredith (Nick Tate) and her lover Burlington
(David Copping) (below).

Mollie on the stage: Molly Dean (Martelle Hammer) under the gaze of
Colin Colahan (Jared Turner) in Melita Rowston's 2002 production
of *Solitude in Blue*.

Mollie 'at rest': the Dean
family plot, Brighton
Cemetery, today.

10

BLOOD IN THE LANEWAY

'They say all the world loves a lover – apply that saying to murder and you have an even more infallible truth.'
– Agatha Christie, *The Murder at the Vicarage* (1930)

As Mollie Dean passed 5 Addison Street at around 12.40 a.m., her assailant came from behind and fractured her skull above the right ear with what was probably a tyre iron; then, as she fell, he hit her again, cracking and exposing the bone above her left eyebrow; her bloodied hair brushed the picket fence. Whether he was the trailing figure, or had lain in wait in the house's recessed gate, the killer made the most of his opportunity; he undertook the rest of his task with similar deliberation, dragging Mollie's disabled figure by the ankles to the west side of the street, leaving marks in the dust, and down a diagonal laneway – the bluestone laneway behind the home of Mollie's uncle Daniel and aunt Emily, by then long abed. Even today it is a dark lane, and about 6 metres in, to the right, a brick wall forms a prow that obscures an old garage door and a patch of concrete from street view.

The hail of blows was furious; they also formed part of a methodical subjection. The killer tried using Mollie's underskirt to secure her hands, and one of her dark stockings, tied in three strong knots, to attempt a strangulation.* He tore at her clothing, leaving a profusion of scratches and abrasions. Then, in a macabre apery of the sex act, he plunged his tyre iron or equivalent into her vagina, inflicting a superficial internal tear. This took time, but he must have felt he had it – until, perhaps, he was disturbed, for he left his victim just alive. Chances are he moved off down the laneway, emerging in Milton Street, from where it was only five minutes on foot to the canal – useful for the disposal of a murder weapon.

At about 12.55 a.m., Beatrice Owen of 5 Addison Street was awoken by groaning. Her mother, Isabella, thought it might be local cats; her brother Fred dismissed it as a dream. But from the veran-dah of the family's bungalow, the human origins of the sounds across the road grew more apparent, even through a screen of cypress trees. Going to the gate, Fred spied the belongings on the pavement. The moans were from the laneway opposite. He threw on clothes and dashed for South St Kilda Post Office to call the police from its phone box. One of Victoria's half-dozen radio-equipped patrol cars, cruising near Luna Park, was directed to the address, and pulled up just before 1.30 a.m. And as Constable Alfred Guider followed the bloody drag marks across the road and down the laneway, his eyes made out a shadowy supine form.

Mollie Dean lay prone on the concrete, legs spread-eagled, dress and chemise pulled up to expose her breasts, bleeding from her head and vaginal wounds, and exhaling further blood with every insens-ible noise. She was clearly in urgent medical need. Having summoned

---

* There is disagreement about which stocking was used to strangle Mollie Dean. Constable Alfred Guider insisted that 'the right stocking was missing' and she was 'wearing left one'; hospital orderly Carl Burroughs recalled that 'the right-hand stocking was still on'.

the civil ambulance, Guider drove to 26 Broadway, surgery of Arthur Crowley, the local GP; while the doctor hastily dressed, the constable also knocked up his near neighbour Percy Lambell, a detective in Russell Street's Criminal Investigation Branch, who lived at 1 Broadway. In the interim, Guider's colleague had draped Mollie's coat over her; she had fallen ominously silent.

When he arrived just ahead of the ambulance at 2 a.m., Lambell examined items from the victim's handbag. Purse; powder puff; clippings about rooms to let; geography papers to mark; letters pending reply. One of these, from Betty Davies, which had contained the tickets to *Pygmalion,* was addressed to 'Mary Dean' at 86 Milton Street, Elwood. Once Mollie had commenced her journey to the Alfred Hospital, the detective rounded the corner in search of the address. The house was dark. A car was parked outside beneath a covering. A dog barked at Lambell's knock.

Detective Jeremiah O'Keeffe: 'Does any man visit this house?'

Ethel Dean said later that scrabbling at the gate had disturbed her at about 1.15 a.m., and that she had lain awake since, expecting Mollie any tick of the clock. The policeman surprised her – and also did not, for she had, she would claim, always worried about her daughter's hours. 'My name is Senior Detective Lambell,' said the policeman. 'Is there a girl named Mary Dean who resides here?' Ethel said yes.

'Is her father in?' Lambell asked.

'No,' said Ethel. 'He is dead.'

'Well, your daughter has met with an accident in Addison Street and we want you to come to the Alfred Hospital,' Lambell explained. 'Does anyone else live here with you?'

'Only my son,' Ethel answered.

'Where has your daughter been tonight?'

The reply was edged with iciness: 'I do not know. She has not been home since Wednesday morning when she left for school. Go and ask Percy Leason or Fritz Hart. They very likely will be able to tell you. I know nothing about her doings.'

Lambell asked if the car outside, covered by a carpet, belonged to Ethel's son – the idea of a woman of Ethel's age driving being clearly absurd. When she reported that it belonged 'to a man who lives up the street', Lambell offered her transportation to the Alfred. Ethel walked down the passage to the back verandah where Ralph slept and roused him. By the time the patrol car arrived, her mood had deteriorated: she was, said Lambell, 'very aggressive', insisting that everyone squeeze up to accommodate Ralph, and rummaging in a bag containing Mollie's effects. Advised that this was evidence, she asked crossly: 'Well, what have you done to find out who did it?' Lambell explained patiently that the vicinity was being searched. He noted that Ethel had moved unconsciously beyond her information that an 'accident' had befallen her daughter, that she was assuming an offence and an offender.

Mollie was admitted to Ward 7 of the Alfred 'unconscious and extremely shocked'. Her clothing was removed, her head shaved, the stocking round her neck cut away. Her eyes still reacted to light, but she was bleeding from multiple wounds, and the extent of her head injuries was shocking: *Truth*, ever picturesque, would liken the state of Mollie's skull to 'an eggshell when it is crushed by a spoon'. Her breathing was stertorous, a broken bone in her trachea having caused one of her lungs to deflate. Her face was bruised and swollen, her pulse thready, her blood pressure weakening. It astonished medical staff she had survived at all. She should be dead already. They monitored her fight for life as best they could.

When she and Ralph arrived, Ethel's condition was also closely monitored. The duty doctor and night sister noted that Mollie's mother never asked what had happened to her daughter, or to see her, remaining in the visitors' room. She asked the latter only whether Mollie was 'disfigured at all'. Her concerns were allayed. Otherwise, attempts to involve her in conversation elicited a jumble of impressions. 'I have not seen her [Mollie] since Wednesday morning, but I believe she was with friends she has stayed with before,' Ethel complained to the sister. 'I do not know where she was. I have been worried about her for some weeks. She made friends with people I don't know and she wanted to go and live with them, but I told her I would always prefer her to come home and sleep.' Even when Ethel was informed of Mollie's death just after 4 a.m., she asked nothing about its cause.

People in extremity often behave unpredictably. They can become hysterical, operate mechanically, grow garrulous, subside into silence. Ethel's instincts were self-protective. 'Oh, those dreadful men,' she said to the sister at sight of the police. 'I will be asked all sorts of questions.' Yet she still remembered, when the police deposited them at home, to tell Ralph to pull the cover from Adam Graham's car.

Though still unaware of the vehicle's ownership, Lambell noticed this when he returned to the crime scene just before 6 a.m. When he and his colleague Detective Jeremiah O'Keeffe knocked on the door of 86 Milton Street later that morning, it was on their list.

Ethel explained that she had not seen Mollie since Wednesday morning, and had no idea where her daughter had spent the intervening period. 'She has been leading a bohemian life lately with an artist crowd and I know nothing about her doings,' Ethel said. 'But if you see Mr Skipper of the *Bulletin* office or Percy Leason they may be able to tell you.'

'Does any man visit this house to see Mollie?' O'Keeffe asked.

'No,' said Ethel.

'Who took the covering off the car in front of your place this morning?' asked Lambell. 'I noticed it was covered at four o'clock and at a quarter to six the covering was off it.'

'My son Ralph took it off when he came from the hospital about 5.30.'

'Has he ever done that before?'

'No, except on one or two occasions on a Sunday.'

'Why did he do it this morning?'

'I told him to do it.'

Unaccountably, according to his notes, Lambell did not at this point ask the obvious follow-up: *whose car is it?* Instead he solicited details of the night before. Ethel repeated that she had gone to bed about 10.45 p.m., and been awoken at 1.15 a.m. by what she took to be Mollie returning by the side gate: 'She has sneaked in before without me hearing her and I got up to chastise her.' Then, according to Lambell's notes, Ethel said something decidedly odd: 'I wish you would not make any inquiries into the matter at all. So far as I am concerned, you can let the matter drop.' From an angry demand the police 'find out who did it' to a professed indifference: O'Keeffe, taken aback, stammered about the matter concerning 'the general public' and necessitating 'the fullest enquiries'.

With a growing sense of domestic tensions, Lambell raised the subject of Mollie's clippings about rooms to let. 'Was Mollie intending to leave home?' he asked. Ethel noted that Mollie 'often talked' of doing so, but claimed ignorance of any recent plan. There seemed a lot Ethel was unaware of: she was barely aware of Mollie's friends, and professed to 'know nothing' about them. Lambell must have taken his leave with a degree of bafflement. A murder less than ten minutes' walk from his front door, everything looking so familiar yet sounding so strange.

At first the news was incomplete, the crime having occurred too late for the morning newspapers. When Mervyn Skipper rang Norman Lewis at 8 a.m., it was to convey a partial message. 'Have you heard the news?' he asked. 'Last night Mollie was attacked and outraged. Would you go and break it to Colin as she is dangerously ill?' Lewis was shocked. 'Good God,' he said, and asked his mother, Florence, to accompany him. They arrived at Pangloss to find Colahan in the course of being informed, by a telephone call from Justus Jorgensen's doctor wife Lil, although she, too, seems to have been unaware that Mollie had died. Colahan looked 'very distressed' all the same. He had had, he would say, a foreboding. After his telephone conversation with Mollie, he had gone into his studio to look over some canvases, and *Sleep* had caught his eye. 'I had a horrible feeling of fear,' he would say. 'I turned out the light so that it should not be visible.' He would tell Lewis that morning, in fact, that in their last conversation Mollie had 'seemed to be restless and uneasy'.

As Florence Lewis left, Sue Vanderkelen arrived. It's unclear whether this was in response to a message, or by prior arrangement. In any case, here she and Colahan were, suddenly closer to a proto-couple than part of a baggy threesome. Norman Lewis stepped discreetly into the lovely garden, bathed in morning sun, while they communed. Others arrived as news travelled: John Farmer from Olinda, Jim Minogue from Malvern, Reg Ellery from Kew. Ellery, medical officer at Mont Park Mental Hospital, took Lewis with him to the Alfred, where Ellery learned of Mollie's death from the medical superintendent. Still thinking to palliate the blow, Lewis on his return to Pangloss told Colahan: 'I am afraid there isn't much hope.' He finally told Sue when she came into the garden again. From inside he then heard the sound of Colahan weeping. 'When I saw him a few minutes later,' Lewis would tell police, 'he looked absolutely broken up.'

By the afternoon, Colahan had composed himself sufficiently to present at the Detective Office. CIB had recently moved from a dingy muster room on Mackenzie Street into fresher quarters on Russell Street across the road from the City Court, but it was nowhere an artist would conceive of lingering: with the time noted at '3.20 p.m.', he gave a terse, euphemistic statement, detailing in 300 words how he had met Mollie 'twelve months ago', become 'very friendly with her' and been 'frequently in her company', including on the night before with its telephonic epilogue. Did his retelling convince police? They would have come across few like him. Lambell was a returned soldier, O'Keeffe a former bread carter. Colahan was fey, spry, an aesthete and epicure. It was hard to visualise his association with the prim and prickly household into which they had walked in the morning. Seven years earlier, Lambell had achieved a certain renown for arresting Squizzy Taylor. Yet what faced him now was not a case requiring bravery or nerve under fire; rather did it involve the close reading of human natures. The police returned with Colahan to Pangloss, and took some of Mollie's possessions – perhaps at this stage the manuscript of *Monsters Not Men*, which would disappear for good. But from Colahan, all police would obtain was that terse one-pager.

Word was now spreading quickly. Children at Mollie's school were sent home for the day. The Education Department wired Ethel: 'MINISTER DIRECTOR AND OFFICERS DEPARTMENT EXTEND DEEPEST SYMPATHY IN YOUR SAD BEREAVEMENT'. Whispers round Elwood had brought rubberneckers to Addison Street who encircled the slick of blood in the laneway – one of them, shockingly, was Daniel Blyth, Mollie's uncle, drawn to the scene of what he first took for an accident. Finally a man arrived with two buckets of sand to 'stop the ghouls'. This, of course, was not so easy. For afternoon papers such as Sydney's *Sun*, Adelaide's *News* and Melbourne's *Herald*, Mollie Dean's death was manna. *The Sun* had its best man on the job, the ubiquitous Hugh Buggy, whose opening paragraph left nothing to the imagination:

Early this morning Miss Molly Dean, aged 25, of Milton Street, Elwood, a teacher at a North Melbourne school, was criminally interfered with, battered about the head and body with a blunt instrument, strangled with her own stocking, and dragged unconscious across Addison Street to a lane within 200 yards of her home and left there to die.

At auction last year, from among a great quantity of papers belonging to Buggy's descendants, emerged a notebook containing his notes of the 'Molly Dean Case', the same pad also containing notations about 'Mena Griffiths' and 'Robert James McMahon' – murder investigations came pretty much alike to the reporter who claimed to have covered more than two hundred. The notes mingle handwriting, including complete words such as 'outraged' and 'shockingly mutilated', with Buggy's famously super-slick Pitman shorthand – a script largely archaic, and now requiring translation. They show Buggy coming quickly to terms with the killing's disturbing mix of frenzy and calm. 'Why should stocking have been taken off and tied around throat as it was not possible she could have cried out after first blow was struck [?]' he asked himself. 'Why should underclothing have been removed and fastened around her arm [?] It is thought Dean's murder was actuated by jealousy to point madness or that he deliberately wished convey impression attack was a sex crazed [sic].' These theories would compete for the remainder of the police's investigation.

The telephone had rung early in the Leasons' hallway in Eltham, the children observing their father draw their mother into the bedroom for whispered confidences. Now Percy, too, spoke to Buggy. The expression 'marked literary ability' went into the journalist's notebook: in his story, he would introduce Mollie as a 'scholar' and part of 'a Bohemian circle'.

The cartoonist hazarded crudely how the murder seemed to have been conducted so noiselessly. 'Knowing the girl and the confidence she had in herself, I do not think that if she had been suddenly confronted by a man she would scream, or that if she had screamed her cry would be very loud,' Percy said. 'She was the type who would have calmly said, "What do you want?", and if attacked would have put up a terrific fight without uttering a sound.'

The Sun reported Ethel as 'prostrate'. Yet Buggy could charm and wheedle into the securest citadel – he would be the only journalist to interview Captain Francis de Groot, the Sydney Harbour Bridge's ribbon-cutting rebel – and seems to have found a way. Certainly, he reported impressions that can have come only from the household, that her mother believed Mollie heedless of danger, and had herself experienced a presentiment about its consequences:

> Miss Dean's mother . . . had a strange premonition last week that her daughter was likely to be injured in some way. When told that her daughter had been seen to alight from a tram late at night and walk home alone, she said that her daughter had no fear. She added that her daughter would walk anywhere alone at night, and said: 'I know that one of these days the police will come to my house and tell me that she has been killed.'

Chief among reasons for Mollie's frequent walks home alone, of course, was Ethel's volatile responses to other visitors, such as Hubert Clifford and Louis Lavater, and a desire to elude her mother's surveillances. But Buggy was not to know that: Ethel was, as yet, the mother of a martyred daughter.

By late afternoon, the story was rippling across Melbourne on the front page of *The Herald,* adorned by no fewer than three illustrations. That portrait photograph of Mollie, to prove so ubiquitous, made its first appearance; chaos was embodied in a snapshot of the murder scene, order in an image of Lambell and O'Keeffe's CIB superintendent. 'JEALOUSY THEORY IN ELWOOD MURDER' was floated in the headline, although an alternative was also mooted: 'It was even suggested that Miss Dean was killed by the same fiend who killed Mena Griffiths, a 12-year-old schoolgirl.' The inference available was that police had no clue. Imagination, meanwhile, was inflamed by the euphemistic intelligence that there was 'no evidence of criminal assault', but that the victim had been 'outraged in a most dastardly fashion'.

The shock was electrifying. Bookseller Frank Wilmot, who wrote his poetry as Furnley Maurice, shared his *Herald* with Nettie Palmer when she visited his little bookshop after lunch. She gasped. 'In town in afternoon Furnley showed me a newspaper report of a girl who was strangled on her way home last night, and said it was Molly Dean, that bright little thoughtful girl,' she wrote in her diary. 'Awful for Colahan. She was with Skipper, Leasons and Colahan at the theatre, then went home to Elwood.' Such things normally never befell 'people you know', she noted; it left her able to 'think of nothing else, but in a numb, shattered way'.

Colahan was no less shattered, perhaps more than he knew. Regrouping at Pangloss after police left, he began to feel he was being watched, and thought he saw through a half-curtained window a man's legs running across his lawn. Feeling the need to do something, he became possessed with the idea that it might be the decent thing to express condolences personally. 'Come with me, Johnny,' he said to Farmer. 'I don't want to go over by myself.' The decision to visit the Deans as a pair, noted Farmer almost four decades later, proved 'just as well'. When they knocked on the door of 86 Milton Street that evening, Ethel Dean's initial shock and later prostration had worn off. Here was a representative of that 'bohemian crowd'; here was the very man who had been with her daughter on her last night. She flew at him in fury. Farmer faltered in his retelling: 'She made sure he . . . It was really dreadful.' Colahan, shaken, was reluctant to return to Pangloss alone, so Farmer drove him to the Jorgensens' in Brighton, where they all stayed overnight, joined by another Meldrumite in August Cornehls. Their artistic sect had always revelled in attention; now it was drawing together in hopes of inconspicuousness.

*

Colahan craved the company of friends. On Saturday morning he called the Skippers from the Jorgensens', asking them over. Lena Skipper, ever practical, brought macaroni for lunch. She was also preoccupied with a comment of the detectives in *The Herald* that the murderer was likely 'a jealous hand who wanted revenge'. Lena found this inherently plausible: Mollie's sauciness, she felt, was bound to drive a man to violence. While Colahan lay on the Jorgensens' couch, she taxed him. Who might be jealous? Who might know? Norman Lewis, perhaps? Colahan sat up, pale and serious. 'I know Mollie better than anyone,' he said firmly. When Lena went on, he elaborated: 'There are letters of Mollie's at my house that if the police found them would implicate another who was right out of it.' Lena could think only of Hubert Clifford, by now safely in England and betrothed. But not even Colahan seemed to have the full picture. 'There are other letters but I don't know whose,' he said.

In fact, Colahan's mind was racing. He was going back obsessively over his last conversations with Mollie, his sensations of disquiet afterwards, his involvement in precipitating her final walk and, not least, his possible implication as a suspect. How those police had looked at him. He was convinced they had searched Pangloss surreptitiously in his absence, even that they had insinuated a dictaphone into his chimney. When the detectives had stood before a wardrobe in which Mollie's letters were kept in a shoebox, he had not mentioned them. Ethel Dean was not the only one, then, loath to make investigators welcome, or suddenly impressed by their own powers of prophecy. Mollie's fate had confirmed Lena in earlier views: that she had been a usurper, a succubus; that she was an inevitable victim of risks she had incurred:

I did not like her [Mollie], she was obsessed with herself
and Colin. She was no doubt an extraordinary character, but
I had no patience with her . . . Only in all her actions some
monstrously selfish aim. I felt she would do anything to gain her
own ends. I often knew what she would do beforehand. I felt
she would get some sort of fixation and go straight ahead and
defeat her own ends. I thought she may end in gaol. I thought
her abnormal and too interested in sex and I did not know
exactly what the end of it all would be but I wished she would go
to England and leave us all in peace.

Already, in fact, there had opened a curious divide in attitudes to
the death of Mollie Dean. As always, there was a fearful fascination
with the possible perpetrator; but in the absence of an obvious suspect, it became as though she had been slain not by an individual but
by forces dark and inscrutable, the same as had overwhelmed Mena
Griffiths. Some saw the decay of society preceded by a collapse of
hope. 'Everyone deeply shocked about Molly Dean,' diarised Nettie
Palmer that Saturday. 'It means that the whole civic life is uncertain.
She herself is a definite personal loss as she was a little like Iris +
so irreplaceable.' The reference was to Iris Macmahon Ball, the
sharp-minded first wife of the political scientist William, victim of
tuberculosis in July 1926, aged twenty-six – an exalted comparison,
as Nettie had idolised her. In her journal, Nettie confessed to feeling
turned outward from her inward-looking life, to seeing Melbourne's
underside and the world's implicit horrors anew:

I have had no contact with violence before, never imagined it
entering my world . . . Somehow I can't help feeling that the
meaningless tragedy is part of the cloud that has been lowering

'Deeply shocked': Nettie Palmer's diary

over the city this past year – the sense of wheels running down ... The shabby hawkers drifting from door-to-door ... The line of men sitting on the Post Office steps. This isn't a rational feeling. The murder is surely one of those inexplicable crimes that might be committed any time. But it makes shadowy figures in the street outside seem more sinister, awakens a distrust of life in you, sharpens your sense of violence sleeping beneath the unrevealing surface of these days.

Others saw the case as reflecting the tide of moral laxity. Premier Ned Hogan's Labor government was wont to commute death penalties – Victoria had not executed a murderer for six and a half years. In that Saturday's *Age* featured the first of several letters to see this as more than coincidental with the 'revolting outrage' against Mollie Dean. 'I have grave fears that these outrages will become common for the reason that the principles of the Labor Party are against capital punishment,' insisted 'Justice'. 'The sexual offender is obviously a moral coward, and the fear of the rope holds many of his type in check.' 'Periodical floggings' would also be morally efficacious. The National Council of Women passed a motion deploring 'recent horrifying crimes' and demanding life sentences for perpetrators of sex offences. Following so soon on the Griffiths case, the death of Mollie Dean also cast doubt on the Hogan Government's curtailment of police recruitment. *Truth* called for the urgent conscription of '50 extra constables' to restore the metropolitan force to strength.

Certainly, the world suddenly looked different. Leason and Skipper, for example, found themselves in a predicament. They had as usual collaborated on a weekly cartoon for *The Bulletin*, posting it on Wednesday for publication a week hence. It was inspired by tensions in the caucus of federal Labor, led by Bendigo's Richard Keane MHR, about management of the economic crisis, including the extension of relief to the unemployed and the release of credit by the Commonwealth Bank. Keane had just chosen a menacing metaphor for the intent of his faction, against the will of prime minister and treasurer: 'The gun is loaded, and it is going off this time.' Leason duly portrayed a gang of masked desperadoes disgorged by a car labelled 'Caucus' menacing a young woman in a virginally white dress bearing the legend 'Australia's Credit' as she walked fearfully down an unlit street. The caption read: 'FEAR. "If they don't mean any harm, why do they say such dreadful things?"' Checking with editor Prior, however, they found it too late to substitute an alternative. It was too late, now, to do many things.

11

NIGHT TERRORS

'You people at the Yard ought to know, with your experience of Jack the Ripper'.
    – Anthony Berkeley Cox, *The Silk Stocking Murders* (1928)

While Colin Colahan sheltered at the Jorgensens' that Saturday, Mollie Dean was laid to rest. At 11 a.m., a crowd of about 200 gathered round 86 Milton Street, within which Reverend George Philip Bray of St John's Congregational Church in South St Kilda held a brief service. The only member of Mollie's artistic circle known to have attended was the novelist Bernard Cronin, of whose Australian Society of Authors she had been a member. There were wreaths also from Mollie's teaching colleagues, and Ralph's co-workers at Auto-Car Service Company. Fifty followed the cortege to the graveside for Mollie's interment in a family plot among the Methodists in the north-western corner of Brighton General Cemetery.

After the scene at Milton Street the night before, Colahan would hardly have been game to attend. But he was able that day to make one gesture towards Mollie, issuing a 'special statement', duly reported in Sydney's *Sun* and interstate editions of *Truth* the next morning:

'Mr Colahan states that he was engaged to Miss Dean and the date of the marriage had been undecided because of economic conditions. He described her as an extraordinarily intelligent girl with great literary talent.' Launching a further untruth and half-truth, *Truth*'s Perth

'Savagely, fiendishly brutal': *Truth* reports

edition reported Colahan to have been divorced 'twelve months ago', the co-respondent being a 'woman unknown'.

Colahan's statement also served *his* purposes. Not only did it engage public sympathy but it drew his relations with Mollie within acceptable bounds. Bohemianism notwithstanding, he was a man of some stature – even *Truth* deferred to him as 'son of a surgeon and leader of the most advanced thought in Melbourne's art circles'. There followed on Monday further favourable news. After reviewing records of the Windsor Exchange, the Postmaster-General's Department confirmed consecutive calls from the telephone box at St Kilda railway station to 'Hawthorn 5176' shortly after midnight Friday. From this point, in fact, Colahan was no longer a suspect, having hardly fitted the frame anyway – the myth that later enveloped him was mainly of his own making.

For the police, this was bad news. From the very beginning, their investigation was skewed, by an abundance of information and a paucity of suspects. Hundreds of letters were received. Scores of eye-witnesses came forward. There had actually been a number of attacks within the triangle of St Kilda, Brighton and Elwood during 1930, including one across the road from the Deans at 73 Milton Street just before midnight on 31 July. Teenage housemaid Dora Phillips had been followed into her employers' backyard by a dark-complexioned man with centre-parted hair and belted overcoat, who had first kissed her forcefully, then thrown her to the ground and sexually assaulted her; two weeks before the attack on Mollie Dean, sisters sharing a single bed in a sleep-out on Grey Street had been bludgeoned by an intruder whom they were unable to describe. Descriptions now forthcoming were likewise unhelpful, based on glimpses in darkness and retrospective sensations of suspicion. The man seen to follow Mollie was in a suit of blue or dark grey or wearing fawn trousers, with a hat or without, maybe in an overcoat but maybe not.

A man *was* reported to have been loitering at the corner of Southey and Mitford streets at 11.15 p.m.; a man *was* reported to have stepped in front of a woman at the Dickens Street tram stop about 11.50 p.m., but turned and walked away at the approach of another pedestrian. Four days after Mollie's death, Police Commissioner Blamey received an anonymous letter from a woman referring to a disturbing encounter at the same stop a little later, a man trying to make conversation as he followed her. To ward him off, the woman had told the man she was 'a married woman with a son as big as you are', quickly walked down the garden path of an unlit house and waited in the shadow until she was convinced he was gone. But her identikit was hardly precise: 'Short and thick-set wearing a dark grey suit, not wearing a hat, hair brushed back'.

As news about the phone calls came through, Lambell and O'Keeffe were at Queensberry Street interviewing Mollie's former colleagues. They then widened their inquiries to her friends past, such as George Browne, Sadie Fields, Joyce Pyke, Clara Behrend and Teddy Sell, and present, including the Leasons, the Jorgensens, the Skippers, Norman Lewis, Sue Vanderkelen and Betty Davies. The latter group squirmed, Lena being typically cagey: 'They also asked me the cause of Colahan's divorce, if Molly was fond of the boys, did I see her often, when last. I could not remember that. I hope I gave the impression I knew very little but I know a great deal which I have been told and second to third hand and from what I have observed.' Sue found it more traumatic. In the heated emotions of the moment, Colahan had apparently blurted out a marriage proposal to his other 'other woman'; Sue had equivocated and, after her brush with the detectives, repaired to Mornington, where she stayed with a widowed aunt, Rose Pitt, in her home, 'Marina'. Even Betty, though she had been far away, found it disturbing to be accosted at her South Yarra apartment: 'If I had not been away and Molly had not gone to the theatre, the whole ghastly tragedy might not have happened. I could not shake off a feeling of having contributed to her death.'

Skipper was resolved, nonetheless, that the best face on matters be put. Any *Bulletin* reader disquieted by that Leason cartoon on Wednesday would have come a few pages later on an old cartoon of Colin Colahan by Dick Ovenden. It adorned a rather otiose biographical paragraph about the painter dropped in at the last minute:

> Colin Colahan, engaged to marry Molly Dean, the literary girl who was brutally murdered in Melbourne last week, was more than half-way through a medical degree before he decided to take up art as a career. He had done some very promising black and white work for *The Bulletin* before he came under the spell of Max Meldrum. On his advice Colahan, who had inherited some means from his father, a well-known Melbourne doctor, went to Paris and studied steadily for four years, before returning to Australia. It was through their devotion to Max Meldrum that he and Leason came together; Colahan and his fiancée were at a theatre party on the evening of the tragedy. As an extreme coincidence, Leason's drawing for this week's *Bulletin*, mailed on the afternoon before the horrible affair, shows a young woman ('Australia's Credit') in terror of assault.

The Bulletin had run the same cartoon and a similar paragraph about Colahan's university studies at the time of his April exhibition. But what now was the relevance of the medical degree; of Colahan's cartoons; of Colahan's father; of Meldrum; of Paris? And what was a 'literary girl' anyway? The paragraph drew attention even in seeking to deflect it. And there was ample attention already.

The night after *The Bulletin*'s publication and a week after Mollie's death, Skipper found himself at the scene of her last night, the Bijou, watching the Gregan McMahon Players follow up their *Pygmalion* with *Right You Are (If You Think So)* by the Italian farceur Pirandello. The play, he thought, was showing its age, yet its sibilances of gossip and clashes of contradiction had a sudden thematic relevance. 'If the playwright had actually set out to write a satire on present-day Melbourne he could not have made his piece more perfectly *à propos*,' he wrote in his review. 'It is safe to say that the majority of the house had been engaged for the past week or so in amateur-detective work on a certain local crime much after the manner of the puppets on the stage.'

Speculation was aggravated by seeming inertia of the police, following their abortive inquiries in the Mena Griffiths case. Lambell and O'Keeffe never seem to have seriously explored the possibility of their having the same perpetrator, and only fringes of the media entertained it: *The Age* commented caustically that the sole similarity was the 'baseless optimism of the group of leading officials . . . that somehow, some day, the offenders will be apprehended'. But the deaths ran together easily, coincident in an unfathomable violence. 'A horrible presence', editorialised *Truth*, seemed to be stalking Melbourne womanhood.

As to the nature of that violence, *Truth* and its rackety weekend rival *Smith's Weekly* had a melodramatic meeting of minds. 'What kind of fiend is the slayer of Molly Dean?' asked *Truth*. 'Contemplating the awful details of this latest and most fearful of Melbourne's sex outrages, there advises the vision of some mad murderer abroad: some modern Jack the Ripper slashing and smashing with his weapons of death, slavering with bloodlust, eager to mangle and destroy.' *Smith's Weekly* could not but agree, throwing in a reference to 1924's 'trial of the century' for some contemporary relevance:

> What else, except the homicidal mania of a Jack the Ripper could have inspired such an act of bestial ferocity, the murderer raining blow after blow upon the victim, taken unawares, dragging her by the feet a distance of 30 yards across the road, knotting a stocking round her throat to silence her moans, handcuffing her with one of her undergarments, mutilating her breasts and finally, with a tyre lever or some such instrument, committing an unspeakable outrage. A fiendish act so redolent of horror, that upon reflection, it is hard to credit the possibility of the murderer, even if endowed with the super-culture of one of the Loeb brothers [sic], having been able to gain an acquaintance with such a keen student of psychology as Molly Dean, whose work, as a special teacher in the Education Department, was especially directed to the study of mental processes. Would not such a keen perception as hers have recognised such a degenerate, however brilliant and well educated, if such had crossed her path and picked him out for an epileptiform type that lies near the borderline of insanity? For by the testimony of friends and acquaintances, Miss Dean was a particularly discerning young woman who gave the impression of studying men with personal detachment, making no light surrendering of her heart.

That Mollie Dean's sensitive antennae would have detected the degeneracy of her murderer was just one of a variety of claims made about her in the murder's aftermath. In some outlets, she went from being part of her circle to a leader, from a scholar to a renaissance woman; in others, she had been drawn into danger by her romantic inclinations. Sydney's *Truth* was more indulgent than Melbourne's. 'Molly Dean was a prominent member of Melbourne's famous Bohemian set,' reported the Sydney edition. 'Her boon companions were artists and newspaper men. She was clever, a prolific writer, a painter of sorts, perhaps a little unconventional but wholly lovable.' Its Melbourne stablemate wondered more soberly if Mollie's 'desire for the unusual' had 'coloured her life', whether 'the role of litterateur' encouraged by 'the adulation of associates' had not spoiled 'a brilliant career' in education. In fact, neither perspective was accurate. Mollie had never fitted comfortably in her circle; she had received little encouragement from them in her writing; that she was threading her lonely path through Elwood so reluctantly was an outcome of isolation rather than involvement. But in the month to Christmas 1930, rumour was on the wing. 'Mothers are seen everywhere leading little children to school by the hand,' reported *Smith's Weekly*. 'And the most independent of flappers, who, in ordinary times would laugh at the idea of being afraid of the dark, are now particular about going out unescorted.'

One man the police were never able to interview was Clarence Weber – whom Colahan, of course, suspected of an assignation with Mollie during his absence in Adelaide. As Mollie had been walking into the Bijou on the night of 20 November, nature's supreme specimen had suffered a lethal coronary occlusion while washing his hands before dinner. As it does when public figures perish abruptly, speculation surrounded his death. It would recur when Weber's ambitious widow became the first Victorian woman to win a parliamentary seat at a general election in 1937, and persisted decades more: when Weber's grandson Ron was at school in the 1950s, a sportsmaster told him authoritatively that Clarence had opened a vein in the bath. One of those helping spread the whispers was Colahan, perhaps exacting a small, delayed revenge on a romantic rival. He breathlessly told Eric Westbrook of the coincidence of Weber's 'extraordinary' death: 'Then came this strange suicide. There may be no connection. The police gave me one day a very indiscrete word, half a hint there *was* a connection.' About it there was never anything extraordinary – heart disease ran in the family. And as alibis go, being dead might be deemed close to unimprovable.

Another man police suspected strongly was well and truly alive. At 11 a.m. on 3 December, twelve days after Mollie's death, detectives Lambell and O'Keeffe banged on the door of a house in Broadway let by George and Alma Goodwin, demanding to know the whereabouts of Alma's brother Ernest William Frederick Wilson. Unsatisfied with her vague answers, they forced their way in and found him in bed. Wilson, twenty-six, was the definition of a scapegrace, describing himself as a 'musician and architect' but actually a licensed horse trainer – not that he had done much in the 1920s except jail time in three states for theft and false pretences.

In June 1928, Wilson had gone on trial in Sydney with four others for perpetrating 'the Darlinghurst Outrage' – the alleged gang rape of 26-year-old Ada Maddocks. Maddocks, a disarmingly well-spoken and resourceful woman who seems to have been turning a few tricks to keep herself and her two children where a violent husband had failed, told police that she had been abducted and sexually assaulted in a flat by men who had picked her out on Bayswater Road. *Au contraire*, said Wilson blithely, in what *Truth* described as 'the most candid testimony ever heard in a criminal court': Maddocks had offered herself to him, he had promised her 'a couple of quid', then after partaking had decided he was 'a little bit short' and left without paying, whereupon she had made allegations in retaliation. It was a lurid tale, involving threats with razors, brushes with drugs, a visit to a movie theatre appropriately screening the noir thriller *Underworld*, and several 'abominable offences', but the accused were cleared. Wilson moved on to Adelaide, where he was swiftly banged up for nine months after lifting a fur necklet from Myer.

Since arriving in Melbourne in June 1930, Wilson had been an obtrusive nuisance to women in the area – accosting them, following them, plaguing them with propositions and lecherous remarks. Lambell and O'Keeffe had studied him in action before moving in and, as Alma Goodwin later told a St Kilda magistrate, were in no doubt of their suspicions:

> The detectives were in a threatening attitude, and they talked of nothing else but the murder of Molly Dean in Elwood. They kept saying that my brother answered the description of the suspected murderer, and they had hundreds of letters about him accosting and annoying women and girls in the St Kilda district. In fact, from their bullying attitude and the way they spoke about the Elwood murder I really thought I would find my brother charged with the murder when I came to this court today.

By the time the case made it to court, however, the detectives had had to back away. 'This man is a sexual pervert of the worst kind,' O'Keeffe told the magistrate. 'No woman is safe from insult when he is about.' But Wilson seems to have had an alibi – as, self-representing coolly, he persuaded a chagrined Lambell to concede.

Wilson: Aren't you in charge of the investigation in the Elwood murder case?

Lambell: Yes, but I am engaged with Detective-Sergeant O'Keeffe in that matter.

Wilson: When you rushed and blustered about the house, you practically told my sister that I was responsible for the murder at Elwood.

Lambell: I did not say you were responsible. I said that a lot of people in the district thought you were.

Wilson: Well, do you think I had anything to do with it?

Lambell paused grudgingly. 'From my enquiries,' he said at last, 'I know you have nothing to do with it.' Wilson could not keep the smugness from his voice: 'I thank you, Mr Lambell.' The magistrate could do no better, or worse, than imposing a twelve-month stretch for lacking visible means of support.

A wilder theory was first tentatively mooted by the normally sedate *Age* on the morning after the murder: 'The fact that a stocking was used recalls an exactly similar crime in London, known as the Silk Stocking Murder.' This epithet had actually been conferred on two murders, one in 1926 (solved), one in 1929 (unsolved), partial inspiration for a bestselling novel. In *The Silk Stocking Murders*, Anthony Berkeley Cox had set his dandified detective Roger Sheringham, aficionado of Freud and wearer of mauve silk pyjamas, on the trail of a serial killer: 'He's mad, of course. His only possible motive . . . is murder for the love of killing . . . The victim's own stocking, for instance. And I imagine it would have to be silk. Yes, that brain of his must be full of strange twists.' Yes, it must be, agreed *Truth* on 6 December, including emigration, positing that the still-unknown strangler of clerk Mary Learoyd in a lane 100 metres from her Ilkley home might have carved a transcontinental swathe: 'There are remarkable resemblances between this sinister affair and one that thrilled England with horror about fifteen months ago – resemblances so striking as to give reason for wonder whether the same person might have been responsible for the two crimes. Far-fetched as this might seem, criminologists know that in their particular profession there are times when truth proves to be stranger than fiction.' Which perhaps went for *Truth* also.

Smith's Weekly, most probably Harry Maddison, renowned as 'The Gimlet of Gun Alley' since his vivid reportage of the 1921 murder of Alma Tirtschke, took a few weeks over its double-barrelled reply. First, *Smith's* claimed, police inquiries revealed Mollie to have been followed on the night in question not by Colahan but by 'an earlier admirer', a university student who had been deflected from his earlier attentions by the 'anonymous letters' of a 'jealous woman', but whose 'affections had not swerved'. He, at the last moment, did: 'Arrived home he sat brooding in the car for some time as though impressed by the shadow of a tragedy that, all unknown to him, was soon to be enacted.' Teddy Sell? Another presentiment? No further detail exists.

Still more extraordinary was the echo of an unsolved murder case a year earlier – that of 29-year-old Norma McLeod, found in her Toorak bedroom with a fractured skull, having seemingly disturbed an intruder. Police had subsequently been plied with letters from an anonymous seer signing themselves 'Asmodeus' – one of the seven princes of hell, identified with lust – containing otherwise undisclosed details of the crime. Now, *Smith's* reported, police had been aided in their investigation of the 'Elwood murder mystery' by 'a middle-aged woman to whom a revelation of this tragedy seems to have come in a dream'. This woman's 'strange divination' was that the killer had erupted from the gate, disabled Mollie in order to drag her across the road, then as an afterthought 'returned and committed the final abomination, perhaps to divert attention from the real nature of the crime and make it appear the work of a sadist'. For additional titillation, *Smith's* reported the dreamer in question to have shared with Mollie an earlier lover: 'Love is a strange potion, especially when two drink from the same bottle.'

Yet, promisingly as it adorned its despatch with the illustration of a spectral assassin over a prone body, *Smith's* brought its readers no closer to a solution than *Truth*. In fact, 1930 was expiring with investigators seemingly no closer to decrypting the mystery than on the night it occurred. An old enigma had resurfaced, with what appeared a satisfyingly ready-made solution.

No sooner had police released Robert McMahon, their number one suspect in the murder of Mena Griffiths, than they wanted him back. The reason was that a swag had been found in Temora's railway shed, including clothes and undergarments stained with blood. It took some weeks to catch up with McMahon, working in his brother Frank's bottle yard in St Peters. Dragged back to Melbourne again, he admitted that the clothing was his, while explaining the blood as resulting from an attempt to circumcise himself – seemingly unsuccessful. Now, however, new eyewitnesses picked McMahon out of line-ups. On remand at Pentridge, he wrote plaintively to Frank: 'I must prove to my fellow countrymen that I am innocent.' It was too late to do so to Mena's mother, Alice. When the inquest commenced at the City Morgue on 30 December, she threw herself at McMahon with cries of 'Let me get at him! Let me get him!' Mena's sisters had also changed their minds and identified him, as did a majority of those testifying. Coroner David Grant found that McMahon had caused the girl's death 'feloniously, unlawfully and maliciously', and committed him for trial six weeks hence. Victoria Police walked a little taller – but only for a week.

Parents in Melbourne had lately been more circumspect. Frank and Sarah Wilson had always been fairly blasé about the late-night absences of their sixteen-year-old daughter, Hazel, with her friend Lucy Hogan: Frank, an unemployed labourer who was surviving by using his front yard in Ormond to graze racehorses, had enough on his mind. One night Hazel and Lucy slept in an abandoned home, another in a phone box. That had changed after the death of Mollie Dean: the Wilsons began insisting on their daughter keeping more respectable hours, and on waiting up for her return. 'The Elwood murder was discussed in our house,' Frank recalled. 'We all had a fair bit to say about the murders.' On the night of 9 January 1931, however, their regime slipped: the Wilsons thought Hazel was staying with the Hogan family, but learned the following morning that the girls had separated at Glenhuntly railway station. As Frank narrated, they next discovered a girl's shoe by their own front gate: 'I recognised it as Hazel's shoe, and the wife also said: "My God that is Hazel's shoe". The Dean case then flashed through my mind, and also how she was carried away . . . The wife then picked up the shoe up and said, "My God she has been killed".' Hazel's body was discovered in couch grass 30 cm high on a nearby vacant lot. She was lying on her stomach, hands tied with a patent-leather belt, feet tied with her bloomers, a stocking in her mouth. She had been strangled.

Hazel Wilson's death, with its similarities to the two preceding murders, struck a heavy blow to the case against Robert McMahon, who, of course, had been safely in custody at the time. Though investigators were as yet unaware, worse was to come. A few days earlier,

Truth had resolved, as police had not, to test McMahon's alibi. With the assistance of his solicitor Roy Schilling, the newspaper's journalists located as many as fourteen people in the vicinity of Leeton who were prepared to swear that they had interacted with McMahon on the weekend of Mena Griffiths' abduction. A cross-section of rural life, they included farmers, carters and labourers, a blacksmith, an insurance agent, and a schoolgirl who confirmed overhearing his offer to play euphonium for a Salvation Army band. They would turn the prosecution case to ashes.

The police already seemed helpless, forcing the populace to occasional excesses of zeal. The week after presiding at Mena Griffiths' inquest, coroner David Grant was closing the morgue at dusk when he saw a man holding the arm of a crying ten-year-old girl. He asked the girl if she knew the man: when she, confused, said no, he snatched her away. The man grabbed her back, punched Grant twice in the face, and boarded a tram. Doing well for a man of nearly sixty, the coroner went in pursuit, and cajoled a constable into arresting his assailant: labourer Patrick Britt, it transpired, was the girl's uncle, although he would have to cop to a fine for assault. In two months, it seemed, Melbourne had been dissolved from an orderly modern metropolis into a huddle of nyctophobic neighbourhoods with premonitions of violence and dreams of murder.

12

THIS IS THE MAN WHO DID IT

Whenever I have in all humility, moved
Amid dire forests of fact, unproved and overproved,
Then only the incomprehensible thing has vividness of hue
And only the unutterable is true.

— Furnley Maurice, 'Whenever I Have'

As the persons of interest dwindled away in the weeks after Mollie Dean's death, detectives Lambell and O'Keeffe turned back towards another figure. Nobody knew quite what to make of Adam Graham. Thirty years old, with rusty hair, a florid complexion and a laconic manner, he lived with his widowed mother Bella and seamstress sister Catherine in a two-bedroom bungalow with sleep-out in Gordon Avenue, Elwood; they enjoyed the slight social edge of the services of a domestic, Mary Beveridge. Most evenings, of course, he spent at the Deans, which Bella called his 'second home', in spite of unexplained distance that had opened between the other Grahams and their former hosts.

Graham's job as a mechanic still had vaguely artisanal charac-teristics: he visited clients to tune and repair in situ, at a time before carports and driveways when vehicles were often garaged away from homes. And here, police believed, was something. A customer of Graham's for fifteen months, 31-year-old clerk Gladys Healey, lived six doors from the Deans in Milton Street, but stowed her Overland automobile in number two garage on the laneway off Addison Street – out the front of which had the murder of Mollie Dean been committed. In fact, Graham had worked in the garage all four days that week, while helpfully driving Gladys and her parents about. Mechanic was on friendly enough terms with client to have asked her out that Thursday evening, although she had 'other plans'. It was after that he had returned home for tea, shed the day's grease in a bath, slipped on his brown suit, picked up a battery he wanted to charge, and stepped out without needing to mention his destination to his mother and sister for they already knew it. Five minutes later he would have been parking his Amilcar out front of the Deans.

As described earlier, the police had at first been so incurious about Graham that they noted his car at 86 Milton Street without troubling to establish its ownership. He looked initially like part of the mourning circle: he drove Ralph to the morgue to identify Mollie's body; he acted as a pallbearer at Mollie's funeral. The police were told he was a regular visitor to the Deans. What puzzled them immediately were Ethel's evasions around this fact. When Lambell and O'Keeffe revisited her on Monday, the former took note of a bizarre conversation.

Ethel: It is no good you coming to see me. You will never catch him now, and I hope you never will.

Lambell: What makes you say that? I thought you would be only too anxious to see the man caught.

Ethel: His conscience will be sufficient punishment for him for the rest of his life.

Lambell: Surely you are not satisfied with the murderer of your daughter being allowed to go with his own conscience being his punishment.

Ethel: If it is a case of jealousy I don't want his mother to suffer for anything he has done, but if he is a maniac I hope you get him.

Understanding themselves to be handling a woman in mourning, the detectives did not press for elaboration. But Ethel then began deflecting questions, obstructing where she was not outright lying.

Lambell: Does any man ever visit this house?

Ethel: No.

Lambell: Are you sure there is no man coming here to see either you or Mollie?

Ethel: No, there is not.

Lambell: We are told there is a man by the name of Adam visiting this house nightly and that it is his car that was in front of your place the night Mollie was murdered.

Ethel: Oh him. He knows nothing about it. You don't want to go bothering him.

Lambell: Where does he live?

Ethel: I won't tell you because I know he knows nothing about it.

Lambell: We must see him and you had better tell us where he lives.

Ethel: I will not.

Lambell: Will you tell us where he works?

Ethel: No.

Lambell: We will have to see him whether he knows anything about it or not.

Ethel: I won't tell you where he is.

At last, Lambell pursued his ends by indirection – with some success.

> Lambell: Where is your son working?
> Ethel: He is working for motor people in Little Lonsdale Street near Russell Street.
> Lambell: We would like to see him this evening. Do you think he could come into the detective office to see us about 7 this evening?
> Ethel: I will tell him.
> Lambell: Will you tell Adam that we want to see him? He could come to the office with your boy.
> Ethel: Yes I will do that.

But just when the strangeness appeared to have abated, Ethel renewed it. 'How will I go about getting Mollie's death certificate?' she asked as the detectives were leaving. 'She was insured for £200 and I suppose I will have to produce a death certificate before I can get the money.' Ethel confirmed that she held the City Mutual policy herself. The detectives advised that she would receive the certificate 'later', and must have withdrawn wondering what they had struck. At least she conveyed the police's message. Adam Graham duly accompanied Ralph Dean to the Detective Office that evening.

The pair had essentially parallel stories. Graham explained that he had remained at the Deans until about 10.30 p.m. then walked home, had a cup of coffee and gone to bed. Ralph recalled that he had spent the evening painting a vessel at the seaside quarters of the Elwood Canoe Club, arrived home at 11.15 p.m., had a cup of tea and gone to bed. The stories were confirmed by family members – except in one minor respect. Unknowingly contradicting her brother and mother, Catherine Graham told police she remembered her brother sleeping on the fateful night not in the house but in the sleep-out ('No person slept in the second bedroom that night. I am certain Adam did not sleep in his bedroom. I know he slept in the sleep-out'). This raised the possibility of his slipping out late at night to lie in wait for Mollie. Police were then informed by the Deans' neighbours, the Goldsteins, that they had seen Ethel outside after she claimed to have gone to bed at 11 p.m. – walking, half an hour later, with her dog along Milton Street from the direction of Broadway, and re-entering her gateway.

The wider police interviewed, and the more they heard about the tensions of Mollie's home life, the stranger Ethel appeared and the larger Graham loomed. Ralph conceded that Mollie and her mother 'were more or less always quarrelling', that 'occasionally Mother has struck Mollie when they were quarrelling', and that Ethel had 'followed Mollie when she left home of an evening'; Sadie Fields said that Mollie was unable to bear being in the same room as 'very dour, silent' Graham; Clara Behrend said that Mollie had told her of Graham's habit 'of carrying information about her to her mother'. Two weeks after Mollie's murder, both Ethel and Graham were brought into the Detective Office to give official statements. Lambell and O'Keeffe did not think they were simply friends, although in that respect neither gave anything away, even when Lambell, in an attempt to shake her composure, showed Ethel her daughter's blood-stained handbag. Graham overheard one of the detectives confide in the other: 'This is the man who did it.' From a search of Gordon Avenue, police retrieved Graham's grey suit. It had perhaps as many as fifteen tiny specks of blood, which he could not explain, although he insisted that on the evening in question he had been wearing his brown suit.

Another late-night stroller, printer Eldred Dyer, then offered a hesitant but potentially significant sighting in the laneway at 1 a.m. on 21 November. If the time was right, he may even have glimpsed the killer – or *killers*. 'I was going into the lane to urinate and when I saw the figure I turned on my heel and walked away to Ruskin Street [where he lived],' Dyer told police, rather haltingly. But the police addendum to his statement, noting that Dyer was 'known to Mrs Dean', suggests some doubts as to his reliability and impartiality: 'This witness told his friends that he saw a man and a woman in the lane when he arrived there about 1 a.m. When interviewed by police he was very reluctant to say anything in connection with the matter as he did not wish to be mixed up with it. Believe witness did see a man and woman as stated by him to his friends immediately after the death of Molly Dean.' *A man and a woman.* Lambell and O'Keeffe had in mind two who answered that description. Two days before Christmas, Adam Graham and Ethel Dean were again brought to the Detective Office for interviews – long interviews.

Lambell and O'Keeffe, decorated police officers, were under pressure; likewise their force. They had sensed undercurrents from those very first moments with Ethel; Graham seemed similarly secretive. Now the pair were in separate rooms, each knowing the other to be there. Each was told of the other making admissions. One, police would claim, appeared to budge.

Ethel spent five hours at the Detective Office, and was first shaken by questions about her actions slightly before and after the murder. She was asked about the neighbours' late-night sighting of her, which first she denied any possibility of, then any memory of. She was asked about the evidence of the nurse at the Alfred that she had asked about Mollie's disfigurement, admitting she did not 'know what made me ask it', as she was unaware at that stage how Mollie had come to harm. Her demeanour at the hospital was made an issue. Lambell, Ethel alleged, upbraided her: 'You are a callous woman; you have a heart of concrete.' But according to O'Keeffe, she caved in to questions about her relations with Graham.

O'Keeffe: He is in the habit of visiting you nightly and leaving his car in front of your house nightly.

Ethel: Yes.

O'Keeffe: Did not Mollie frequently complain about your friendship with Adam Graham?

Ethel: Yes she has spoken about it.

O'Keeffe: She accused you of being intimate with Adam Graham.

Ethel: Yes she did but she withdrew it shortly after.

O'Keeffe: You know you did not set Mollie a very good example the way you were carrying on with Graham.

Ethel: I know I never. I know I have done wrong.

O'Keeffe: How long have you and Adam Graham been having intercourse?

Ethel: For years.

O'Keeffe: Where did intercourse take place?

Ethel: In my bedroom.

O'Keeffe: Would he sleep with you all night?

Ethel: No, he has stayed with me till one and two in the morning but never later.

O'Keeffe: Did Mollie know you and Adam were having intercourse at your place?

Ethel: I don't think so.

O'Keeffe: Did she ever catch you?

Ethel: Not that I know of.

O'Keeffe: You know you and Mollie were not on friendly terms. Mollie had left home on two or three occasions lately and she was thinking of going away again.

Ethel: I admit we did not agree. I did not like the crowd she was mixed up with.

O'Keeffe: Did you want Mollie to marry Adam Graham?

Ethel: No.

It was not a confession to murder, but it *was* a confession – and it continued. Ethel admitted to having followed Mollie with Graham to 'see who she met, and where she went, because I thought she may get into trouble', to having undermined her daughter's relationship with Teddy Sell, to having assaulted her daughter in front of Hubert Clifford, even to having brandished a carving knife at her ('Yes but I would not do her any harm'). Ethel backtracked so far from her earlier certitudes that, at least on the face of it, she moved from denying any part in her daughter's death to denying any *recollection* of involvement in it: 'If I did anything to my daughter to bring about her death on the early morning of November 20th 1930 [sic] I cannot remember doing it.' To this, however, a caveat should be added: Ethel did not make a second statement. Her admission to relations with Graham remained in the form of O'Keeffe's record of their interview, meaning it lacked the weight of a document she had signed after having it read to her.

Despite being fetched at 8 a.m. and not released until after 9 p.m., Graham was made of sterner stuff: even his inquisitors had to concede that he 'consistently protest[ed] his innocence'. Yes, he had slept in the second bedroom that night; no, his sister was mistaken in recalling him in the sleep-out. 'I know she said that,' Graham said.

'But it is a deliberate lie.' Yes, he had on occasions followed Mollie; no, he had not done so on his own.

> Lambell: Did you ever follow Mollie when she went out with a young man named Sell to the Victory Theatre?
> Graham: No.
> Lambell: She says [sic] you did and Mrs Dean also told us you followed Sell.
> Graham: They are both telling lies. I have only followed Mollie on about four occasions and each time Mrs Dean was with me.
> Lambell: Why did you follow her at all? What is it to do with you who she went with?
> Graham: I only followed her because her mother told me.

Yes, he was close to Ethel Dean; no, he was not *that* close to Ethel Dean.

> Lambell: How long have you been having intercourse with Mrs Dean?
> Graham: I have never had intercourse with Mrs Dean.
> Lambell: She says you have, and you and she have been having intercourse in her bed for years past.
> Graham: That is a lie.

The certainty was impressively solid given the duration and tenor of the interrogation, of which Graham would give a firsthand account:

> When I got there I was taken into a large room. A detective sat on each side of me, and one was seated at the table, apparently writing.

They stared into my eyes, pushing their faces up close to mine. One of them said, 'I want you to confess.' I asked him what he wanted me to confess to and he then said, 'You killed Molly Dean.' I said, 'It's a lie.'

The detectives asked me if somebody else had killed Molly, and suggested that I had held her while she was struck. They kept shooting questions at me, one question following the other so quickly that I was unable to answer properly. They had me crying for three hours, and I don't mind admitting it, although I am a grown man.

Graham was made to dress in his grey suit and blue overcoat, and to parade up and down the police yard, while a selection of eyewitnesses looked on. The enfilade of questions in the interview room ceased only in the superintendent's presence. When it resumed, it threatened to turn physical:

Another detective came into the room and asked if I have confessed yet. When he was told I had not, he said, 'We have had murderers and the worst type of criminals and liars in this room, but the worst of all is you. You are the biggest liar that has ever stood in this room yet.' He stood up in front of me and said, 'I have a good mind to knock your block off.' I said, 'Have a go.'

When Graham added to his previous statement, the contradictions were entered as accusations: 'The statement of my sister that I slept in the sleep-out at our house during the night of 20 November . . . is a deliberate lie and the statement of Mrs Dean that I was intimate with her for several years is a deliberate lie, although I visited her regularly.

I cannot account for her making such a statement.' His responses otherwise were matter-of-factly transcribed.

> Lambell: A man of your description was seen following Mollie Dean in Dickens Street the night she was murdered. Was it you?
> Graham: No.
> Lambell: A man similar to you was seen at St Kilda railway station about midnight the same night. Was that you?
> Graham: No.
> Lambell: Did you do anything to bring about Mollie's death?
> Graham: No.

Suspects under questioning: public interest quickened again. Without naming them, a reporter from *The Sun* watched Adam Graham and Ethel Dean depart the Detective Office separately: 'The man seemed unaffected by the long interrogation, but the woman showed signs of fatigue. She walked unsteadily to the police car, in which she was driven home.'

For the Meldrumites, Christmas 1930 also passed solemnly. The Skippers drove to Lakes Entrance for a week. Betty Davies was staying in nearby Kalimna; Sue Vanderkelen remained at Mornington. Colahan was withdrawing from Pangloss to a fifth-floor studio in the Dudley Building, at 527 Collins Street – location of Max Meldrum's first studio. When they returned from their holiday, Lena Skipper and her daughter Helen came to assist his packing and cleaning before the house was signed over to Vi. While they were there, Colahan was startled by an unexpected call preluding the arrival of detectives. 'They may be going to arrest me,' he said gloomily. In fact, they asked more questions of Lena, including whether she had been jealous of Mollie for having accompanied Mervyn to the theatre on occasion. Lena responded tartly that her husband was a man of 'many tickets and many friends', and hoped that 'this would satisfy them'.

It must have, because nothing from the Skippers formed part of the brief the police forwarded to Coroner Grant on 14 January. Nor were statements handed up from the Leasons, the Jorgensens, Fritz Hart, Sue Vanderkelen or Vi Colahan – all caught up in the charivari of Mollie's love life. There *were* mentions, hints, parts savouring of a greater whole. And as rumours circulated, the inquest's possibilities were widely foreshadowed, even in interstate newspapers like Sydney's *Sun*, Brisbane's *Telegraph* and Perth's *Daily News*. Adelaide's daily *Mail* foretold 'remarkable disclosures' that would 'cause surprise in art, literature and music circles', with mention expected 'of the association of prominent men with Miss Dean'. Adelaide's weekly *Observer* included an ear-witness account of a *sotto voce* conversation between two men about 'a recent court case', beginning with a 'filthy jest':

'Have you heard the other one, the . . .' the whispering continued for half a sentence.

'Yes I know that. Extraordinary how they make 'em up, isn't it?'

In turn the tall man became the whisperer. 'I suppose you've heard what they are saying about . . .'

They were now wallowing in the Mary Dean 'case'.

'Yes,' said the elderly man. 'I heard that. People will say anything, won't they?'

'They say,' said the tall man, 'that she . . .'

He whispered an appalling libel of the dead girl.

'Yes,' said the elderly man. 'I heard that . . .'

After 'fifty yards of silence', noted the eavesdropper, the conversationalists 'began to complain about the appalling quality of yellow journalism'.

In photographs of crowds surging through the gates of the City Morgue to attend the inquest when it began on Thursday 29 January, there are many expectant smiles to be seen. News was bleak, times grim, circumstances straitened. The basic wage had just been slashed 10 per cent, and beef withdrawn from the dole ration. The coroner's courtroom at the morgue was bare and poky, unused to the pressure on its bar table from learned counsel, and on its seating from a public audience. But it would host for a couple of days the town's most popular and least expensive theatre. *Truth* reviewed it in terms that would have flattered a stage production: 'two days' tense gripping drama' and 'two days of deep allegation and violent denials' in which 'the mounting pile of evidence paled stories of previous crimes into the very shadow of mediocrity'. And what a plot: 'Like a winding stair it climbed – ever towards sensation. Each step added its new phase; its new angle and its astonishment.'

For the Meldrumites, the inquest proved a good deal less salacious than might have been feared. Some of them were photographed as they arrived, but only Colahan and Lewis had to testify, and they were expertly shepherded by Jim Minogue's younger brother Henry, a barrister with a speciality in libel that would not have been lost on the attending reporters. In July 1929, Minogue had acted for a self-styled hypnotist, herbalist, spiritualist and psychometrist whose claims he could read souls by pressing flowers against his head had been called a fraud by *Truth*: despite this seemingly unpromising brief, he had won his client windfall damages of £3500.

Colahan was reinforced by solid ranks of supporters. Mervyn Skipper sat up the front with him and Betty Davies, who enjoyed flirting with one of the detectives; Lena Skipper kept Norman Lewis company at the rear; the Jorgensens and Leasons joined in debriefings at Colahan's new studio, holding their nose at the newspaper coverage. 'How far from the truth these papers get!' scoffed Lena. 'I can't take them seriously at all.' But if they were objects of curiosity, they also occasioned a good deal of sympathy. As *Smith's Weekly* observed, Melbourne's 'Bohemia' did not emerge at the inquest as so *à rebours*:

> 'Bohemianism' was the keynote of the colour scheme. One felt that whoever the individuals whom circumstance forced into its pillory, and whatever the outcome, 'Bohemianism' so called was indicted. But 'Bohemianism', of the kind that answers to the name in Australia, is not among the steep places that lead to destruction; nor is it a classifiable disorder, like cirrhosis of the liver, to be regarded as an extra life insurance risk.
>
> During the two days' inquest there were in attendance at the Morgue (and not only in the seats reserved for prospective witnesses), several quite authentic 'Bohemians' as 'Bohemianism' is locally understood; and, with two or three exceptions, the only external signs to distinguish them from ordinary mortals seemed to consist of heavier bi-focals and an extra inch or two of hair. Mr Colin Colahan, slender and weedy and ascetic, with pale blue eyes gazing mildly through heavy glasses, with the serene expression of a bronze contemplating the Gautama Buddha, must have been a sad disappointment to any whose riotous imagination had pictured Molly Dean's hero as a colourful sheik.

No: from the opening of proceedings, Llewellyn C. Jones, counsel assisting the coroner, was stimulated by the more conventionally tawdry. The Crown was in headlong pursuit of Ethel Dean and Adam Graham, at first through the flustered Ralph Dean, who strove none-too-subtly to tone down the statement he had given police.

Jones: Your mother and deceased sister were friendly?

Ralph: Yes.

Jones: Always?

Ralph: Well, they had rows.

Jones: You mean frequent quarrels?

Ralph: No.

Jones: But they were nearly always quarrelling.

Ralph: No.

Jones: Did you tell the police they were always quarrelling?

Ralph: They had a few good quarrels. I cannot remember what I told police.

Jones: Did your mother object to the life your sister had been leading?

Ralph: Yes, she had been leading a rather bohemian life, and my mother objected to the man friends she had been meeting.

Jones: Your mother has struck at your sister?

Ralph: Yes, my mother has hit her.

Jones: Did your mother once threaten to do away with herself?

Ralph: I believe so.

Jones: A man called Adam Graham used to frequently visit your house?

Ralph: Yes.

Jones: Your sister was not friendly with him?

Ralph: She never went out with him.

'Of course she did not go out with him,' said Sadie Fields when
her turn came. 'She did not like him.' Mollie's friends held nothing
back. Sadie told the coroner of Graham's unwanted attentions, of
the surveillance that Mollie had endured, of the bruises that Mollie
had worn. Teddy Sell reported some of Mollie's remarks: that Ethel
disapproved of everyone she knew; that Graham lay at the bottom of
the trouble; her reaction to the letter Ethel had sent Teddy: 'That's
just like her.' George Browne remained unmistakably confounded by
Ethel's visit in April 1929: the way Ethel had complained of Mollie's
invoking her professors in argument at home; the way Ethel had
rejected Browne's offer to relocate Mollie to the country because she
needed her money; most mournfully, how Mollie seemed to be 'going
to pieces' when last they had met. Also on the first day came the
eyewitnesses, including James Nankivell, who believed it could have

'Grim-lipped': Ethel Dean at the inquest

been Graham following Mollie down Dickens Street, and boarding house proprietor Henry Coles, who consented that Graham and Ethel might have been the man and woman he saw near Mollie at St Kilda railway station.

On advice from counsel, respectively A. L. Read and Leo Cussen, neither Ethel nor Graham testified; Graham even started holding a protective hand in front of his face as camera bulbs flashed. But while this precluded the risk of self-incrimination, it also surrendered the second morning to Lambell's lengthy recitation of his evolving investigation, and candid view of his quarries: Graham's maintenance that 'everyone was lying but himself'; Ethel's having 'never cried in my presence, or shed a tear since I first saw her'. Read raised the predictable spectre of admissions under duress, and even falsification of the record of interview.

> Read: Did you say [to Ethel] 'tell us all about it and nothing will happen to you'?
> Lambell: No.
> Read: Did she admit intimacy with Graham after a lot of persuasion?
> Lambell: No, not a great deal.
> Read: Do you know now that Mrs Dean emphatically denies ever admitting any intimacy with Graham?
> Lambell: That surprises me. I didn't think she would deny it.

But who could tell? In the absence of their direct testimony, onlookers fell back on grading the accused from their demeanours. *Truth* thought Graham 'stoic' and Ethel 'grim-lipped', while sympathising with teenage Ralph: 'Tears often welled into his eyes and coursed down his cheeks, and at the end his head dropped to his mother's shoulder in a spasm of weeping.' Betty Davies remembered Ethel as a 'black-eyed old witch', Graham as 'a great bull of a fellow' cursed by his complexion: 'He was one of these very, very red-headed people with very florid skin. Poor lad he'd had an attack of boils in his youth.' Lena's views remained characteristically unreconstructed:

> Mrs Dean was a mass of emotion and whispered to herself 'it's a lie, it's a lie' to all evidence against her. She looks a crazed woman. Certainly Molly's home life must have been awful. Apparently, the mother and this young man joined forces against her but Molly loved sensation and probably caused them to act as they did without really any motive for the crime.

As the second afternoon wore on, the gaze on Graham hardened, notably when he appeared to prompt an answer by his mother, Bella. 'Who is this young man?' Coroner Grant asked her.

'My son,' said Bella sheepishly.

'Stand away!' the coroner said testily. 'He has no right to suggest words to you. He must go and sit in the body of the court. If you are nervous I will get a policeman to stand beside you.'

As the coroner beckoned Lambell, Bella held up a horrified hand. 'Oh no!' she cried. 'Not that man!' As Graham resumed a seat in front, Betty Davies enjoyed the tension: 'I could see his neck swelling, getting more and more purple with his blood pressure going up. It was a dramatic moment.' More was to follow. When Llewellyn Jones told the coroner that he had no further evidence, Graham was called on to stand and in a faltering voice uttered his only audible words of the two days: 'I plead not guilty and on my counsel's advice reserve my defence. That's all I have to say, Mr Coroner.' Grant then pronounced his

'Gripping drama': the crowd surges towards the inquest

finding that Mary Winifred Dean had died from injuries feloniously, unlawfully and maliciously inflicted: 'And I find that Adam Graham murdered her.' There was uproar.

13

A CHILDLESS CRADLE

'And so the ghost of Molly Dean was laid and, sadly, no-one
seemed to mourn her.'
— Betty Roland, *The Eye of the Beholder* (1984)

Thus Betty Davies — by then Betty Roland, after the elapse of half a century, in her memoir of the Meldrumites. As the inquest concluded, in fact, the circle of which Mollie had formed part was readying to reassert itself. Through January, perhaps in an effort to buck up his friend's spirits, Percy Leason had been preparing a lavish tribute to Colahan for *Art in Australia*, invoking Rembrandt, Constable, Velázquez and Corot, but arguing further that his friend's work was 'beyond the range of a writer on art'. Only a painter could hold a view on Colahan, insisted Leason, and only in paint — a claim no less extravagant for its utter sincerity. The purpose, no doubt, was rehabilitative. The pair chose, defiantly, to illustrate the article not only with a streetscape but with the *Standing Nude* that Colahan had exhibited in April 1930, referred to in Chapter 6 — whose subject may well have been Mollie Dean.

Some who had undergone an experience like Colahan's might

have craved a period of contemplation, in seclusion or even obscurity. He appears to have felt nothing of the kind. On the Tuesday after the inquest, for example, he posted a letter to the secretary of the Crown Law Department.

Sir,

I was required by the police department to attend the coroner's inquest on January 29th and 30th. As a result of this my work was held up for two days. At the coroner's court I was informed that being a professional man my application for reimbursement of loss thus entailed should be made to your department. I calculate this loss as at least one guinea per day.

Yours faithfully

Colin Colahan

Probably rather taken aback that a man should seek to be compensated for attending a procedure to resolve his lover's murder, the secretary referred the letter to David Grant, who confirmed having receiving a similar inquiry from Colahan:

The writer of the written letter attended the inquest concerning the death of Molly Dean which was held on the 29th and 30th ultimo and gave evidence.

He asked for expenses and was told that as he had not suffered any loss in wages he could only be allowed out of pocket sums expended in necessary travelling and meals. As he walked away without saying whether this allowance was acceptable it was assumed he did not press his claim.

It was suggested by my orderly that he might communicate with the law department if he was dissatisfied.

> Mr Colahan is an artist who lost two days from his studio but we could not express this loss in terms of money.

The department's acting secretary was advised to inform Colahan that he was 'not entitled to any expenses other than fares'. But if you've the effrontery to seek payment for attending your murdered girlfriend's inquest, using her nude in *Art in Australia* hardly seems so bold.

The Meldrumites were then emboldened by controversy. On 11 February 1931, *The Herald* reported that National Gallery director Bernard Hall had 'incensed' many painters by decreeing the removal of Max Meldrum's *A Peasant of Pacé* in order to accommodate the newly acquired *Sweet Nell of Old Drury* by W. B. McInnes – a portrait of actress Nellie Stewart that had appeared alongside Colahan's *An Autumn Bunch* in the Christmas *Table Talk*. *The Herald* quoted Leason as describing the decision as 'scandalous', and the gallery's further indifference to the work of Colahan and Jorgensen as 'deplorable'. As the journalist noted: 'Probably no painter in recent times has caused more controversy than Max Meldrum.'

The Herald left the Meldrumites' recent notoriety unmentioned, but Lena Skipper noted Leason's conviction that Hall's Machiavellianism was on show: 'Percy said Bernard Hall put it away because the Meldrum school are in bad repute, one of its members being connected with the Molly Dean murder, as the lady passed her last night alive at the home of one Colin Colahan.' Jim Minogue organised a strategising luncheon with the Skippers at a Chinese restaurant, probably the Chung Wah in Heffernan Lane, where Vance Palmer drafted a letter of protest. After Louis Esson and Donald Thomson appended their signatures, Colahan, Jorgensen and Farmer had the clever notion of cajoling McInnes himself into signing, and embarked for the artist's home in Alphington where he obligingly did so. The initiative had a comic sequel when the artists arrived at the Heidelberg residence of Clewin Harcourt, a portrait artist just returned from Europe, followed soon after by McInnes, who had changed his mind, fearful of offending the powerful Hall; Harcourt felt the same way. The *Herald* letters to the editor column ran a number of complaints about Hall's heresy, although only one, Fritz Hart's, from outside Meldrum's acknowledged acolytes. If unavailing, the campaign was at least vitalising: Lena enjoyed the 'excitement and humour' of the situation, while feeling that it 'really goes back to the Dean murder case, as Hall took that opportunity to thrash a dog when he was down'. They were determined not to be down long.

The day the gallery trustees upheld Hall's decision to demote *A Peasant of Pacé* marked another end: the Crown Law Department confirmed that Adam Graham would not after all go to trial. It was not in the end so surprising. That detectives had let the coroner lay the charge; that a bail surety of only £1000 had been sought; that the force was itself in disarray: these had all convinced the accused's solicitor, Percy Tully, that the Crown knew its case to be weak. He turned attention on the force: 'If we are to believe in the well-known principle of British justice that a person is deemed innocent until he is found guilty, it is time a public outcry was made against such practices of the police.' When Graham was interviewed by the *Weekly Times*, these practices were made the stuff of melodrama:

> When I was last interviewed at the Detective Office on January 9, one of the detectives said: 'You know you killed Molly Dean. Her ghost will haunt you all the days of your life.'

He picked up my right hand and was looking at the back of it when the other detective came in the door. He grabbed me by the left arm and examined my left hand. One of them said, 'Yes, these are the hands that killed Molly Dean.' Apparently a man has no redress for this sort of thing.

When Ethel was interviewed by *Smith's Weekly*, she was apoplectic:

'The cruel, heartless treatment to which I have been subjected by the detectives,' Mrs Dean said. 'The manner in which I was made by them to appear in the worst possible light, the awful, malicious lies that have been circulated about me – my life has been made a hell. And by what? Lies, lies, all lies. When I think of what I have suffered, of what I am still suffering, is this our much proclaimed justice?

This suffering, jarringly, consisted entirely of what she had undergone at the hands of police. Of her daughter the piece contained little more than a postscript: 'Mrs Dean went on to say that although she had been accused of treating Molly harshly, she had never done anything other than exercise the just rights of a parent.' There was, however, evidence for her chief complaint: 'God knows, even an innocent person has little chance when the Melbourne police are after convictions. Recent events have proved that.'

Crown prosecutor Clifford Book would have nodded ruefully. His 27 February 1931 recommendation that the Crown Solicitor file a *nolle prosequi* in *R v Graham* is missing from the department's files, but his reasoning was hardly opaque. Nine days earlier he had filed another *nolle prosequi* in *R v McMahon* after reviewing the police's work on the murder of Mena Griffiths. To check the counterclaims

'Lies!': Ethel Dean protests

collected by *Truth*, Book had taken the unusual step of visiting Leeton himself, Senior Detective James Bruce driving him there with McMahon and McMahon's counsel. Witness after witness picked McMahon out of line-ups. When the schoolgirl put her hand on his shoulder, identifying him as that aspiring euphonium player, McMahon burst into tears. Detective Bruce's eyes may have moistened too.

The police's failure to make the case against McMahon had been a humiliation – 'a stigma', said *Truth*, 'which is going to affect it unpleasantly for a long time'. Looking at the wholly circumstantial and inferential case against Graham, Book would have been loath to risk a repeat. It was bad enough two weeks later when the inquest into Hazel Wilson's death proceeded. In the absence of a suspect, police here had fixated on Hazel's father, Frank. Frank had been violent towards his wife, at least until his mother-in-law's death six years earlier; the family had also, it was acknowledged, been financially stretched by Hazel's tuberculosis. But nothing connected Frank to the murder except the dogmatism of none other than Senior Detective James Bruce, so described:

> There is something I would like to say and I am going to say it. It is that in the Detective Office, Senior Detective Bruce said to me: 'Look I will tell you, you damned old fool, just say you caught her by the neck and she went out, and you will be walking about the streets after.' I said 'Why would I say that?' He said 'You know.' When I am spoken to like that in the Detective Office I have to put up with a lot, and it is bad enough to lose a little girl. That was after the statement was made. I kept alluding to the statement and he turned to me 'they are only bloody lies'. He said that to me after I signed the statement. There were only the two of us in the room.

Bruce subsequently sued for defamation when *Smith's Weekly* aired allegations he had pressured McMahon to confess. In October 1931, he was awarded damages of £650, as was always likely – who would accept the word of a convicted sex offender over that of an experienced policeman? But there was no avoiding that the preceding year had been a disaster for the force: abject failure in three of the ghastliest murders committed in Victoria, to go with the ceaseless wranglings about its resources and industrial relations. The Wilson inquest showed the police haunted by their failures, still unsure whether they were looking for three murderers, two or even one. 'Asked did I find any point of resemblance between the mode of death [of Hazel Wilson] and that in the case of Mary Dean,

I say there was a certain resemblance in that the violence had been directly applied to the throat,' said the government pathologist, Crawford Mollison, in his statement. 'Asked could the death of Mary Dean have been similarly caused, I would say that in her case there were additional injuries to the head, but there was a definite injury to the throat as well.' In other words, he had not a clue.

It remains possible that Adam Graham killed Mollie Dean, and that Ethel either knew or feared it. Mollie had rejected them serially, and with good reason, after their petty and puritanical interferences in her life. On balance, it's also probable that Graham *did* have a sexual relationship with Ethel, and that it was the latter's shame about its possible discovery that made her such an uncooperative witness. What had happened two years earlier to mar the previous family friendship was never explained, but it was evidently serious. When Bella and Catherine Graham were interviewed some weeks after the murder, they admitted having not yet visited Milton Street to express their condolences – rather more, one imagines, than an oversight.

Yet for Graham to have prepared the ambush to which Mollie fell victim would have required some uncanny intuition. He would have needed to be aware she was returning home *that* night, on *that* train, would miss *that* tram, and would end up on *that* walking route – one must also bear in mind that he only visited the Deans on the evening of 20 November because Gladys Healey was otherwise engaged. Graham knew the lie of the lane from it being Gladys's garage, but that knowledge was available to anyone, not least an offender already roaming the streets and taking opportunistic advantage of unaccompanied women, of whom we know at least one and possibly more existed.

That precious prosecution brief, which had eluded Mollie's previous chroniclers, seemed at times a veritable marvel – a window on the streets of St Kilda and Elwood as the characters crisscrossed beneath the same stars. Yet it was a misted pane, a persuasive rather than an objective chronicle, weakest of all when it tried to confirm sightings of Graham as following in Mollie's tracks by reference to a distinctive gait. Police had lined up a score of eyewitnesses to identify Robert McMahon from sightings in Fawkner Park in broad daylight. Almost all had been wrong. The reliance on a handful of late-night glimpses of shadowy figures in poorly lit streets to finger Graham showed a misplaced residual faith. Before the modern snares of DNA and CCTV, of course, police could do little better – fingerprints, in this case inconclusive, and post-mortem examination, here unenlightening, were the limits of their science. Bracketed as it was by the murders of Mena Griffiths and Hazel Wilson, then, the pursuit of Mollie Dean's killer evinced desperation for a conviction rather than for justice.

Five years later, those brackets would be unexpectedly removed. On 2 December 1935, the bound, gagged and suffocated body of six-year-old June Rushmer was discovered lying face down in sword grass outside Leongatha in Gippsland. The killing resembled another recent local murder, that of twelve-year-old Ethel Belshaw, who had been found on a patch of scrub near the pier in Inverloch, 27 kilometres away, at the start of the year. When the talk of a road gang having a smoko at nearby Dumbalk turned to the Rushmer tragedy, one workmate joked to another: 'Wasn't it you I saw riding your pushbike near there the other day, Arnold?' Had 36-year-old Arnold Sodeman deflected the jest with another, it might have passed without notice. Instead he barked: 'No, you bloody well didn't.' He stood up, discarded the rest of his tea and walked to his tent. When the gang contacted police, the detective sent to interview Sodeman, who had lived with an unsuspecting wife and daughter in Inverloch for the past five years, was none other than Detective Sergeant Jeremiah O'Keeffe. Unlike Adam Graham, this suspect folded quickly. When O'Keeffe commented that his alibi for the killing of June Rushmer was 'as empty as a childless cradle' and invited his confession, Sodeman replied: 'There is not only this one . . .'

The psychiatrist Dr Reg Ellery, who five years earlier had ascertained Mollie Dean's death for Colahan, was an expert witness

'Not only this one': Arnold Sodeman

at Sodeman's trial for his four murders. There was a good case of diminished responsibility: Sodeman had been monstrously abused in childhood; his father and grandfather had ended their days in mental hospitals; he was suffering, it would be learned from his autopsy, from leptomeningitis, a degenerative brain disease aggravated by the alcohol associated with all four murders. But Sodeman, waiving appeals for the sake of his family, went compliantly to the gallows in June 1936, the first of six hangings in Victoria in the next six years cheerfully waved through by Premier Albert Dunstan of the Country Party.

In the case of Mollie Dean, no such serendipitous discovery awaited. Perhaps it had already been brushed past. Evidence had been given sparingly, grudgingly, on all sides. Newspapers were actually a good deal more successful at presenting Mollie in the round, treating her sympathetically, even seriously. 'The little group of literary and artistic lions that every big city possesses are a sure attraction for a type of girl with a certain mentality, but Molly Dean was no notoriety hunter,' reported *Smith's Weekly*. 'She moved naturally into the circle with its triple link of interest, in music, reading, and painting.' What eluded the journalists was the ambivalence about Mollie within that circle, a principality of bohemia whose protocols she flouted as a woman by expressing desires and ambitions. But then, the Meldrumites hardly understood this about themselves.

There would surely have been more to glean at Milton Street, but no-one would concertedly revisit the crime in the lifetime of those involved. For the police, it was a site of failure; for family and friends, it was a locus of shame. Rumour was, therefore, allowed to flourish without correction. In addition to the canard about Clarence Weber and the speculation about Ernest Wilson, whispers

suggested a cover-up by police commissioner Thomas Blamey and/
or chief secretary Tom Tunnecliffe, probably because they refused to
endow a reward for information about her killer. Another persistent
story achieved the permanence of print in *The Eye of the Beholder*:
'Shortly after the inquest Adam Graham and Mrs Dean were married
and, as a wife cannot be compelled to give evidence against her husband in a capital case, the Crown was deprived of its chief witness and
the case collapsed.'

Credulously republished in several places, the story is quite
erroneous, although it mangles fact rather than concocting it,
springing most likely from whom Adam Graham *did* marry, some
seventeen years after Mollie Dean's death: Gladys Healey. The family
story is that Adam and Catherine Graham felt unable to wed until
their widowed mother died, which she did not until May 1946. Adam
at last married Gladys on Boxing Day 1947 at Holy Trinity Church,
Balaclava, looking in photographs decades older than his forty-eight
years, heavily set and white-haired: his once-red barnet, he would say,
had greyed rapidly under the stress of suspicion. Catherine married
two years later. Neither marriage yielded children.

Eric Westbrook would complain that Adam Graham had
'disappeared'. In fact, he spent thirty years living with Gladys at
98 Milton Street, in the same block in which Mollie was murdered.
Does a murderer do that? Perhaps one chillingly cold-blooded.
Does a woman marry a man she knows or fears has killed another?
Perhaps one very docile and tractable. Yet this seemed a little more
difficult to credit when, with the help of the will Graham lodged
before his death from heart disease on 3 September 1980, I traced
his niece Deanne, born the year after Adam married Gladys, who
was her father Ivan's sister. She had nothing but fond memories
of her indulgent 'Uncle Scotty' and 'Auntie Gatt'. Deanne and

her husband, Michael Carroll, still owned her uncle's crystal cabinet and large camphor box. Could the man who married her aunt have been a murderer? Well, the Carrolls agreed, with people who can tell? But, naturally, it was hard to square with a perception rooted in a child's upward gaze at an imagined adult perfection.

Ethel Dean, meanwhile, never remarried. Three years to the day after his sister was killed, Ralph married Joyce Millar, 22-year-old daughter of a master builder. To raise a family they moved to Oakleigh; to recuperate from hers, Ethel sold Milton Street in November 1947, moved to Malvern, then St Kilda, then Surrey Hills. They would be re-entwined by the passage of years: Ethel's twilight was spent with Ralph and Joyce in Belmore Road, Balwyn. By the time she died of breast cancer in Westbury Private Hospital, Deepdene, on 12 October 1962, Mollie Dean's 85-year-old mother had been a widow more than half her life. As mentioned in the introduction to this book, Ralph's children preferred not to divulge such recollection or information as they may or may not have had. But what a gash for a family to bear – the suspicion of involvement in a daughter's bloody death, the knowledge that at the very least their fears, resentments, actions and inactions had contributed to it. And if the Deans were less than candid with investigators, people forget, omit and even lie for reasons other than that they are guilty of a crime.

No murder, it has been said, is ever completely 'solved'. The world never returns to the way it was; the absence of the victim goes on ramifying; the handling of the killer will ever be contentious. But at least the sentencing of a perpetrator generates a sort of narrative arc. When nobody is punished, the reproach distributes itself more widely, less predictably – over individuals, systems, societies, even the victim themselves, for incurring what can come to be felt as foreseeable danger. Instead of arcing, the narrative fans. Which is why although her former companions thought that they had finished with Mollie Dean, she had not quite finished with them.

14

ADVANCE, RETREAT, WITHDRAWAL, SURRENDER

*I was frightened but at the same time I felt elated – I, too,
I thought, am persecuted and misunderstood.*
— Mervyn Skipper, *A Pressman's Soul* (c1936)

Colin Colahan was a prolific artist. Hundreds of his paintings are known to exist; hundreds are in private hands; hundreds more would have been lost or destroyed. These must include most of the canvases for which Mollie Dean posed. *Standing Nude* may be of Mollie, but the provenance is uncertain. Only one work is absolutely guaranteed as her – that last collaboration as artist and model, mentioned in Chapter 9.

In *Sleep*, Mollie is folded gracefully into Colahan's plush armchair, head canted sideways, feet nestled cosily – not an easy pose to maintain, and hinting at prior experience. It makes of her a beautiful object, but there seems more to such a frankly and sympathetically sensuous realisation – could it be called a lover's view, with its savouring of the body's curves and corners, the sitter's repose and abandon? The skin is as fresh and pink and quiveringly alive as the night the paint was applied to the 71 cm by 50 cm canvas – the night, and there is no escaping it, before Mollie's death. You are gazing at the painting of a woman doomed to die, of a body a killer was driven to ravage and mutilate little more than twenty-four hours later: one could surely find no tenser overlappings of 'the male gaze', when one man must destroy that which another has sought to celebrate.

Sleep veils its subject's identity. Garry Kinnane speculated that Colahan 'could not give a thought to finishing it' after Mollie's death. Yet Colahan, incomparably swift, never overworked a canvas – Mollie's fear of being recognised is the likelier influence. Referring in her diary to Mollie 'standing for a nude for Colin and the face is in shadow', Lena recalled refraining from the taunt: 'Have you heard Colin is doing a nude of Mrs Eve, she is quite recognisable by her hip?' What's destined for permanent incompletion is not perhaps the canvas but its focus: the viewer aware of the sitter's identity cannot escape contemplating the life not led, the words not written, the loves not experienced. Which may be why, as Kinnane noted, Colahan 'could not bear it', and, as he cleaned out Pangloss in January 1931, disposed of it.

Though born seven years after her death, Robin Bradley grew up with Mollie Dean. He is a son of the violinist Reginald Bradley, and member of a fecund musical family: Reginald's siblings were soprano Aileen, violinist Leo, pianist Kevin, cellist Norman; his wife Eunice was a concert pianist; their first son, Desmond, was for two decades among the world's outstanding lead violinists, starring with the Royal Philharmonic Orchestra. Reginald was a friend of Max Meldrum, knew Colahan, and acquired *Sleep* for a princely £15. It went up, after Reginald and Eunice married, in the family music room in Essendon, and Robin grew to adore it. He sold the painting twenty years ago to a private collector, and part of him remains regretful: 'Very much. I miss it very much. It is a very beautiful picture.'

Here, it might be felt, is the likeness of Mollie that makes up for the monochrome flatness of that solitary photograph, endlessly and pointlessly reproduced – a likeness not identifying but nonetheless biographical, enfolding her youthful vitality that had enticed Colahan, his artistic gift that had exhilarated Mollie, and even the unresolved furtiveness of their relationship. To this day, *Sleep* has never been publicly shown. In the painting's uniqueness lie both the splendour and the practical limits of Colahan's art, which by this stage had come fruitfully to an accommodation with impressionism while ever tabooing expressionism. The arrest twelve years later of the soldier strangler Private Edward Leonski would call forth Albert Tucker's *Memory of Leonski*, and his cascading *Images of Modern Evil*; Colahan's dedication to the objective science of appearances afforded him no scope to revisit a tragedy in the midst of his own life. Nothing in tonalism left energy over from the relentless transcription of nature and interrogation of surfaces. The preference was for subjects that stayed still and at safe distance, while life sat in temporary abeyance to one side.

One could not always be painting, of course. Life had to resume. But they must sometimes have passed within touching distance. Among Colahan's best-known later works are the result of a 1940 encounter with George Bernard Shaw. Colahan the raconteur relished relating how he first approached the playwright about painting him. Shaw was friendly but dismissive, trying to ward the artist off by proffering a postcard photograph. 'While we've been talking I could have completed a couple of portraits of you!' Colahan jested – a sally with which Shaw was so enchanted that he acquiesced, on condition that he could keep working throughout. Each kept his bargain. In his minimal time at the playwright's Whitehall flat, Colahan completed two paintings, reflecting Shaw's moving between two positions:

head down and writing, head up and thinking. What were Colahan's thoughts? Did his mind traverse the experience of *Pygmalion* at the Bijou Theatre on the night of 20 November 1930? *'Are you a man of good character where women are concerned?' 'Have you ever met a man of good character where women are concerned?'* Having once joked about finding himself 'a rich wife', Colahan had just remarried, to a comely actress, Ursula Marx, whose financier father had relieved all his new son-in-law's money concerns. What was Mollie Dean to him now except a memory? Except that memories have ways of making themselves felt.

On 14 March 1931, the day it emerged that Adam Graham would not go to trial, the Meldrumites had scheduled a joint birthday party for Percy Leason and Mervyn Skipper at the former's home. The disclosure, depriving them of finality in the murder of Mollie Dean, muted festivities: Colahan arrived late and left early. Both the Skippers and the Leasons thought they had detected a coolness from neighbours since the inquest, and were striving towards a sort of normality. The Skippers left that day with Clarice Beckett, who stayed with them overnight, and painted six studies of Eaglemont the following morning; in the afternoon they drove to the Botanic Gardens, where Fritz Hart was conducting one of his popular outdoor concerts. There was an Easter camp at San Remo on Westernport Bay where talk continued of the group's quarrel with Bernard Hall; news had by now also been received, via Alma Figuerola, that Meldrum planned returning to Australia. But one detects in the group a deepening inertia, reflected in a desire to refight old battles – overtly to assert their continued relevance, less consciously to roll back time. Art historians today sift the 1920s and 1930s for the seeds of modernism: from paintings like Grace Cossington Smith's *Rushing* and

Margaret Preston's *Implement Blue* to the linocuts of Dorrit Black and the textiles of Michael and Ella O'Connell. Just round the corner now was Sam Atyeo's *Organised Line to Yellow* and his invocation of Schopenhauer: 'Art is only art when it is not nature.' Yet Meldrum's antithetical belief that 'all great art is a return to nature' positioned his followers at an impossible angle to the coming torrent. Perhaps they still smarted from their brush with notoriety, were looking inward, marking time.

Colahan had been reconciled with Sue Vanderkelen, though he had rescinded his stammered marriage proposal, and she was never to enjoy a more serious commitment than Mollie. He accoutred his studio-cum-living-quarters on the fifth floor of the Dudley Building with rich tapestries, a handsome armoire, an oak refectory table, and a host of items raffishly displayed; a makeshift kitchen and amply cushioned bed completed its domestication. But his circumstances were unmistakably diminished, along with his reputation. Before the murder, he had been among the four or five most successful painters in Australia; now came few commissions and fewer sales, until the National Gallery bought a small early work, *The Little Aphrodite*, using funds from the Felton Bequest. Not even Meldrum's return, after the brief euphoria on reunion at Victoria Dock, relieved things. His certainties were as adamantine as always. In his first interview, he decried modern art as a 'conspiracy between the artists and the dealers of today'. In his first public act, he sued a critic who on radio had maligned 'the cult of Meldrumism' as composed of wartime shirkers. The £100 he was awarded was a rare payday. The school that Meldrum opened on another floor of the Dudley Building was in competition with those of three former acolytes: Jorgensen, Colquhoun and Shore, whose partnership with George Bell was the first in Melbourne to transact in the tenets of modernism.

The Mollie Dean case had also affected the order of precedence among the Meldrumites. That Mervyn Skipper had 'defied public opinion in order to defend them', observed Betty Davies, left him a 'fully accredited member of the fraternity'. Colahan painted his portrait; Jorgensen gave his eighteen-year-old daughter Helen painting lessons. In a building at 363 Little Collins Street, Mervyn and Lena redoubled their commitment. Adjacent to a small second-hand bookshop that they endowed for Helen to run was opened a tiny gallery, named for Meldrum, with Jim Minogue in charge.

The movement, however, was ever more incestuous – something made almost literal in February 1932 when, around the time his wife Lil was bearing him a son, Jorgensen deflowered Helen. Mervyn was thunderstruck. He had readily decried bourgeois respectabilities; now his own were affronted. The relationship also exposed the variances between Colahan, the accomplished seducer, and Jorgensen, the aspirant, which the former noted with practised amusement:

> I remember once, at dinner, he looked around and said, 'Who's the most beautiful girl of our circle?' I quite innocently said, 'Of course, Sue [Vanderkelen].' He hit the roof – Helen was. Well, Helen was the most bouncy, the most gorgeous, but for pure beauty, Sue was unique. He was furious. He had to have the most beautiful girl.

This was a hinge point in the group's evolution. Jorgensen's suddenly plural love lives, coming after the growth of classes at his school at 127 Queen Street to about fifty students, further stimulated his desire to become in his own words 'a thinker who sometimes painted rather than a painter who sometimes thought' – indeed, to become the centre of his own circle. The whole Skipper family came growingly under

Jorgensen's influence; despite naming his new son Max, he slid away from Meldrum; he made Sue Vanderkelen a proxy in his rivalry with Colahan by plying her with idiosyncratic relationship advice, such as that she should bear her lover's illegitimate child, which had the effect of confusing and depressing her. 'I've hated all this free love,' admits her character Paula in 'Sue's Story'. 'I've been like a woman who wears an unbecoming hat just because it's fashionable.'

In the meantime, indeed, Colahan had rejuvenated himself, as he was wont to, by a new affair, or the resumption of an old one. Mireille Wilkinson returned to Melbourne in mid-1932, with their love child Marc and her obliviously cuckolded husband. 'Sue's Story' dramatises the consequences. Sensing Miranda Martin (Mireille) as a rival for Simon's love, Paula knows she will be found wanting: 'But Miranda, with her superficial brilliance and all the glamour of looks and wealth and a certain inaccessibility, was just what Simon would fall for in a big way. He was a sexual snob, Simon, wearing his women like [carnations in his] buttonholes, impatient when they became wilted.' She perceives, too, Simon's need to feel the superior of Sven Janssen (Jorgensen):

> 'If he [Janssen] liked a girl he'd take five years at least to win her, but they fall for me like ninepins. It only takes me . . .'
>   'Overnight,' said Paula maliciously.
>   'No,' said Simon modestly. 'No, a week. I leave the overnight achievement to Clark Gable.'

Colahan's second affair with Mireille reprised the first: she again fell pregnant with his child. François was born on 28 May 1933, around the time of Colahan's first one-man show since Mollie's death. And by now, whether despite or because of the presence of their uxorious inspiration Meldrum, the whole group seems to have been possessed by a contagious sexual carelessness. Betty Davies finally fled her marriage and 'saw no reason why I should not indulge my sexual needs with any man who happened to excite my interest', taking a 'rather vixenish delight in seeing how far I could entice them': she had flings with both Colahan and Mervyn Skipper, as well as 'a number of my erring husband's friends', before at the Jorgensens meeting Guido Baracchi, and fleeing with the incongruously wealthy communist activist to Leningrad and Moscow. A protégé of Colahan and Jorgensen, 24-year-old John Busst, was then engulfed in a bitter divorce when Chica Boileau finally cast off her hapless doctor husband, inquiry agents laying out a gaudy trail of infidelities: in a tent at an artists' camp at San Remo, at the Meldrum Gallery 'or one of the rooms adjacent thereto', in a 'single-seat touring car' on Williamstown Road, and in a doorway on Swanston Street then departing 'in a taxi cab with the blinds drawn down'.

What did not eventuate naturally could also be manoeuvred. Colahan and Jorgensen, for example, tried mischievously to manipulate an affair between mutually admiring Percy Leason and Clarice Beckett – their respective biographers differ about its consummation. Even Colahan's ex-wife, Vi, enjoyed her liberation, leaving their son with her mother to pursue an affair with the poet John Thompson, then departing Melbourne for London where she married engineer James Boyle. The group may not have mourned Mollie Dean, and would certainly not have seen themselves emulating her. But her kind of sexual insouciance had steadily become their norm.

Mollie Dean's shade fell elsewhere. Elwood residents pointed out her home in Milton Street by day, quailed superstitiously from walking

Addison Street by night. And not only did the press periodically recall the undispelled mystery of her death, but at the end of 1932 she was even published. Louis Lavater had probably scheduled Mollie's 'Subject and Content' ('A work of art is distinguished from mediocrity not by its subject but by its content') for publication two years earlier then withdrawn it on her death. As *Verse* reached the end of *its* lifespan, having exhausted Percival Serle's resources, Lavater squeezed the essay into the magazine's last edition, identifying the author as 'Mary Dean'. He was on his own now, his irascible wife having one day summoned a carrier and moved out, never to be seen again – they would divorce soon after. The loss of that pretty young poet who had written him so vivaciously must have cut deeply.

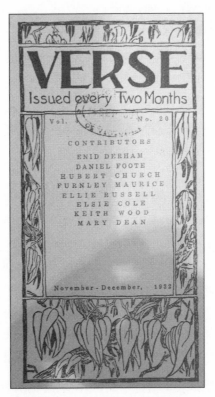

Deadline: the late Mollie Dean writes

As one publication perished, another was being conceived. Since his joining what he saw as Melbourne's artistic vanguard, Mervyn Skipper had chafed ever more against journalism's inhibitions and compromises. He saw the death of editor Samuel Prior in June 1933 as preluding *The Bulletin*'s further decline, and determined at last to strike out on his own. But when he announced his decision one evening in the Meldrumites' usual upstairs room at the Latin, Skipper was not accorded the reception he expected – Jorgensen and Colahan mocked his giving up such a cushy job as the Melbourne editor of a prestigious weekly. Skipper flushed with rage, a scene dramatised later by Betty Davies:

> 'Why do you never understand me? Why do you ridicule everything I do?' he shouted at his tormentors.
>
> 'Because you are ridiculous,' said Jorgensen. 'Look at you now, red in the face and behaving like a child. How can you expect me to respect you when you go on like that?'
>
> 'Damn you, you bastard! Damn you!' Mervyn shouted, rushing down the stairs.

Mervyn dragged Lena home in a fury and slammed a door behind him, mind swirling with suicidal thoughts. It was probably at this time he wrote a melodramatic letter to Lil Jorgensen requesting a poison draft from her medical supplies. Lil reproached him, and in due course fences were mended. But this clearly concerned more than a career change. *Pandemonium* described the world of the 1930s and its publisher's state of mind, his ambition and his despair.

The Skippers gave it their all. They shuttered their bookshop, relocated the Meldrum Gallery to Jorgensen's building, raised a little money by letting their home in Eaglemont and selling their car, then a little more from an improbable backer – Leo Brearley, only son of the inventor of stainless steel, recently arrived in Melbourne from Sheffield. First appearing in February 1934, *Pandemonium* was an earnest journal for earnest people, inky and independent, mixing an unashamedly elitist view of art with a leftward tilt in politics. It espoused pacifism, cosmopolitanism and the Douglas Credit Party, then a reforming voice in the Labor tent, destined to be drowned out in future governments. But it also read as though captive of a clique: Skipper generated much, serious and satirical, in addition to many deft cartoons; he reproduced art by Jorgensen, Colahan, Clarice Beckett and Alma Figuerola; although drawing on established writers like the Palmers and M. Barnard Eldershaw, his most regular contributors were Leason and Meldrum, the latter of whom penned a memorably scathing assault on the collection of his old enemies at the National Gallery ('vulgar', 'degrading', 'worthless', 'inept', 'hysterical', 'vicious pictorial propaganda'). And inevitably, like *Verse*, *Pandemonium* failed, publishing the last of its dozen issues in January 1935. Skipper had to seek his old job back, on inevitably poorer terms than before – humbling for a proud and troubled man. He fell compliantly in step with his confederates' next venture.

A few months earlier, the Jorgensens had acquired 3.6 hectares of bush near Percy Leason's property. Since his travels in rural France with Colahan and Colquhoun a decade earlier, Jorgensen had dreamed of a self-sustaining artists' colony made inspirational by its architecture – so was born the ever-evolving vision of 'Montsalvat', as it would be christened by its tireless cook Sue Vanderkelen after the sanctified castle in *Parsifal* and *Lohengrin*. More grandly conceived than the Boyds' 'Open Country' in Murrumbeena, in the coming vein of the Reeds' 'Heide' and the Pughs' 'Dunmoochin', Montsalvat also reflected something of the group's recent experiences. It would offer respite from the dismaying cycle of painting and exhibiting, and from the prying eyes of press and public.

Jorgensen's first generation of votaries would include Vanderkelen, the Skippers, the Leasons, and students like John Busst, Arthur Munday, George Chalmers, Nell Lempriere and Vida Turner, working with whatever materials were available, whether rammed earth, mud brick, bluestone or salvage. Jorgensen forged a particularly valuable relationship with the city wrecker Jim Whelan, who let him fossick among demolition debris and make off with windows, doors, lintels and flagstones galore. So even as Montsalvat represented a fresh tillage, its creators unknowingly sowed grains of the past. The colony's first building, called Lil's House, with its high-pitched roof and dormer windows, is connected to its first floor by a fine cast-iron staircase, clawed from the remains of the Bijou Theatre, where Mollie Dean began her final night alive.

There were two conspicuous dissenters to this bold vision. The gap opened with Meldrum by Jorgensen's messianic whimsicalities never closed. Although it was rumoured that Meldrum was driven past Montsalvat on a couple of occasions, he never visited the colony whose artistic creed derived so profoundly from his own. Jorgensen had in any case begun going by the title once Meldrum's alone, 'the Master' – and a man proverbially cannot serve two.

Mireille Wilkinson's decision to return overseas with her husband, meanwhile, finally forced Colahan to decide where his future lay – she would be taking, of course, her two sons by him. The siren song of the Northern Hemisphere was strong. Farmer and Polly Hurry were already in London, part of an Australian painting diaspora including Stella Bowen, William Dobell, Carl Hampel and

Roy de Maistre; Sam Atyeo was about to depart for Paris. Certain aspects of Melbourne seemed unlikely to change. As Nettie Palmer noted before she and Vance also headed for Europe, Australian cultural creativity was hobbled less by short supply than by anaemic demand.

There was a further personal consideration. Colahan was increasingly concerned about his eight-year-old son with Vi, David Michel, marooned at a Christian Brothers boarding school. Expatriation, the artist concluded, would resolve all the foregoing at a stroke. It is widely repeated that Colahan quit Australia never to return because of the odium associated with the death of Mollie Dean. But if his public profile had not completely recovered by the mid-1930s, his artistic profile had. Part of his raconteur's repertoire was the story of a benediction from the venerable Sir John Longstaff who – either in the bar at the Windsor Hotel or on a visit to the Dudley Building, depending on how he told it – ostentatiously swept Colahan off to lunch to publicly advertise his support. Indeed, it was a highly successful exhibition at the Athenaeum in August 1934 that made Colahan's departure possible: the £250 he received from the National Gallery for a superb portrait of Dr John Dale, a vision of purpose in a deep-red dressing-gown, would take him most of the way. Dale returned the compliment. In his capacity as government medical officer, he provided a personal letter of approval enabling Colahan to incorporate his son on his own passport. So it was that in May 1935, Colahan collected David from his grandmother, told her they were off to San Remo for the weekend, and fled. With the aid of Leason and Minogue, father and son met the train in Albury, and connected in Sydney with a ship bound for London – where Colahan, never too long tied down, deposited David with his mother. His only contribution to Montsalvat would be selling Cunégonde to John Busst.

The dissolution of the Meldrumites, as it were, was rendered still more complete by the death of Clarice Beckett six weeks later. Alone among her contemporaries, she had never travelled, explaining drolly that she had barely got the hang of painting Beaumaris. Unmarried, in her forties, yoked to her domestic responsibilities, Beckett had been working in ever greater extremity: the pneumonia that took her life developed from a chill when she was doused in a winter storm while painting. *The Age* described Beckett's passing as 'unlooked-for' – at the time, except among a tiny band of admirers, it probably applied to her painting as well. Sales at her shows barely covered the costs of framing. Beckett's mother had died a year earlier, her father would die a year later, and her status as tonalism's only still-celebrated exponent lay generations hence.

This once formidable and companionable alliance, then, had in five years fissured, faded and retreated – the five years, in fact, since Mollie Dean's death. Modernism was advancing, but rather passed them by, Montsalvat's *pisé de terre* walls forming palisades against its encroachments. Grace Cossington Smith had rendered a Sydney Harbour Bridge almost radioactive with colour; Danila Vassilieff and Yosl Bergner were documenting urban deprivation with unsentimental eyes; interior design was being made over by Fred Ward, photography ennobled by Harold Cazneaux and Max Dupain. The Meldrumites registered these buffetings: Skipper put Dupain on the cover of the last issue of *Pandemonium*. But the obduracy of the group's strongest personalities prevailed. History, in retaliation, has relegated them to its margins. In chronicling the 1930s, the National Gallery's 2017 'Brave New World' exhibition could find space for only two Becketts, and two Leasons from 'The Last of the Victorian Aborigines', his series documenting the Indigenous population of Lake Tyers – and these were discounted as 'infamous portraits' rooted in 'salvage anthropology'.

On this the influence of Mollie Dean's death should not be over-stated – the Meldrumites were born *refuseniks*. But it is also detectable. Colahan's eclipse, Jorgensen's ascendant, even Bernard Hall's revenge on Meldrum's *A Peasant of Pacé* – are all in a degree directly related. Then there are second-order effects like Percy Leason resettling his family in the United States out of disaffection with Jorgensen and the Skippers cementing their relationship by supporting Montsalvat financially. 'Don't invest in BHP,' Jorgensen would claim to have told Skipper. 'Invest in BHJ: Big-Hearted Jorgy.' As the years passed, in fact, Skipper would grow ever more biddable, a process foreshadowed in *A Pressman's Soul*.

In this autobiographical novel that Skipper commenced around the time of his agonies about *Pandemonium*, Mollie Dean looms surprisingly large, if not so much her murder as its implications. Though he affixes no name to the crime, 'the murder of the model of one of the painters in particularly atrocious circumstances' is what confirms Skipper's alter ego David Ferling in his conviction 'that the artist stood alone in a hostile environment'. His precis of the murder mixes acuity, sympathy and anti-suburban snobbery in roughly equal measure:

No good purpose would be served if I went into the details of the crime, as far as they are known, and it is likely to remain forever a mystery. Sufficient to say that the version given to the public was so unlike the reality as the rest of its newspaper pabulum. Described by the press as brilliant and beautiful, the victim was neither; but she was striking-looking, with a dark, eager, questing face, anxious and at the same time impudent; she was extremely intelligent and belonged to the petit bourgeois class which produces occasional individuals in whom mean streets, primary education and penury stimulate ambition instead of crushing it. The desire to escape from such an environment, with its accompaniments of envious, economically determined parents, jealous sisters and brothers and importunate but commonplace suitors must be tremendous but it usually finds expression in the cinema or the inner life of fantasy. This girl was of sterner stuff. She had thrust tenacious hands into the society of artists whom she found interesting by making herself of particular service to one; she was just raising herself up to an intellectual equality and more than an equality with her feminine rivals of more fortunate social origin when she was found, mutilated and dying in a dark lane near her home.

There's characteristic insight here, into Mollie's disadvantages of class and scorn of mere escapism; likewise in Ferling's world-weary critique of a city repulsed and titillated by random violence:

During my career I have had, professionally, to pass under review a wearisome succession of such violent tragedies and, so far as the public is concerned, this is what invariably occurs: the public is, at one and the same time, shocked, terrified and pleasurably thrilled. The necessities of commercial competition, not to mention their own natural curiosity, compel the newspaper proprietors to strain every nerve to present to their readers as full a picture of the affair as their limited intelligences and their inhibitions will permit them to. With hats cocked on one side and impudent expressions in their eyes, the reporters invade private homes, accompanied by photographers, and subject the occupants to an inquisition that they would hesitate to impose on their nearest friend; and they are not above bullying a helpless child. The newspapers embroider the details with imaginative fictions culled from the cinema, they speculate on the cause of the crime and demand that all sorts of measures should be taken to prevent the public conscience being outraged by a repetition of such diabolical outrages. The public's mind is filled with sinister – yes, and seductive images, even when the crime is of the most sordid variety. At the same time, some of its emotions are painful and a desire to make somebody suffer for them becomes paramount . . .

If an arrest is long delayed, the police force is attacked, the detectives are accused of incompetence and there is a demand that they should be trained in modern psychology. Dismayed by this criticism, the detectives redouble their efforts to run down the criminal and they are not above using star chamber methods and of making an arrest on evidence that would hardly be sufficient to hang a cat . . . Besides which the entire community turns itself into an amateur detective force of unexampled ingenuity and energy. Soon there is scarcely an adult person in the city who does not know who committed the crime and why. Part of this enthusiasm for crime detection is, no doubt, merely a manifestation of man's love for displaying his ingenuity in a field where neither knowledge nor talent are required; but in the present case it was accompanied with an extraordinary hate and fear directed against persons who were perfectly innocent; and this, it seemed to me, was because they were artists who happened to be unpopular.

At which point the critique subsides into self-justification. Through Ferling, Skipper presents the invasiveness of journalism as serving the interests of the general philistinism. The model's killing becomes almost incidental; the murderer's actual victim, it is inferred, was *art*. 'Her death was a painful shock but what interests me now was the relation which immediately arose between the public and my friends,' Skipper muses. 'Most people have purely sentimental and romantic notions about how artists live. They imagine that their lives are in some way richer but at the same time more reprehensible than theirs.' And so forth, at tiresome length. *A Pressman's Soul* is fictionalised, of course; but it's telling what Skipper chose to exaggerate about its factual antecedents. For his depiction of the press coverage bears little resemblance to its actuality. Even the scandal sheets that reported Mollie Dean's murder – *Truth, Smith's Weekly* et al. – ended up far more fascinated by affairs at Milton Street than among the Meldrumites. Reporters trod delicately around Mollie's relationship with Colahan; the names of Meldrum and Jorgensen were never mentioned. The public *were* intrigued, but by a mystery so dark and unfathomable why would they not have been? In a more cerebral but just as urgent fashion, Skipper also fell under the murder's spell – it afforded a way of talking himself into choices he had already made.

15

A DANGEROUS LITTLE PIECE OF GOODS

'I say Molly, do you try to flirt with everybody?'
'That's not flirting – not really George.'
'You know I – errr – I rather like you, only –'
'Only what?'
'Only you are sometimes such a little devil –'
'Oh thank you George. I wonder why I like you to call me that.'
— Fritz Hart, *Puck and Mr Perkins* (1939)

For a life so brief, Mollie Dean's touched on many others. Those individuals then had lifetimes to think of her. For the sake of completeness I followed many of them through. Not surprisingly, the men did rather better than the women. A member of the Melbourne University Regiment, Teddy Sell joined up ten days after the outbreak of war, rose to the rank of major, married and had three children, one of whom married the boss of Carlton & United Breweries. Hubert Clifford achieved the heights of the BBC's head of light music, and contributed compositions to scores of movies, including *Anna Karenina* and *The Third Man*. George Browne became principal of the Teachers' College, professor of education,

a prolific writer and thinker, then on retirement a television personality: for a decade after his 1956 retirement, *Professor Browne's Study*
was a staple of Channel 9.

The Behrend girls would remain spinsters. At the time Clara was
interviewed by police after Mollie Dean's death, she was the only family member working. 'Three unmarried sisters I decided was enough,'
she recalled, and in August 1933 accepted a job offer from her old boss
at Read's, now running the Perth department store Boans. She became
his advertising manager, the first female fellow of the Advertising
Association of Australia, and for eighteen years the president of the
West Australian chapter of the Advertising Institute, her committee otherwise composed entirely of men. Her attempt to set up a
solo agency in 1951, however, was a failure: foiled by sudden import
restrictions, she lost her capital. Clara ended up an office worker at
a technical college, cushioned in retirement only by the aged pension. Late in life, she commenced a reflective correspondence with her
cousin Gael Hammer, full of dignity, devoid of bitterness. 'I agree it is
a pity none of my sisters married, but in my case at least, I cannot see
any merit in anyone marrying just for the sake of it,' she reflected in
one letter. 'Let me say that my reasons were several and perhaps I did
not have the good fortune to meet "Mr Right". However, I have had
a most interesting, if difficult life and have few regrets. I should have
liked a daughter although not all daughters love their mothers.' There
spoke a voice of experience.

Clara's other University High classmate Joyce Pyke sought to
follow in the path her mother had forged and that Mollie had con-
templated. Six weeks after her friend's murder, she quit teaching to
try writing full time. But something went wrong. Joyce fell ill. On
29 November 1933, aged twenty-six, authorising with a firm, neat
'Joyce M. D. Pyke', she filled out a will: 'It is my wish that my body

'Scattered': Joyce Pyke

be cremated and the ashes scattered to the four winds.' Two years later, it was and they were, after her death in Brisbane's Maroona Private Hospital. The official cause was 'pyrexia and acute delusional mania'. When I was finally able to trace her nephew, he explained the family lore: that Joyce had fallen in love with a married man, never recovered from the severing of the relationship, and perished from what would now be called an eating disorder. Fifteen years after they had stood side-by-side in a photograph of the editorial committee of *The Record*, Mollie Dean and Joyce Pyke were both dead.

Who can say how Mollie's shade bore on those who walked in it? To her funeral, the novelist Bernard Cronin carried a wreath on behalf of the Society of Australian Authors; from her memory, he may have drawn some inspiration. Cronin limned the female characters of his novels like *Bracken* and *The Sow's Ear* with considerable sympathy. The latter work, described by *The Age* on its 1933 publication as 'a testimonial to Australian womanhood', is set in a Tasmanian coastal timber town oppressed by ignorance, religiosity and an 'all-enveloping bondage of sex', in which teenage girls are betrothed to older farmers in order to 'settle early and disarm the devil'. 'I suppose there is such a thing as love,' sighs sixteen-year-old poetry-loving June Windsor when it is her turn. 'It must be more . . . mean something more than . . . than just . . . having babies . . . and slaving . . . and *starving*.' It is not striving June who perishes, however, but her potential rescuer, the progressive 25-year-old schoolmaster. When June hears of his drowning, she is lost in 'Ode on a Grecian Urn' – Mollie Dean's favourite poem. When June is last seen, it is as a middle-aged drab – the fate Mollie was spared. Cronin would later dabble in crime, introducing his glamorous victim in 1944's *The Shadows Mystery* by a painting that nonetheless fails to do her justice: 'There is a portrait of her in the little gallery, painted by a famous artist. All Melbourne has flocked to see it. It is an exquisite thing. But, compared to the Mary Falconer of flesh and blood, it is as the light of a candle to the incomprehensible loveliness of the sunrise.'

That same year, Mollie Dean was killed again – or at least 'Molly Dean' was, in the first reel of the British B movie *Headline*. A pretty ingenue murdered by the playboy villain who has seduced and betrayed her, 'Molly Dean' is then rather forgotten amid the tale of rival reporters on the killer's trail. Brookie (David Farrar) from *The Sun* and Dell (William Hartnell) from *The Record* use all the tricks of their cheerfully amoral trade: there is an effective scene where they try to relieve Molly's widowed mother of the only photograph of her daughter, a duel Brookie loses thanks to an untimely pang of conscience; being played by much the bigger star, however, he

Mourner: Bernard Cronin

ultimately prevails. Although the setting is London, the pair might easily have been Hugh Buggy of Sydney's *Sun* and Harry Maddison of *Smith's Weekly*. Indeed, *Headline* was adapted from the 1933 thriller *Reporter!* by a young Australian journalist, Ken Attiwill, who had recently swapped a job on Melbourne's *Herald* for Fleet Street and Grub Street. The part of Molly in *Headline*, meanwhile, was also played by an expatriate, Sydney's Nancy O'Neil. And if perhaps nowhere else, a proportion of Melburnians who flocked to see *Headline* around Christmas 1944 would have been reminded of Mollie Dean by 'Molly Dean'. It was a strangely suitable name – plain but euphonious, lightly tinged with melancholy – for a murder victim.

There is no pinning Mollie Dean to June Windsor, or Mary Falconer, or even 'Molly Dean'. Writers are bowerbirds of impression and anecdote. Influence is cunning, seldom direct, dotted lines rather than thick arrows. One suspects that 'Molly Dean' was simply a name that *Headline's* makers reached for – even if it is rather poignant that the character was invented then portrayed by Australians drawn to London, a group Mollie had fantasised about joining. But in memory, Mollie Dean had acquired a ghostly quality, on the fringe of aware- ness. The writer most obviously inspired by Mollie Dean, in fact, was not a writer at all. He was a musician.

Fritz Hart was a man of utmost discretion, but even he must have found the summer after Mollie Dean's death stressful. He saw his only son, Basil, wed, after years of ill-health. He learned of the suicide in London of his old friend Philip Heseltine, creatively exhausted and financially ruined. Then, in February 1931, his great patroness Melba died, and was accorded a stupendous funeral, thou- sands filing past the coffin, conservatorium pupils weeping copiously. Hart was a pallbearer; so was his shrewd and patient rival Bernard Heinze. Both were named joint conductors in the ensuing merger of the Melbourne Symphony Orchestra with the Melbourne University Conservatorium Orchestra. But in all but name the latter was taking the former over, and Hart would be outmanoeuvred in the resultant power struggle. He devoted ever more of himself to an annual four-month guest conductorship with the Honolulu Symphony Orchestra, its attractions enhanced by a new mistress, Marvell Allison. When his wife Jessie succumbed to ovarian can- cer in November 1935, Hart decided his future lay in Hawaii: he accepted a permanent role with the HSO and married Marvell in September 1937.

It's not unlikely that Hart's escutcheon was blotted by revela- tions of his brush with Mollie Dean – Heinze was every bit as adroit as Bernard Hall at exploiting weakness. Hart would have been unrepentant. As he told Marvell in one of their love letters: 'Life is at least partly – if not largely – the consciousness of men and women for each other as men and women, physically as well as in other ways.' Mollie's story had certain newly operatic qualities too. The year Hart made his move to Hawaii was the year of Alban Berg's *Lulu*, which opens with the eponymous *grisette* having her portrait painted by an artist lover and ends with her murder by Jack the Ripper. Hart did not write operas of that kind, but he did write fiction, albeit on the quiet, and destined never to see the light of day.

Hart's twenty-four unpublished novels today form part of his papers in the National Library of Australia. They came to my attention while perusing the collection's finding aid. On making inquiries, I could find nobody who had read them. Yet surely at some stage, I reasoned, his mind had wandered back to those inner ordeals of 1930. It was torture finding out. Hart wrote in long but small hand, using every inch of the paper. The object seems to have been entirely his own amusement. Rather than plan, he would simply set in motion a cast of sub-Wodehousian characters – flighty, leggy heroines, tongue-tied but well-meaning young men, wealthy and indulgent elders, plus the odd funny foreigner – and see where they led. This usually involved a lot of 'I say', 'my dear fellow', 'damned nuisance', 'rum thing', 'what the devil', 'I always look askance at people who are afraid of splitting infinitives' and 'that looks like an attractive bus – let's take it'. The backdrops were his – art, music, literature, all of them combined. So were more than a few echoes. In the first, *Puck and Mr Perkins*, dated October 1939, painter George Hooper and minor poet Stanley Perkins find themselves in a convoluted tug-of-love with a serially flirtatious soubrette named Molly. Molly Fairbrother even has writing aspirations, although unlike Mollie Dean can afford them: her father, Jonas, is 'a successful something in the city', and her playground is the family pile in Devonshire, venue for lots of brittle dialogue:

> George re-lit his pipe, looking rather bored.
>
> 'But, my dear girl, where is your common sense?'
>
> Molly wrinkled one corner of a rather whimsical little mouth.
>
> 'Never had any – don't want any. Shouldn't know what to do with it if I had any.'
>
> 'Oh yes you would.'
>
> 'Well?'
>
> And now an attractive right eyebrow wrinkled, evidently intent on remaining so until a question was answered.
>
> 'You'd turn me down, marry someone else – first chap you came along – give up writing, take up art, or philosophy, or try your hand at being a modern Nell Gwynn, or – any old thing.'
>
> 'It's lucky – isn't it, darling? – that we are never likely to fall in love. You are rather nice to flirt with – but you'd make a ghastly husband!'

And much more in the same vein. *Puck and Mr Perkins* rather meandered where it was very obviously going, as did most of the novels, and I had slouched through the possibilities of sixteen when the dating of the seventeenth – 'Melbourne, June 1930' – made me sit up. Honolulu being hardly more than a military encampment after Pearl Harbor, Hart had time to toil seriously on the previously mentioned *James Goes Home to Dinner*, dated March 1942 – even, mercifully, producing a typescript. Transparent too were the characters' drawing from life. Eileen Coote was saucier than Mollie Dean and James Montague more naive than Colin Colahan, but he also deferred to acerbic savant Donald Maudesley (Max Meldrum) and palled around with ace cartoonist Reilly Morgan (Percy Leason) and his wife, Minnie (Belle Leason). But despite the debt to actualities, what was engrossing were the departures from them, where Hart resolved matters to his tastes.

The plot runs so: James Montague has married shrewish Elsa Shropshire (Vi Colahan, with a dash of Jessie Hart) in a fit of absent-mindedness, while still nursing an unrequited passion for an old flame, Sylvia Orpen (shades of Sylvia Vanderkelen), who is married to a brutish businessman. Alienated at home except for his five-year-old daughter, Barbara, he comforts himself away: 'So long as he was conventionally discreet Elsa never attempted to interfere

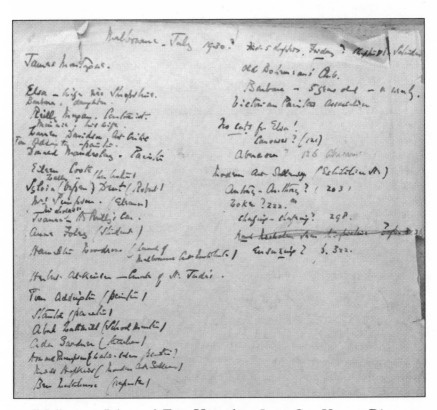

'Melbourne, July 1930': Fritz Hart plans *James Goes Home to Dinner*

with the life he had outside the walls of his own home . . . and, of course, there was generally a girl or two with whom he could fall in love – and he had always been a fool where women are concerned, and knew it.' At a picnic he encounters Eileen Coote, a pretty 25-year-old teacher who bemoans her 'bad time at home'. He is duly foolish: 'I suppose I was decent to her – flirted with her to cheer her up, and all that sort of thing. Of course I did suggest that she should drop up to the studio one night – and – oh damn – I did kiss her . . .'

The 'bad time at home', as Eileen explains it when James draws her into the studio and a compromising clinch after plying her with alcohol, is Mollie Dean almost to the last detail:

> 'I am just tired of everything – teaching in school by day, return-
> ing to a house where I have been slaving myself to death – why,
> I even do the family washing – and my mother pretends to be
> an invalid, with a heart that might give out at any moment if she
> does a hand's turn of work . . . Have you ever been so poor that
> you've been driven nearly mad with anxiety how to meet your
> bills week by week? That has been my life for years . . . Mother
> has an annuity of fifty pounds, thanks to my father's insur-
> ance, but that is all we have to live upon except what I earn as a
> teacher in a state school . . . The last eight or nine months have
> been a nightmare to me.'

That last detail is that Eileen has no intellectual life; she is barely more than a coquette, albeit an accomplished one:

> 'That is enough, Jimmy,' she said with a sigh, partly of tri-
> umph and partly of content. 'Now you must sit over there

again. I know now that I'm a thoroughly wicked girl, and find it rather fun.'

James looked at her with astonishment in his eyes. This was a new side to the incalculable Eileen, he thought. Somehow or other she seemed to have turned the tables on him. In what way he scarcely knew, but he was, a little uncomfortably, aware of the fact . . . Beneath what he had always considered to be her essential conventionalism he discerned a vital, almost elemental woman, warm-hearted and warm-blooded. Dangerous? Very likely, but refreshingly alive.

No sooner has Eileen offered to pose for James than Sylvia reappears, hotfoot from her abusive spouse (modelled, perhaps, on Betty Davies' husband, Ellis). They acknowledge their mutual affection, but Sylvia, hearing of his recent brush with Eileen, convinces James that this is clearly 'the model he is dying to paint'. So he proceeds, in a scene that by Hart's rather staid standards has unusual sexual tension, James painting an exhilarating likeness while also straining to accommodate Eileen's wish to remain anonymous. 'By Jove, that's your pose, Eileen,' he promises. 'Half your face is hidden, and with that ripping hair hanging down your shoulder as it does now, no one will recognise you when you are exhibited – as you damn well will be. I'm going to make a good job of you, young woman.'

The seeming inevitability of their uniting physically as well as artistically is stemmed by the abrupt arrival at James's studio of Sylvia and Minnie. Eileen peevishly flees. Cautious Minnie warns James off ('She's ripe for mischief, if I know anything about the less amiable qualities of my own sex'); suddenly ardent, Sylvia draws James on ('I realise it took Eileen Coote to make me understand that I could not possibly let you go'). Hart's inference is that Sylvia is a far better match for James than Eileen, matrimonial status mattering far less than caste and kind. Nor can Hart concede a woman too much power too long – rather incongruously, he next allows Eileen to be seduced by her married headmaster, Abel Whatmill, an old *roué*.

The nude then becomes the novel's focus. Everyone likes it – 'It is a bloody masterpiece already, damn it,' says Reilly Morgan – save the sitter. Eileen is convinced she can be recognised and that the painting's exhibition will have 'appalling consequences'. She materialises at James's studio while it is being minded by his amiably dim student Tom Addington, who confirms her worst fears by realising who she is: 'I say, d'you think you could ever bring yourself to sit for me? . . . By Jove, I'd like to have a shot at you . . . Why dammit you'll be famous because of this picture.' Eileen, furious, slashes the canvas to ribbons with a palette knife that she then throws at Tom; he slips, brains himself on a heater's heavy iron base, and hovers for a period between life and death, which results in Eileen being charged with attempted murder. Tom survives and Abel Whatmill pulls strings to have the charge withdrawn, but not before Waterhouse, a 'sharp-nosed reporter' commissioned by a 'muck-raking editor', both persuades Eileen to talk and learns from Addington's feather-brained fiancée that James had earlier made a copy of the destroyed canvas. Waterhouse's scandal sheet, representative of the same journalism reviled by Mervyn Skipper, causes Melbourne 'to laugh, to sneer, to wonder, to condemn and moralise over the ways of artists and artists' models'.

Eileen, 'filled with passionate anger and burning resentment', has a nervous breakdown. This allows James to couple within his class with Sylvia, before she nobly returns to her beastly husband with the intention of settling overseas out of consideration for James's bond with his daughter, Barbara. In her farewell note, Sylvia completes a transformation from Sue Vanderkelen to Mireille Wilkinson: 'For, Jimmy, we are going to have a child. And it will be mine – mine! And I'm its mother – his mother, of course. I waited until I was quite sure. Yes, you did not know, but I had to make up my mind that this had to happen. It was the one thing that kept things right between me and my conscience.' James glumly goes home to dinner, where Elsa pettishly chastises him one last time: 'Really James, you might try to be punctual for meals. It is very little I ask of you, but I do ask you this.'

So runs the plot – stripped of a considerable number of subplots, and other figures recognisable from the Melbourne arts crowd of 1930. The missing event is the murder: Eileen goes the way of many a hysterical fictional woman before her, into a vague seclusion, where she can no longer offend delicate sensibilities. The missing character is the writer: Hart has, as it were, shown just as much care as his female protagonist not to be recognised. Perhaps accounting for his own role in Mollie's life required too much self-disclosure, even in the medium of private fiction; certainly it would also have called on a more complete character than Eileen Coote to have explained their attraction. As it was, Hart ended up writing of his femme fatale with considerable sublimated hostility. Eileen goes from being a 'nice kid', a 'poor kid' and only a 'potential little bitch', through description as a 'naughty girl', 'little minx', 'little spitfire', 'little virago', 'little bitch', 'dangerous little piece of goods', 'disgruntled piece of goods', to concluding as a 'really disgusting little baggage' without doing very much more risqué than sense James's attraction to her. For Hart, I observed, this was extreme language – another of his manuscripts, *Alice and a Scruple*, hinged entirely on the shocking nature of the word 'bitch' in polite company. Perhaps, after all, Hart *did* blame rumours associating him with Mollie for his stymied career in Melbourne. Certainly he had some sport at the expense of the tabloid hack Waterhouse, last seen covered in paint and thrown down the stairs by a revivified Tom Addington. As it is, *James Goes Home to Dinner* shows a remarkable knowledge of Colahan's relationships with Sue Vanderkelen and Mireille Wilkinson, including of his children with the last, which for many years was a secret in his own family. Was he going on rumour? Did the men discuss it? Was there a late-night conclave between these former lovers of Mollie where they shared their embarrassments, how this 'really disgusting little baggage' had nearly brought them both to grief?

I completed Hart's literary canon without much more to show for it but with many further questions, all probably insoluble, and one overriding impression – how much Mollie Dean needed scaling down, even travestising, to suit the male imaginations making use of her. Unlike Skipper, Hart had at least given her character a name and a certain beguiling vitality. But Eileen was never other than déclassée, and the instant she declined to be brushed off became a nuisance to be disposed of. Homicide being too strong a draft for happy-go-lucky Hart, he had murdered Mollie with mockery instead.

16

I COULD FEEL THE NOOSE
AROUND MY NECK

*The man who killed Jess was never apprehended, you see, and
I think there is some terrible worm of stark terror that keeps
crawling around in his brain, behind that bald, brown, ordinary
little face with the hurt bulging eyes and the sunken jowls.*
— George Johnston, *My Brother Jack* (1964)

The northern winter was lifting. The Continent and the Festival of
Britain beckoned. As they arrived in London in March 1951, George
Johnston and Charmian Clift felt at last where they belonged. After
years of personal turmoil and professional toil, Australia's most
charismatic writing couple were joining a colourful community of
expatriates, for whom self-exile had afforded freedom and opportunity: Peter Finch, Lloyd Lamble, Sidney Nolan, Donald Horne,
Robert Helpmann, Paul Brickhill, Russell Braddon, Albert Arlen,
Cedric Flower, Leo McKern and others. 'I used to think that the most
desirable state of being that could be imagined was to be a young and
talented Australian in London,' Clift would recall.

Johnston and Clift also encountered some veterans of the journey
'home'. Colin Colahan had been in London more than a decade and

a half. He and his wife Ursula were cosily settled at 35 Tite Street, Chelsea, a house built by James McNeill Whistler. Colahan's son with Vi, David Michel, had been killed during World War II, crashing his motorcycle in Ireland while serving as a despatch rider. Otherwise, the years had been kind. Colahan had been a prolific official war artist and become a fashionable portrait painter; Ursula had abandoned the stage to bear two beautiful daughters; they had inherited substantial means on her father's death four years earlier.

With his love of company, and of an audience, Colahan was the perfect host for the new arrivals – an intellectual and social will-o'-the-wisp. With him, Johnston felt instinctive pangs of kinship. Like Colahan, he had studied at the National Gallery Art School. Like Colahan, he now enjoyed a certain comfort and prestige. As boss of the London bureau of Associated Newspapers, Johnston was entitled to a chauffeured car and a plush flat on Bayswater Road. He and Clift had big plans for extracurricular writings, for novels, short stories, scripts, magazine articles – plans that grew to incorporate the Colahans. Johnston, for example, bought a Standard Vanguard to whisk everyone off on a vineyard tour of Bordelais. If the illustrated travelogue they had anticipated producing never eventuated, the trip was hugely convivial, and led to others.

The couples were not long acquainted when Colahan divulged the circumstances preluding his coming to London. More than twenty years having elapsed since Mollie Dean's murder, Colahan's retelling had evolved into a chilling tale, in which the innocent artist had been harried almost to death row by the baying hounds of the press. The tale invested Colahan with the qualities of both martyr and mystery; the families' deepening friendship was seasoned with a certain melancholy. While Clift sat for a portrait, Colahan played mood music on the gramophone. Without fail, Mozart's *Requiem* would cause her to brim with tears – on at least one occasion, she fled the studio with eyes streaming. The tensions were not imagined. The marriage of Johnston and Clift was abidingly strained by his doing too much writing, thanks to journalism, and her too little, thanks to mother-hood. Colahan, now fifty-five, still quietly yearned for Mireille, for whom his first-born with Ursula was named; he also maintained his roving eye, which had alighted on a handsome 38-year-old model, Monique Bornoff.

So fascinated was Johnston by his new friend that he soon folded Colahan into a short story. Its narrator, Brian Burton, is an archae-ologist. Exploring Etruscan tombs beneath the walls of Orvieto, he encounters the effervescent Sefton Halliday, a wealthy painter and cultural tourist. Burton enjoys his ceaseless, erudite, epigrammatic conversation; he is no less transfixed by Halliday's startlingly beau-tiful, serenely quiet, much younger wife, Erica. It emerges that Erica had been an actress enjoying a brilliant career until its curtailment by her domestication. But as Burton's relationship with this enigmatic couple unfolds, it grows clear that she is still playing a role, unreach-able and impenetrable, accepting everything 'good and bad, pleasure or privation, with an unruffled calm that sometimes seemed close to indifference'. The only hint of her inner anguish is when she listens to the *Requiem*. 'I can honestly say I've never known her not to weep,' muses Halliday. 'What is it? Something psychic possibly.'

For his part, Halliday is increasingly restless, ever questing, insati-able for experience, exuding at times a 'faint but unmistakeable flavour of hysteria'. He was, Burton learns, previously married to a model of whom he was 'frightfully ashamed'; he worries now about a waning of his creative spirit, and a weighing-down by comforts. 'He is like a child,' Erica finally confides in Burton. 'He lives always on the surface of his life. And he must forever move across it very quickly . . . In those

deep parts, you see, he cannot swim . . . and of course, he hates me.'
Then, one day, the Hallidays are found dead, poisoned. The police propose a suicide pact. Burton privately demurs: they lacked the necessary
'sense of oneness'. Finding the *Requiem* on the turntable at the scene,
he concludes: 'I am sure that it was Halliday, that it was he who poisoned her and then similarly destroyed himself.'

The story, 'Requiem Mass', went unpublished in Johnston's lifetime. His agent could not sell it; perhaps it was also a little close to
the bone. Of course, it hardly implies that the writer felt his friend
capable of murder. But it is sensitive to the waft of mortality around
Colahan, and to general anxieties of surfeit in the life of art. Johnston
then did, almost certainly, publish about Colahan. In its edition of
6 May 1953, Associated Newspapers' glossy magazine *People* contained

Local boy makes good: Colahan in *People*

a long profile of the painter, unsigned but flavoured with a warm acquaintance.

'The Australian Artist in Whistler's House' opened with an anecdote about a visit to Tite Street by a young Australian artist who met its opulent furnishing and appointments with 'aggressive scowls and scarcely veiled criticisms', as though he 'demanded to know what right Colahan had to live in such luxury'. This boor was unaware, said the writer, that Colahan had known 'deeper poverty, harsher privations and more personal misery than the younger embittered artists who now resent his standing'. As evidence the writer provided a truncated version of Colahan's travails in the years between his phases abroad:

Colahan returned to Australia [in 1927], partly because he felt himself ready to become a painter and partly because the marriage which he had undertaken before he left Australia had 'gone wrong'. His divorce cost him all his money and all his 'independent income'. But his return was completely encouraging. His first one-man show was successful and established him immediately in the front rank of Australian painting. It was at this moment that a tragic irony picked up his destiny.

A young artists' model, the attractive and peculiarly magnetic Molly Dean, was brutally murdered one night at St Kilda. The last person with whom she had been seen alive was Colin Colahan who had taken her to the theatre the night before. Next day detectives called on him and subjected him to a rigorous cross-examination. Colahan insisted that he and the girl had parted in town, he returning to Hawthorn, she to St Kilda, and in fact shortly after midnight she had phoned him twice from a public callbox in St Kilda. As it happened a PMG direction was then in force that all telephone calls emanating from public telephones in the St Kilda area after midnight had to be checked and logged by the telephone exchange. Police investigation showed no record of the two calls to Colahan which he insisted had been made by the murdered girl.

'It was a most appalling experience,' says Colahan. 'I had no other alibi and although I was perfectly innocent I felt as if the whole web of circumstantial evidence was wrapping itself about me. I could feel the noose around my neck and there seemed nothing I could do about it.'

Meanwhile the Melbourne Press was publishing columns on the early stages of what was to prove one of Australia's classic murder mysteries and Colahan's name was tossed from headline to headline. And then, a couple of weeks later, his alibi was proved. A man working at the St Kilda telephone exchange on the night of Molly Dean's murder casually announced that the phone calls from Molly Dean to Colahan's studio had been made. He said he had been thinking of the vacation he was to begin next day, had jotted the record of the calls down on the back of an envelope and had forgotten to log them in the official sheets. On such a trifling incident as this, a man's life may sometimes hang.

Anyone can misremember, but this sequence of events has only the merest connection with fact. Colahan's marriage to Vi may have 'gone wrong', but it was their parenthood that drew the couple back to Melbourne, and their divorce lay years hence. Mollie Dean's role in that divorce – indeed her entire relationship with Colahan – is excluded. Most notable is the invented drama of the 'couple of weeks' time-gap between Colahan's claim about the telephone calls and their confirmation by the vagrant telephonist. The uncertainty lasted no more than the weekend; the calls had been appropriately

logged, as was standard for all phone-box traffic. There was no tossing of Colahan's name from 'headline to headline'; where his name
appeared, he was delicately referred to as the bereaved 'fiancé'.
Colahan was certainly penalised for proximity to the scandal, but
such suspicion as surrounded him was less of involvement in the
murder as of a haphazard personal life – and barely the half of that
haphazardness was known. But when Johnston swept up Colahan's
narrative in the saga of *My Brother Jack*, it would be that of the
hounded, vilified, deracinated artist first presented by *People* in May
1953. Mollie herself was also to be reconsidered.

Countrymen who had heard little of Colahan in nearly twenty years
would have enjoyed 'The Australian Artist in Whistler's House', with
its air of local-boy-made-good in a London gilded by the imminent
coronation. One imagines a rather different reception at Montsalvat,
which had sealed up its entrances against the glamorous art world
of which Colahan remained part. Jorgensen now dismissed his old
friend as an artist; Sue Vanderkelen had written out her torments in
'Sue's Story'; Mollie Dean was nobody's business, if somehow still
everybody's. 'Perhaps the most fiendish murder in Australian history,'
thought H. H. Cox, tireless chronicler of true crime in Sydney's *Sun*,
when he recapitulated the story in his columns. 'Many theories,
no solution' read the subheading to his torrid retelling.

The times themselves were growingly conservative. Australia
was settling into the Pax Menziana. Sexual mores were stabilising
after the national aphrodisiac of American servicemen in World
War II, domestic life condensing around the stock character of
the stay-at-home wife, with the home a bulwark of normality.
Intrigued by Colahan's recollections of the Dean case in the previous

edition, *People* went back for more, and the anonymous writer of
'The Molly Dean Mystery', run over three well-illustrated pages
on 20 May 1953, imparted a contemporary spin to this curio of the
recent past: 'The killing itself had no particular significance, but the
story it brought to light creates a vivid picture of the kind of moral
conflict that was going on in those strange years. It is a tragic picture
of the clash of beliefs between the old and young.' Scouring of the
clippings library, in fact, had generated a curiously staid rendering
of events:

> She [Mollie] liked to mix with the bohemian crowd of her time
> and discuss art and literature and philosophy until the small
> hours. If it were late she saw no reason why she should not stay
> overnight at the house of a friend – man or woman – instead of
> obeying the rather rigid convention of the time.

That Mollie might have done more than 'stay overnight' was never
entertained. The article conceded no more than talk, which it was
prepared to condone up to a point: 'By what outdated dogma was it
wrong to engage in frank discussion of sex? What Victorian prude
claimed it immodest for a girl to pose in the nude for an artist? She
revelled in the mental freedom of the intellectual, delightedly condemned the "old", "outworn" and "conventional" tenets of society
and behaviour.' Mollie's writing went unmentioned. Her relationship with Colahan was reduced to a solitary muffled sentence: 'Colin
Colahan, an artist and close friend, said he had known Mary about
twelve months and was friendly with her.' The Deans' 'trouble at
home' was presented as arising not from Ethel's obsessively controlling temperament but from Mollie being so 'aggressively "free"' and
'ultra-consciously shorn of inhibitions and taboos':

Her widowed mother rightly became disturbed and worried. It concerned Mrs Ethel Dean that her daughter should flout the conventions by staying at a man's house overnight or going into the country on weekend hikes. Faithful to her daughter, driven by a desire to protect her from harm, she became suspicious of some of Mary's set, objected to them and condemned them as a Bohemian crowd.

Perhaps most tellingly, the story excluded any reference to Ethel's physical and emotional abuse, her relations with Adam Graham and their stalking of Mollie – Graham was not introduced until the fourth-last paragraph, as a 'friend of the Dean family', in the context of his being charged with the killing when it was 'abundantly plain' he must be 'innocent by every legal tenet'. The writer took the view that Mollie's 'allegations' of 'disturbed home life' were 'the outpourings of an overwrought girl who was inclined to exaggerate in her role as a frustrated intellectual', quoting her opinion, recalled by Ethel, that Milton Street was too cluttered with furniture and carpet. Here, thought the writer, lay 'the real tragedy', which was 'the desire of both mother and daughter to meet on common ground and view things from the same standpoint'. But the reader would have been left to conclude that this tragedy was grounded in irreconcilable tastes in interior decoration.

In telling one story, then, 'The Molly Dean Mystery' told another, of a society still half in love with the 'outdated dogma' it affected to deplore. If Ethel took *People*, it would have afforded her a certain comfort: she had been right all along that girls 'too brainy' got what was coming to them.

*

This, of course, was the voice of the narrow and censorious Australia that Johnston had fled, which he would backdate to the 'mental deserts' in which he had spent his adolescence and youth in the 1920s and 1930s. These, his alter ego David Meredith would argue in *My Brother Jack*, were 'the real enemy', worse than Hitlerism and Stalinism – 'this awful fetish of respectability that would rather look the other way than cause a fuss, that hated "scenes", that did not *want* to know because *to know* might somehow force them into a situation which could take the polish off the duco and blight the herbaceous borders and lay scabrous patches across the attended lawns'. It's why Johnston was instinctively credulous of Colahan's narrative of the artist as the victim of a vindictive press and vulgar public; it's why Johnston turned back to the story as he commenced the novel sequence that would make his name.

By 1962, however, his own circumstances had changed. Johnston and Clift had forsaken London's cosmopolitanism for the unsullied simplicity of life on Hydra. But the family's Aegean idyll had soured. Now fifty, Johnston had been ravaged by tuberculosis; Clift, nearing forty, was casting about for romantic distraction; they were undergoing their own crises rather than partaking of anyone else's. As Johnston plunged into a planned autobiographical fiction, the underlying unease skewed and sharpened the sense of his own failings. In prose his mother grew more selflessly stoic, his father more physically sadistic, his brother more nobly resourceful, and he more timid and cowed – 'the good trier' but 'the near-miss, the also-ran', as Johnston explained Meredith to himself. The painter Sam Burlington, who provides a roof when Meredith is turned out of the family home, is similarly outsized, handling words 'with the comic skill of a vaudeville juggler tossing Indian clubs', and warning his guest that he may have to look away 'from our scenes of licence and depravity'.

Burlington drew on Johnston's memories of a combustible student contemporary at the National Gallery School, Sam Atyeo. Burlington is not a Meldrumite but the 'authoritative rebel on modernism', a merry prankster who puts jockstraps on Laocoön and a fringed cocktail dress on *Diana of the Chase*. But the plot owes everything to the sequence and flavour of events as outlined in Colahan's interview with *People*, and anyone acquainted with the facts of Mollie Dean's murder would have recognised their reuse in *My Brother Jack*. *Pygmalion* became *No, No, Nanette*. Mollie the teacher daughter of a headmaster became Jessica the art-student daughter of a bank manager. But Jessica and Sam part at Flinders Street station after an indeterminate disagreement; she calls him after midnight from a St Kilda telephone box to 'patch it up'; he being 'rather impatient and irritated' says that they will 'talk about it later'; she is strangled walking home, with the city's press a voyeuristic accessory after the fact to 'the Jessica Murder':

The world of half-tone blocks is peopled by strangers: the kidnapper, the murderer and his victim, the absconded embezzler, the jilted sweetheart, the unscrupulous financier, all these are people *we* never know. So it was a long moment before I could take it in: as if the machinery of cognition had slowed down to deliberately postpone comprehension. Yet the bold captions on the blocks left no doubt as to identity. The single-column block said 'Samuel Burlington'; the three-column block above it, showing a pretty, nymph-like girl in a striped bathing costume, with long fair hair blowing in the wind and a canoe paddle in her hand, was marked 'Jessica Wray'. And at the top of the page, across what for the *Post* was the sensational splash of a four-column headline, the black Cheltenham Bold capitals said: 'STUDENT HELD

FOR QUESTIONING ON JESSICA WRAY MURDER', and below this, in smaller type, 'Intimacy Admitted: Startling Studio Disclosures'.

I was appalled . . . I felt dazed and sick and stunned. I hardly remember getting off the tram; with my fingers clenched around the unbelievable newspaper I walked to the railway station as if in a dream.

Johnston swiftly looks away from the death to emphasise the prejudices of Melbourne's moral middle class. Jessica is described as having been killed 'in a desolate area of suburban parkland', as though the crime scene itself is responsible. Meredith staggers back from the headlines at the newspaper kiosk – 'STUDENT HELD IN MODEL SLAYING', 'GIRL MURDER SENSATION', 'WE WERE LOVERS SAYS ART STUDENT' – onto a train 'rushing headlong into horror'. In a famous sequence, he overhears a spontaneous kangaroo court in session:

I was in a second-class smoking compartment. Women never rode in smokers in those days, and at each station more men would get in, and they were all discussing the murder, some of them with gravity, but mostly with coarse jokes and comments, and with lechery in the hard bulging eyes that seemed to roll along the headlines, and across the grey-black stippled facsimile of the girl I knew as Jess. Their words, lively and seditious, jumped from door to window, twined around the smoke wreaths and the chipped mahogany and the string mesh of the luggage racks and the dead matches and empty cigarette packets beside the cuspidors and the old blotched tourist photographs of Porepunkah and Toolangi. 'They arsk fer it, these young ones, the way they carry on. It's no bloomin' wonder . . .' 'Wouldn't 've minded if she'd arst *me*; I could've given 'er an inch or two!' – 'Ha, ha, ha!' – 'Spare me days, she sounds as if she was a real *one*, though!' – 'You know wot t'expeck wiv these bo'emian types, though . . .' 'Humdinger, I'd say, didn't mind strippin' it off, neither . . .' 'Yeah, but jist fancy a pretty sheila like that . . . dunno wot the world's coming to, fair dinkum I don't . . .' 'These days they think they kin get away wiv any-think, that's the trouble . . .'

The callousness, the ignorance, the lechery: it is all here, as the train clatters on 'through the grimy deserts of suburban rectitude'. In revisiting the murder story in *My Brother Jack*, Meredith claims to be sifting the contents of a 'huge old trunk' in which thirty-year-old clippings are tucked away in 'dog-eared note-books', enabling him to cite paragraphs like those by 'Our Special Reporter' describing Burlington's apartment: 'One sensed in those flamboyant and almost foetid surroundings the atmosphere of the seraglio and a taint of young depravity and irresponsibility that seemed to bear no rela-tionship to the decencies and dignities of Australia's proudest city.' Yet, as we have seen, for all the coverage's occasional melodrama and eccentricity, nothing of this kind was published in even the yellow-est organs of the press after Mollie Dean's death. Johnston's telling expressed his despair at the country he had abandoned and the craft from which he was estranged.

Like Mollie's, Jessica's murder remains unsolved, with a further allusion to the deaths of Mena Griffiths and Hazel Wilson when a twelve-year-old is assaulted soon after in the vicinity of the crime scene, replenishing the supply of headline hysteria: 'SEXUAL MANIAC AT LARGE?' The significant departure from actuality was Johnston's exaggeration of Burlington's endangerment, due to his adoption of Colahan's story of the telephone calls. In *My Brother Jack*, Burlington is not cleared of suspicion until confirmation of his alibi, as reported by the *Morning Post*:

> Selwyn Grant, an employee on the switchboard at St Kilda tele-phone exchange, yesterday testified that on the night of the Jessica Murder he monitored a call made from a public call-box to the number listed for Sam Burlington at 12.34 a.m. Grant was to begin his annual holidays at the end of the shift. Inadvertently he wrote the data on a slip of paper, which he put into his pocket, intending to enter it in the log before knocking off. He forgot to do so. The following afternoon he left with a party of friends to spend a week camping and trout-fishing. It was some days before he saw a newspaper and remembered the report which he had overlooked. He communicated the information to police at Buxton when he visited the township to buy provisions, and Russell Street CIB was informed accordingly.

It echoes the story Colahan would tell Eric Westbrook in 1969 ('Two weeks later, a bloke came back from his holidays and said oh yes, the story's true, perfectly true') and Garry Kinnane in 1983 ('after four days the operator . . . returned from a holiday in the country'); the switchboard operator would even obtain a tourist destination in Betty Roland's *The Eye of the Beholder*, his holiday consisting of 'a fishing trip deep in the Gippsland mountains' (actually her husband's favoured recreation). But it was a complete invention. Why did it persist? It made a better story. It engaged the interlocutor's sympathy by making Colahan a kind of secondary victim of the crime. It braced the image of Melbourne as a bastion of moral piety with a hypocritical lust for sensation. And its appeal is timeless. Sketching Mollie Dean's murder in 2005, *The Age* reported confidently: 'George Johnston used an accurate version of the murder in his novel *My Brother Jack*.' But it was an accurate version only of itself.

The irony of the book so imbued with Johnston's sense of failure was its commercial and critical success. *My Brother Jack* was an instant best-seller and won the Miles Franklin Award. It also enticed its creator and Clift home, she in August 1964 to a fresh commission: the task of adapting her husband's novel to the small screen. This was more than usually difficult. The ABC wanted ten half-hour instalments, poten-tially stretching the plot's limited action rather thinly, and requiring Clift to expand sections of the story. Partly because of the popular-ity of actor Ed Devereaux, Jack grew considerably, from the outline of an archetype into a full-fledged working-class hero. To a lesser but still noticeable extent, so did Jessica Wray, even turning back into a brunette for her portrayal by 31-year-old Tessa Mallos, making her screen debut. She became spirited, volatile, independent, more than

SAM BURLINGTON'S APARTMENT. THE STUDIO. This is the typical Bohemian decor of the late twenties and early thirties, an uneasy mixture of Futurism, Cubism, the florid and romantic naturalism represented by Norman Lindsay, and leftovers of Art Nouveau. Furniture is a big divan, a table littered with art magazines and Davey's big typewriter, decorative leather poufs, Sam's big easel with the uncompleted nude study of Jess, stacks of gramophone records and a rather elaborate panatrope. Lampshades and cushions are fringed and fantastic, general decor is a garish orange and black, elongated formalised nudes in the Aubrey Beardsley manner. There are paintings and reproductions on the wall, also a Mexican hat and draped Spanish shawl, some exotic and erotic sculpture. It is very young. There is an exuberant desire for decadence everywhere displayed. It is the sort of place that will embarrass Davey, startle Jack, and shock Mum almost out of her wits.

'Typical': Colahan the tonalist becomes Burlington the modernist
in TV's *My Brother Jack*

a match for Sam Burlington (David Copping), and enticing to David Meredith (Nick Tate).

Most notable were scenes in which Jessica's frank sexuality and liberated ways unsettled David during his stay with Sam. 'Slatternly wench,' Sam chides her. 'Trollop. You do look very decorative, dove, but you mustn't trade on it. And you mustn't tease David. I won't have it.' Clift was more engaged than Johnston with David's 'mixed desire-dislike' for Jess, developing as Jess's relationship with Sam deteriorates – as could be heard in Sam's invitation to David to 'a little shindig' in Toorak.

> David: No thanks Sam. I'd rather work. Honestly. Besides [casually] Jess going?
> Sam [looks at him sidelong]: No, Jess isn't going. [Slowly, very busy with tie] To tell you the truth, Davey boy, I'm just about up to the neck with that young vixen. I'm no Spartan boy to let her gnaw out my vitals. When a woman starts making scenes it's time to . . . well, anyway . . .

Scene eight of episode three is a hinge point. Jess arrives at the apartment and pours herself a drink while Sam paints, and a row develops.

> Sam: Do make yourself at home. Don't mind me at all. I am only working. [Goes on with it]
> Jess [trembling]: You were glad enough once to have me round while you were working. When you wanted a free model.
> Sam: A lovely model too, dear. Most accomplished. But you see, Jess, at the moment I don't need a model. Free or otherwise. [Looks at her] In any case I've come to the conclusion that you are rather more expensive than I can afford.

Jess: Poor little rich boy! I might have known! Make sure you enter up this drink in the ledger, won't you? And there was a meal last week. And I suppose you charge taxi-fare in that show-off car of yours . . .

Sam: You're being tiresome, Jess. I meant expensive in an emotional sense.

Clift seemed to understand, as her husband had at least not spelled out, that Mollie's relationship with Colahan was a failing one. What had in the novel been a generic 'quarrel' originated on television in a confrontation about the lovers' respective roles. Interestingly, Clift had laid aside her own autobiographical novel, *The End of the Morning*, to effectively burnish her husband's reputation. In the rancour between Sam and Jess, there is a trace of feeling about gendered divisions of creative labour: when the woman complains of being picked up and put down again, she is being 'tiresome'. David's guileless arrival at the height of the discord then reveals his influence as a further source.

Sam: Come in, dear fellow, come in. You are interrupting nothing of the least importance.

Jess: Hah! As if that would make any difference to little pussyfoot?

Sam: Now look here, Jess!

Jess: You're such a dishonest swine. [Mimicking him] 'Dear fellow', 'old chap', 'Davey boy'. Why don't you tell 'old chap' here some of the things you've said on the rare occasions he's been dislodged from the cosy triangle? Why don't you, Sam? Or shall I? Somebody should. The poor boy doesn't know what you really think of him . . .

Sam [furious because there is some truth in this]: You bitch!

David: I'd better go, Sam.

Jess: Don't let me stop you.

David [with dignity]: You're not stopping me, Jess . . .

Sam: Why not stay here until you do find something?

Jess [to David]: He hasn't always been so anxious for your company, let me assure you of that.

Sam: No, Davey. You're right. This is too nasty for words.

Jess: It's going to get nastier, I promise you.

Jess's breach of lovers' secrecy confirms their misalignment. It also sharpens the 'shadowy sense of involvement' that Meredith feels after the murder in the novel into a specific complicity: he had inflamed the row that caused Jessica Wray to leave, and in due course to come to harm.

Clift's other significant enrichment of the plot is that Jack, who in the novel is in the Wimmera when Jessica is killed, appears in the adaptation in the role of quasi-detective. He alone believes Sam's story of the telephone calls, and embarks (off camera) on shoring it up. He nobly defends Sam when Dad at the breakfast table denounces the licentious bohemians ('Touch pitch and you'll be defiled'); he is there for some 'I-told-you-so' exposition when Sam's exoneration is announced.

Jack: It looks as though you were wrong about that young student bloke, pop . . .

Dad: Funny thing about that phone call. Just goes to show the devil looks after his own . . .

Jack: Goes to show that people make mistakes, that's all. Codger at the post office was in a hurry to get off shift, just shoved the piece of paper in his pocket without writing it in the book, then went off on his holidays in the bush and didn't see a newspaper. Well that's cleared now, so the rozzers can start chasing someone else. Loony most likely. Escaped from the bin.

Jack lets it rest there, for neither Johnston nor Clift showed any interest in complete resolution. An unsolved murder better suited both their purposes, leaving blame diffuse, available for creative apportionment. But it's a shame in some ways that their only guide to the story was Colahan's, for the stunting of Mollie Dean would surely have struck a chord with Clift, both of them being involved in works they could never complete. Just as *Monsters Not Men* disappeared with Mollie's murder, so Clift's *The End of the Morning* was left as a fragment when she took her own life in July 1969, a year before Johnston's death. For female writers, rooms of their own remained ever elusive.

Over the last half-century and more, hundreds of thousands of Australians have been introduced unknowingly to the murder of Mollie Dean – while taking fictional form, it may well be Australia's most widely circulated true-crime story. The first television adaptation of *My Brother Jack* was acclaimed as setting a new standard in Australian drama; the last adaptation, a 2001 miniseries written by John Alsop and starring Matt Day as David Meredith, also rated respectably. In its retelling of Mollie Dean's death, the miniseries fell somewhere between the versions by Johnston and Clift, with some modern flourishes. Jessica Wray reverted to blonde, portrayed by English-born Lucy Taylor. Sam Burlington was played by Felix Williamson as an Anthony Blanche-style fop, with lines such as: 'Religion is merely the opiate of the masses. Art is the suppository.' Retained from Clift's conception was the basis of the climactic argument between Sam and Jessica.

> Jessica: I spend days at a time sitting for you when I could be doing my own work. I'm never allowed to express a bloody opinion. What am I to you?
> Sam: When you sit there you are just form, light and colour. You're just a bowl of fruit. A bowl of fruit doesn't have to express a bloody opinion.
> Jessica: How dare you? I'm just as much of an artist as you.

Here, though, the dispute, coming unheralded, is made to seem more like feminine pique, culminating in petulance when Jess flees after throwing a paint pot at Sam's expressionist canvas, then moderated by psychobabble. 'Go after her, will you?' Sam tells David forbearingly. 'Make sure she's all right.' As Jess and David then sit on a tram together, she is contrite, and he constructive, suggesting she call Sam, and invoking his parents' marriage as a caution: 'Because I grew up seeing what happens when two people stop talking to one another. I know how it ends.' In this case, of course, he doesn't. Jess steps off, saying that she will use the post office phone box, dismissing David's offer to accompany her: 'It's fifty yards down the street. I'll be fine. I might even be able to catch a taxi to his place.' Next he knows, David is spying the newspaper headlines ('NUDE MODEL IN ST KILDA SLAYING') and deflecting suspicious detectives ('We hardly even knew each other'), for media sensationalism and police intimidation never go out of thematic fashion. In the end, the tension is quickly alleviated by an identical murder occurring while Sam is in custody, and the sequence concludes by reverting to the novel, with an oedipal twist. Sam packs for overseas, thinking that he might, like his father, end up growing roses. 'Wouldn't that be the ultimate irony?' he asks. 'After all that we strive for we end up becoming our fathers.'

So it was that Mollie Dean, who aspired to writing a great Australian novel, ended up featuring in one instead – not inappropriately, a foundational text in the theme of suburbia's stifling weight, that critique sustained into the present by the likes of David Malouf's *Johnno* and Tim Winton's *Cloudstreet* (also visited by haunting murder). Her diluted spirit even infuses something like A. L. McCann's ennui-laden 2005 novel *Subtopia*, where the narrator, Julian, is gifted a copy of *My Brother Jack*, then lengthily channels David Meredith's horror-struck journey after Jessica Wray's murder on his own homeward train trip: 'The ghosts of tired commuters dozing off with their newspapers and their paperback novels. Lassitude, boredom, a multitude of obstinate details crowding out thought at the arse-end of the working day, lonely wage slaves trudging home to the sluggish rhythms of commerce, goods and services, professional intercourse, mass transport, furtive cravings, gross domestic product and a leisurely game of golf at the weekend.' And had I not picked up my battered old copy of *My Brother Jack* again, my path and Mollie Dean's would never have crossed.

At the same time, the telling can hardly satisfy, for all the writer's well-honed sensitivities. In the matter of Jessica Wray, Johnston's *My Brother Jack* is a curiously muted and bloodless affair. The violence begets no sensations of horror, no beseechings for justice. The lost promise occasions no pathos and no obsequies. There is no feeling of anyone caring much at all, save for themselves. Because Johnston first encountered Mollie as an unfortunate event in the life of her former lover, Sam Burlington and David Meredith are depicted as the crime's greater victims, the tragedy of Jessica Wray washing away in their oceans of male self-pity. Of Mollie Dean, then, *My Brother Jack* is at best a marker, scarcely a memorial.

17

21ST-CENTURY MOLLIE

*'You're twenty-eight years old, live on Broadway in Elwood, drive
a nineteen sixty-seven Ford Futura and your work history's a bit
hit and miss . . . So I'm wondering why you're so interested in the
murder, who you're working for and what you want from me.'*
— Leigh Redhead, *Peepshow* (2004)

I live diagonally across the road from the scene of a notorious killing. At around 3.30 p.m. on 23 March 2004 I glanced out my study
window in Carlton and noticed police swathing the La Porcella
restaurant in crime-scene tape. About an hour earlier, crime boss
Mick Gatto had shot gunman Benji Veniamin, for whose murder he
would be acquitted on self-defence grounds. I have since read that
the restaurant had long been notorious in the underworld as 'Gatto's
office'. I had only ever known it as a quiet place that never seemed to
have many patrons. The venue has since changed hands, and nothing
about the unprepossessing building speaks of its brush with infamy;
it has only been pausing to reflect on murder scenes generally that
has reminded me of the foregoing.

Something similar seems true of Mollie Dean's doomed zigzag
home. Remarkably little has changed about it in nearly ninety years.

St Kilda's history of self-devouring development has altered portions of Grey and Barkly streets. But one still passes by such landmarks as the Village Belle (albeit closed) and the Victory Theatre (albeit renamed), while Elwood's Mitford, Dickens and Addison streets are notably intact. The Dean house sits snugly alongside its double. While flats occupy the site of the Owen house, Knights Court, from which James Nankivell peered down that night and saw Mollie's upturned face, remains. The whole housing wedge seems to have been secured from the passage of time by the scrapping of the Brighton tramline in the mid-1950s. Traffic is light, pedestrians few. The light is dappled, the air of quiet solidity.

Perhaps this subtly sharpens the menace — the feeling that if murder can occur here, it can occur anywhere, befall anyone, in the random unbridling of a pent-up impulse. The laneway that sheers off Addison Street has no name, leads nowhere in particular. It needs an informed eye to discern the meaningful features, like the recessed entry of the garage that sheltered Mollie Dean's killer, so he could not be seen from the street, and the slight concavity in the cobble-stones where pooled Mollie Dean's blood, so it had to be washed away to deter ghouls. Which makes one aware of one's own latter-day ghoulishness.

One day, coming back from Elwood, I got chatting to a fellow tram commuter. Writing and old stories came up. He told me his, then inquired after mine. Me? Well, I explained, I was researching the life of a young woman slain in Elwood in 1930. 'Mollie Dean?' he asked at once. In the 1950s, he told me, his family had owned a local dairy, and his mother was always enjoining her children: '*Never go down the laneway.*' We laughed about the coincidence of our meeting, and that I was now doing, in effect, what he had always been told not to. For here was, of course, a further dimension of the allure of the site, and others like it: their taboo nature. No trip is so transgressive, no destination so inviting, as the tainted or prohibited. There is even a name for this now – the emergent culture of pilgrimage around locations of tragedy is referred to as 'dark tourism' and 'thanatourism'. Indeed, these locations become 'traumascapes' by our coming to them, by the introduction of our own fears and imaginings. Over the years, the laneway off Addison Street had blended back into the streetscape. What after all was to notice about it? But since 2000, as I was to learn, others had been coming, and with serious intent, preluding a rediscovery of Mollie Dean, and a belated female editing of her story.

Around the time of 2001's *My Brother Jack* miniseries, 26-year-old theatre maker Melita Rowston was embarked on her own search for Mollie Dean. A native of Beaumaris, she had been seduced by the oeuvre of local girl Clarice Beckett, whose fame was finally growing after long obscurity, a barn full of her neglected paintings having come to light in a country shed. At a retrospective of the artist she had encountered the art historian Rosalind Hollinrake, whose monographs on Beckett included Mollie Dean as a background character. Into a play Rowston wrote about Clarice, *Night Reflections*, she incorporated Mollie as an interlocutor. Next, Rowston wanted to draw Mollie's liminal figure to centre stage, which meant, among other things, dogging her footsteps, using microfiche copies of newspapers in the State Library of Victoria as a guide. So, one afternoon, she found herself in Addison Street, trying to work out where the crime had taken place.

An elderly man emerged from a small house, introducing himself as a former mayor of St Kilda. He sounded like the sort of chap who might have a feeling for local history. Rowston asked if, by any chance, he happened to know anything about the long-ago death of a young woman called Mollie Dean. The man pointed knowingly across the road to the mouth of a laneway. 'See that spot?' he asked. 'That's where she was killed.' It was as though it had occurred the week before.

The dramatis personae were by now mostly gone: Mervyn Skipper in 1958 and Lena in 1971; Percy Leason in 1959 and Belle in 1989; Justus Jorgensen in 1975 and Lil in 1977. Having made Monique Bornoff his third wife, Colahan had died in 1987, a year after Mireille Wilkinson, nine years before Betty Roland. They had been succeeded by published sources, less intimate, although in some respects more reliable and accessible: not just Hollinrake's works on Beckett, but Kinnane's portrait of Colahan, Jenny Teichman's memoir of Jorgensen, Michael Jorgensen's cameo of Jim Minogue, and a comprehensive survey of tonalism, *Max Meldrum & Associates*, by Peter and John Perry. Yet for all the chronicling, it struck Rowston that Mollie Dean was still seen almost exclusively through male eyes. Even Teichman's *Justus Jorgensen*, for example, scorned to so much as mention her name, simply describing Colahan as 'the most fascinating charmer who ever walked on two legs', and praising his resilience: 'What is more (or so I gathered) this hero had once been on trial for his life, for murder – he was acquitted. There were giants on the earth in those days.'

Rowston's newspaper scourings reported that Mollie had aspired to write. But about what and for whom the sources were silent. Rowston was intrigued to read in Roland's *The Eye of the Beholder* about Mollie's insistence on sitting with the male Meldrumites and participating in their conversations rather than tending to them – and that, in fact, she had been resented for it, mainly by the other women. Rowston was reminded of her own grandmother. Mardi Rogers had grown up wanting to be an artist or a poet. Then, in 1945, Mardi fell pregnant, was marched to a shotgun wedding, and by the time her granddaughter knew her had coarsened into an embittered alcoholic. Rowston saw Mollie Dean as fighting back, clawing her way out of suburban anonymity like a cat in a sack; but just as she had almost extracted herself, an unknown hand had cast that sack into a river.

'*I'm writing a book! I'm bursting with ideas!*' In *Solitude in Blue*, which premiered in full at the Griffin Theatre in December 2002, Mollie Dean at last obtained something like a voice – its small audiences would have had little notion how long that had been in coming. The play introduced her, played by petite brunette Martelle Hammer, fluking an invitation to an exhibition at the Athenaeum by 'this bloke Meldrum', and there coming alive. She sipped proper champagne. She heard a Chopin nocturne. She saw men with strange beards, and intuited that these 'Meldrumites' were 'real artists' – exactly the kind of company she wished to keep. And so for a new century a new Mollie Dean was born.

Rowston's *Solitude in Blue* renders Mollie Dean recognisable for modern sensibilities. Young, bright, questing for an outlet, knowing about her sexuality, she is a feminist *avant la lettre*. One of the play's very simple, perhaps unconscious breakthroughs is that Mollie appears under her own name. She is no longer Mervyn Skipper's perfumed jezebel, Sue Vanderkelen's 'Millie Bond', Fritz Hart's 'Eileen Coote', George Johnston's 'Jessica Wray' or even Kristel Thornell's later 'Jean', but one who objects to aliases, decrying handles like 'Miles Franklin' and 'Henry Handel Richardson': 'There's no way in hell I'm going to write under a pseu-oyd-on-hym!' She is that very contemporary phenomenon, the memoirist/autobiographer, telling her own story, subjectively entitled to replace naturalism and chronology with atmosphere and tableaux.

Having trailed the Meldrumites to a bar, Mollie interrupts Colahan's colloquy, and throws a gauntlet down: 'You're an artist, yet all you do is talk and talk.' They actually have this in common, because Mollie is herself struggling to do better than talk about writing: 'Well, I have about twenty-two first chapters for twenty-two different books and hundreds of other ideas. They're written down on scraps of paper, receipts, bags and clothing tags.' When they commence a volatile relationship, Mollie struggles to make herself heard above the competitive din of the artists' circle, and seethes when relegated to the fringes of Colahan's homecoming party for Jorgensen.

> Mollie: A girl clutching a pencil isn't as romantic as a bloke grasping his big brush.
> Colin: Let's not argue.
> Mollie: Then Lena Skipper grabs my arm and leads me into the kitchenette where she hands me a butter knife and orders me to cut up Justus's cake. I wanted to plunge that thing right through her heart.
> Colin: She was—
> Mollie: So I'm cutting up cake, I'm doing a real shit job of it but Lena's preoccupied with the baby's colic. And there's a roar of laughter from around your easel as you make another witty jest. And everyone shouts 'drink up'. But no-one offers me a drink. And I'm trying to catch your eye through the steam from the kettle, but you were looking towards your own glorious future.

Nor does Mollie take to Jorgensen, a 'dirty little old man'.

> Colahan: He's a genius.
> Mollie: Who cares about a painting of a hut in the woods?
> Colahan: Careful.
> Mollie: You're acting like you're the head boy at Melbourne Grammar and Justus is your wonderful principal . . .
> Colin: What are you? A little tart writing a novel on a bus ticket.

At the same time, Colahan provides Mollie with her inspiration by returning home with news of the killing of Alma Tirtschke – plucked, with literary licence, from 1921. It offends his aesthetic sensibilities: 'Murdered in Gun Alley – what a horrible name.' Mollie, however, is drawn to the scene, almost against her will: 'This is crazy. What am I doing?' Much the same as the playwright that bright day in Elwood not so long before. And as Mollie noses round Gun Alley, there emerges from the shadows a kind of expositor: the saturnine figure of Adam Graham, who derides her fancy ways and conveys her mother's distress at the neighbourhood gossip.

> Graham: I seen you carousing with them bohemians. I heard about their drinkin' and orgies and I ain't gunna sit by whilst you drag your family's name in the mud.
> Mollie: Those bohemians are educated, well travelled, they've seen places you'll never dream of, they talk about stuff that's beyond you. They believe in me.

Except that they don't, quite. In an effective metaphor, Mollie and Colahan have only the one typewriter between them, and he is busy writing *Max Meldrum: His Art and Views*. Mollie is actually trying to coax Colahan from dogmatic Meldrumism ('Is this the muddy mark you want to leave on the Australian art world?'), but he continues deferring to his guru ('Why should I listen to you? You're a second-rate tart in your homemade skirt'). She goes on dreaming of her book ('I just want a typewriter and a few hours of solitude a day'), but when she takes an interest in the deaths of Mena Griffiths and Hazel Wilson again encounters an uncannily lurking Graham, who importunes her possessively. 'I don't know what you want but whatever it is I'll get it for you,' he promises. 'I want MORE,' she barks back. It is not on offer. When Mollie discerns evidence of Colahan's relationship with Sue Vanderkelen ('That's her fucking scarf!'), he retaliates by flourishing his own completed book ('Funny how I made it to print before you did and I wasn't even trying').

During her research, Rowston noticed that 86 Milton Street was for sale, and attended an inspection, finding the 1920s features covered by only a thin 1960s patina. Ethel's kitchen and Ralph's sleep-out remained intact; Mollie might have hung her clothes on the line out back. Mollie's climactic speech is a screech of defiance against suburbia's straitening influences: 'I want to smash their letterboxes, plough up their nature strips, tear out their garden paths! I wanna break their windows, burn their verandahs, rip out their Hills hoists! I wanna fill out the letters of my name – Molly Dean – with my own blood.' And Mollie *is* to achieve a kind of artistic apotheosis – but not on her own account.

Solitude in Blue was a far cry from the science and subtlety of a tonalist portrait. It was loud and vivid and earthy, the lovers consummating in the mud beneath Princes Bridge, and connected only tenuously to primary sources and chronology. Yet it was also the first work to explore Mollie's representative dimensions: what goes to developing, and to silencing, a female voice. For having read a report of her murder, Colahan rings down the curtain by unveiling a canvas of his lover in an attitude of sleep, deathly sleep. 'Finished!' he cries.

If a bold, independent, ambitious, sexy woman writer cut down in her prime made a better emblem in the twenty-first than the twentieth century, Mollie Dean had to make another transition: she had to get, or more accurately be got, online, so that a casual browsing for her name snagged on something digital. Tracing another take on Mollie Dean starts with Travis Sellers, an information technology support worker and member of the St Kilda Historical Society. For a quarter of a century, Sellers has had a consuming fascination with his local cemetery of Brighton, richly sown with history: last resting place of Sir John Monash and Adam Lindsay Gordon, of multiple Baillieus and Boyds, of Albert Tucker and Frederick McCubbin; also of a scattering of murder victims, from Alma Tirtschke to war hero Eric Tulloch, shot by an unknown gunman the night before he was to coach Melbourne Grammar in the 1926 Head of the River. Today Sellers runs a compendious website, brightoncemetery.com, funded by donations. In the 1990s, he was simply seeking fruitful connections. One of his favourite school texts had been *My Brother Jack*, whose author, George Johnston, he knew to be a local. Sellers wondered if he was interred in Brighton Cemetery. As it happened, Johnston was not but Mollie Dean was: Sellers photographed her family's lonely plot to adorn a two-page article in the December 2000 edition of the society's *St Kilda Chronicle*, racily entitled 'The Artist, the Fiancée and Murder at Elwood'.

Four years later, a young architect, Simon Reeve of the Heritage Alliance, was commissioned by the City of Port Phillip to report on the streetscapes of Elwood. To leaven the dry chaff of Edwardian architecture ('symmetrical facade with tripartite casement sash windows that flank a central gabled porch with half-timbered gable ends and stop-chamfered posts'), he went page-by-page through the *St Kilda Chronicle*, and stumbled on Sellers' story. Reeve pinned the laneway down by perusing coverage of the inquest, finding references to the Owen family who first raised the alarm, and locating them in the electoral rolls at 5 Addison Street. He then photographed the murder scene on an appropriately gloomy day in the pouring rain, and recommended that the site be 'interpreted'. 'It wasn't usual to include something like that in a heritage report,' he says. 'But it occurred to me that if it wasn't marked in some way, then the laneway might be infilled with housing without anyone knowing about it.' The report was duly posted on the council website, noting the Dean case as an inspiration both for *My Brother Jack* and, now, for *Solitude in Blue*. Unknowingly, the web diffusing information and misinformation alike, Reeve also spread Betty Roland's inexactitude about Adam Graham marrying Ethel Dean.

After moving into Elwood in the mid-1990s, singer/songwriter Lisa Miller and her architect husband, Ben, had been struck by its incongruous feeling of remoteness. 'Since the end of the tramway, the area has been a kind of quiet pocket where nothing connects,' she says. 'Laneways cross it like the lines on a hand.' One day while they were traversing the web for historic information, they stumbled on both Reeve's report and Sellers' story, now uploaded onto his cemetery site. Thanks to Trove, the National Library of Australia's maid-of-all-work, Miller could plunge straight into newspaper accounts of the crime. Realising with a shudder that she often passed the relevant laneway while dog walking, Miller decided that Mollie Dean cried out for the idiom of the murder ballad: think Lead Belly's 'In the Pines', Marty Robbins' 'El Paso', and such standards as 'Banks of the Ohio', 'Knoxville Girl' and 'Little Sadie'. And, well, while she knew it sounded corny, Miller even felt a little like a 'medium', for the young writer's restless spirit:

> Don't go walking down my street
> If you don't have nothin' for me,
> And you don't go tell my story
> To everyone you meet.

Miller composed 'Molly Dean' in her head while walking the neighbourhood, sometimes thoughtfully, sometimes uneasily, lines swinging from Mollie's point of view back to her own. Having taken at face value Reeve's reporting of Roland's reporting of Adam Graham's marriage to Ethel, she inferred their guilt. But Miller was more struck by the silence of others who might have known, might have intervened, might even have prevented:

> 'Cos somewhere somebody knows
> Oh someone always knows
> Somebody who knows.
> And it wasn't just the brutal hands
> That took the life from me,
> Or the cold and heartless mother,
> But the ones that let them be.

The story had a further contemporary resonance. In St Kilda, there had recently been a spate of unsolved killings among the sorority of working girls, their bodies being found in local lanes. This was not, then, merely a local folktale. The strand of violence against women was dismayingly continuous:

And you can tear down the walls and the gates
But the layout's still the same
And there's another hapless woman
Left crumpled in the lane.

'Molly Dean' became one of Miller's live staples – in a December 2015 YouTube video, she performs it with Shane O'Mara and Charlie Owen at Music on the Hill. On her 2017 release *The Dusty Millers*, with her sisters Loretta and Tracey, it is set between

'Another hapless woman': the Dusty Millers sing Mollie

two country and western classics, Bob Nolan's 'Cool Water' and Dolly Parton's 'Jolene'. A tribute to Miller's craft is that the song sounds as though it, too, was written many, many years ago. Perhaps, in a way, it was.

Even if the murderer of Mollie Dean was merely an opportunist, he found his target with cruel precision, cutting off in her prime a woman determined to advance, to transcend, *to live*. Could her agency be somehow restored? Could her energy be in some way rekindled? A few years ago, these questions came to Katherine Kovacic. Kovacic's undergraduate degree was in veterinary science, her masters in art history; she combined these interests in her doctorate, a study of animals in art, and her work, as a freelance art-historian-cum-dog-trainer. Kovacic had also cultivated specialities in tonalism and artistic expatriatism, curating exhibitions at the Castlemaine Art Gallery of the works of Archie and Amalie Colquhoun, and of Australian artists along the French and Italian coasts. Both threads connected to Colin Colahan, and fed an intrigue with item 12 in the catalogue for his exhibition at the Athenaeum in April 1930: a portrait entitled 'Molly Dean'. The painting, like so many of Colahan's, is lost. Kovacic's whodunit, *The Portrait of Molly Dean*, to be published in May 2018, imagines its rediscovery.

The milieu has itself been in a phase of rediscovery: Kristel Thornell's *Night Street*, winner of the Vogel, was followed by Emily Bitto's *The Strays*, winner of the Stella, also set in the Melbourne art world of the 1930s, also offering a female slant on a mainly male enclave, a cell of self-involved avant-garde painters identified as 'the circle'. Though it was in preparation, Kovacic, slim, self-contained, with smiling eyes and a red Pre-Raphaelite mane, generously shared with me her manuscript and thoughts. She had always been intrigued by the impenetrability of the mystery around Mollie Dean; she had noted Eric Westbrook's conjectures about the paucity of evidence; she had retraced Mollie's footsteps on her final walk ending at the laneway, and been struck, like Melita Rowston and Lisa Miller, by how lightly time had touched it.

The tradition of drawing on factual crime for fictional inspiration stretches back to Poe's 'The Mystery of Marie Rogêt', based on a sensation of the moment in New York: the July 1841 slaying of 'the Beautiful Cigar Girl', Mary Cecilia Rogers. In Australia, homicide has headed straighter for the screen: the backpacker murders in *Wolf Creek*, the bodies-in-barrels murders in *Snowtown*, the deaths of Sallie-Anne Huckstepp in *Blue Murder*, Anita Cobby in *The Boys*, and Leigh Leigh in *Blackrock*. Mollie Dean was by contrast historically obscure. But no longer inaccessible: Trove now returns more than 1000 hits, including some that would have eluded the most assiduous analog explorer; six years ago, one of the database's industrious text correctors helpfully daisy-chained many of the most useful stories. And like the murders of Ethel Griggs in 1928 and of Shirley Collins in 1953, inspirations recently for Reg Egan's *Lottie* and Janice Simpson's *Murder in Mt Martha*, nobody was convicted of Mollie's death – an open invitation to find one. The historical characters, then, provided Kovacic with her palette; the indeterminate conclusion offered a blank canvas.

In Kovacic's novel, the Dean portrait comes to light in 1999, identified only as 'Lot 186 Australian school' in an auction-house catalogue. The painting falls beneath the gaze of feisty art historian Alex Clayton, who recognises it at once. She bids successfully, despite a mysteriously determined underbidder. For the portrait contains a secret, which it would be unfair to reveal, but which is teased out in a switching back and forth between 1999, as Alex unravels the clues, and 1930, as Molly Dean leaves them, the latter in the attempt to make her name as a reporter in the face of her mother's desiccated rectitude:

> 'How ridiculous. You can't stop me from associating with my friends. They're creative and imaginative enough to understand me and my writing. Unlike you. You have all the artistry of, of . . . a dead fish.'
>
> 'I'm not prepared to watch you throw away a perfectly good job for some ridiculous fancy. Besides, if you carry on like this, no man will look at you, let alone want to marry you.'

There is a suitably sinister Adam Graham, a fetchingly bitchy Betty Roland, and a disarmingly sympathetic Colahan, whose girlfriend assumes the unillusioned modern stance that he is 'a good fit' and 'certainly enjoyable' despite his vagrancy. For the moment anyway: 'Being a wife was not part of Molly Dean's plan; she had a career to build and fully intended to become famous. It was only a matter of time.' It *is* a matter of time – the eighty years since her first incorporation into fiction. In *A Pressman's Soul*, Mollie was a mistress and a model without a name, her death an excuse for Skipper to complain about his journalistic contemporaries. In *The Portrait of Molly Dean*, her name appears in the title, she is comfortable in a non-exclusive relationship with Colahan, and *is* one of Skipper's journalistic contemporaries – a crusading one at that. There is also, reflecting the author's other life, an appealing canine, named Hogarth. The solution? It's a blend of police corruption, corporate depravity and novelist's licence, says Kovacic: 'A nod to the conspiracy theorists, really. Thank you, Eric Westbrook.' But the further development, perhaps the ultimate development, is that a modern seeker enables Mollie Dean to essentially finger her killer. No wonder Mollie was drawn to the power of fiction. It can offer something not in my gift: a form of posthumous empowerment.

EPILOGUE

As 1966 began, the Homicide Squad of Victoria Police received an anonymous letter postmarked Brisbane of which at first they could make no sense. 'Dear Sir,' it commenced formally, in a neat cursive script. 'Would your department still be interested in some information that will lead to an arrest regarding the Molly Dean case?'

'Molly Dean case'? Nobody at Russell Street could recall any such crime. The homicides then obsessing the state were those of prison warder George Hodson and tow-truck driver Arthur Henderson, for which recently recaptured Pentridge escapees Ronald Ryan and Peter John Walker would shortly go on trial. Then someone with a longer-than-average memory recalled that schoolteacher, that laneway and that unsolved mystery. Acting on the writer's request to do so before 14 February, Homicide chief Frank Holland insinuated an advertisement into the personal columns of newspapers in Brisbane soliciting further information.

When no response was heard, police went public. Dusty draw-
ers were rifled for that one old photograph, memories for ancient
impressions. 'MURDER STILL RANKLES . . . EVEN 35 YEARS LATER' read
a headline in *The Herald*, whose John Craven had located 76-year-
old Percy Lambell, still in Elwood, sixteen years retired. 'I've thought
about the Molly Dean case for years,' he said. 'I followed every lead at
the time and I came to a dead end. I can't think what this letter writer
could say that wasn't uncovered in the past. But I hope the police
hear from him again.' The term 'bohemian' now ringing quaintly,
Melbourne's *Sun* updated the 'brilliant schoolteacher with a vivacious
personality' with a word now in common coinage: 'She was a feminist and refused to conform to some of the strict ideas of "a woman's
place" in the 1930s. She believed in going her own way, and liked the
company of artists for whom it is believed she posed in the nude.' That
the anonymous correspondent had mentioned their failing health
conjured visions of a deathbed confession:

> Detectives at Melbourne CIB are waiting on tenterhooks today
> for word from Brisbane.
>
> They still believe the letter may be genuine. If so, a macabre
> and baffling riddle many be solved in a sensational manner . . . by
> a voice from the long past.
>
> Police do not believe the writer of the letter is yet dead. The
> writer indicated that his (or her) health was failing rapidly. But
> the writing has been studied carefully and it does not seem to
> have been written by a sick person.

It is, still, a captivating notion. The conventions of the police procedural
have conditioned us to the idea that all crime is soluble, usually within
the extent of 300 pages or an hour of television. Since popularisation

of the 'cold case' concept, it seems that no evidence is beyond retrieval, no clue beyond elucidation. Writers such as Kate Summerscale, Erik Larson and Sinclair McKay have burrowed centuries into the past. In some instances, previous verdicts have been spectacularly vacated. Mollie Dean's generation imagined Colin Ross to have been safely convicted of the murder of Alma Tirtschke: Kevin Morgan's *Gun Alley* suggested otherwise.

Yet only the merest fraction of cold cases ever warm. The relentless pace of hot cases melts them away; memories falter, wounds heal, trails go dead. So it proved with Mollie Dean. From the nameless letter writer, no more was heard. Police found other priorities; the media mind, faintly jogged, moved on. The offer's provenance and sincerity had been doubtful anyway, the artifice of the advertisement in the personal column a jarringly coy touch in the context of a claimed urgency. It remains just possible a revelation is out there. Documents have ways of surviving unless their destruction is specifically ordered – like Hugh Buggy's notebooks. But Buggy himself passed forty-three years ago. And with the passage of nearly nine decades, all we know for sure about Mollie Dean's killer is that he is also dead, swallowed up like Poe's 'Man of the Crowd':

> There are some secrets which do not permit themselves to be told. Men die nightly in their beds, wringing the hands of ghostly confessors, and looking them piteously in the eyes – die with despair of heart and convulsion of throat, on account of the hideousness of mysteries which will not suffer themselves to be revealed. Now and then, alas, the conscience of man takes up a burden so heavy in horror that it can be thrown down only into the grave. And thus the essence of all crime is undivulged.

In any event, a solution is not the same as justice. The obvious tragedy of Mollie Dean's death contained another less obvious, which
is the way others turned aside from it. There is no eluding that the
opportunity to murder a young woman alone after midnight on a
deserted street arose out of her undeserved estrangement from both
friends and family, with the probability that this ambivalence also
complicated the hunt for her murderer. The quicker she then faded,
the better for all involved, a process arguably beginning with her
burial: interred in the Dean plot, she received no marker. The only
headstone is for George, tactfully describing him as a 'beloved husband' and 'loved father' above a nearly illegible footnote: 'At Rest'.
Nothing for Mollie: she is quietly folded back into the family that
had begrudged her every step away.

Among her former circle she dwindled to a source of dinner-table
chitchat. The conversations with Colahan and Betty Roland recorded
by Eric Westbrook from the late 1960s show their memories to have
become hopelessly confused, mainly by tendencies to self-protection
and self-dramatisation. 'I know this so clearly,' Roland insisted before
launching into a rendition of events erroneous in almost every respect.
Invited to reflect on Mollie herself, they cryptically quoted others.
Said Colahan: 'Percy Leason, when he heard of the murder and so
forth, his reaction was: "How completely in character." Which is one
summing-up.' Said Roland:

> Now here's a . . . Sue Vanderkelen, who was very subtle, very witty,
> made a beautiful remark. That Molly . . . It came out that Colin
> had promised to marry Molly.
> Colahan: That's not true.
> Roland: I know it's not true. But the press did that, you see.
> Colahan: I know they did that.

Roland: That you had promised to marry her, and that she was
a talented novelist, and Sue said: 'Poor Molly, both the things
she wanted most in life she achieved post mortem. That she
was the future wife of Colahan, and that she was a talented
young novelist.' So I think that's a nice sort of tagline to the
whole thing.

One summing-up. A nice sort of tagline. An ugly death polished into
aphorisms, with a last supercilious reference to 'the press' – even
though they had not concocted Colahan's 'promise' to marry Mollie,
but trustingly reported his lie that they were affianced. Just a girl. Just
a murder. Just a story.

Perhaps we should not be too judgemental. Perhaps Mollie's story
lies closer to what might be called 'real crime' than true crime. The
idea that murder can be 'solved' comforts the crime consumer, free-
ing us to revel in the dispelling of mystery by the force of reason and
the quelling of violence by order, and to take a share in the therapeutic
solace of 'closure' and the pleasing ring of 'justice'. For those in emotional proximity to murder, there is no closing the book on the note
of a well-formed denouement. Grief is one emotion among many. As
the case of Mollie Dean remained yawningly open, the only way to
turn was away, with a set of laundered 'facts' at the ready just in case.
In the future of the Meldrumites lay searchings in sharply disparate
directions. In the future of the Deans, what an eerie hollow was left.

Unburdened by the same shames, Mollie's recent discoverers have
been free to offer overt reinterpretations. A theatrical two-hander.
A murder ballad. A whodunit. Journalism too – for my version
of her story, while drawing on recoverable fact, is likewise a work
of imagination, differentiable perhaps by Gide's famous distinction
between fiction as 'history which *might* have taken place' and history

as 'fiction which *has* taken place'. And it's arguable that the times rather suit Mollie Dean. She modernises so easily that it's as though we have caught up with her rather than she catching up with us. Colin Colahan, Justus Jorgensen, even Max Meldrum – who are they today? Yet we *are* receptive to stories of female creative adversity – Plath, Woolf, Claudel, Dickinson et al. The recent 'Zeldamania', when Zelda Fitzgerald was played by Jennifer Lawrence, Scarlett Johansson and Christina Ricci in three separate screen projects, was essentially an argument that the under-acknowledgement and thwarting of her writing were as important as her actual writing. Of this, Mollie's story offers an extreme example: the under-acknowledgement was nearly total, the thwarting lethal.

Nonetheless, I'm not sure Mollie Dean would have wished to be remembered as a martyr. On the night she was brought into the Alfred Hospital, the medical staff were astounded that she had not already succumbed to her injuries, given the damage and defilement she had suffered. She did not go gently – she fought for hours. And though it was her death that alerted me to Mollie, it was her hunger for life, defiant of gender and class, art hierarchy and family expectation, that would not let me rest until I had looked as hard as I could. It presented, at first, as the tiniest of targets: a handful of factoids, a forgotten faction, a silent family, a single photograph. And nothing, really, could be changed or fixed by my looking. Yet what were these challenges compared to hers? Always one must try, even if there is no telling how things might end. All I could offer was this modest measure of restorative justice – that of treating Mollie Dean as more than a mere victim. But it testifies to the power of her spirit that it should have endured and outlasted, long enough to finally find a sympathetic echo in the present.

ACKNOWLEDGEMENTS
AND BIBLIOGRAPHY

The research for *A Scandal in Bohemia*, involving quite a deep dive into the past, loomed as a mainly solitary endeavour. In fact, it became a task with many companions. Indeed, I would hardly have advanced an inch but for the professionalism and goodwill of staff at Victoria's Public Record Office, an unsung but indispensable institution that fulfils its mission ever better thanks to the efforts of such as Kate Follington, Rebecca Young, Tara Oldfield and the estimable Charlie Farrugia.

I commenced this research journey with visits to Garry Kinnane, biographer of George Johnston and Colin Colahan, and thank him for his hospitality and generosity. Morag Fraser helped me negotiate some tricky shoals at Montsalvat, where Anthony Aspridis made me welcome. Thank you to Sue Thomas for permission to quote from the diaries of her grandmother-in-law Lena Skipper; to Adam and Ruth Callander for permission to quote from the memoir of

Lena's daughter Sonia; to Margaret Ringersma, for guidance to her aunt Sylvia Vanderkelen's 'Sue's Story'; to Gilda Baracchi, who allowed my use of her mother Betty Roland's papers and works; to Max Leason, who allowed my use of his father Percy's art and photographs. The Art Gallery of South Australia consented to reproduction of Sidney Nolan's *Brighton Road State School*, the Art Gallery of Ballarat to reproduction of Sir John Longstaff's portrait of Betty Roland. Jim Tzannes, executor of the estate of the late Tessa Mallos, kindly lent the wonderful photographs of her playing Jessica Wray in the 1965 adaptation of *My Brother Jack*, winkled from her own scrapbooks.

The State Library of Victoria permitted quotation from the works of Fritz Hart; HarperCollins and Jane Novak from the works of George Johnston, Charmian Clift and Norman Lindsay; Allen & Unwin from Leigh Redhead's *Peepshow*; Sue Milliken from her company's 2001 adaptation of *My Brother Jack*; Taylor & Francis and the Bertrand Russell Peace Foundation from the works of Bertrand Russell; Kristel Thornell from her *Night Street*; Carmel Kenny of Equity Trustees from the works of Nettie Palmer. I was further assisted by other descendants and friends of several of my main characters: Lisa Barmby, whose great-aunt Nora married Colin Colahan's brother Fred, discreetly delved into family lore as I could not have; Robin Bradley, son of Reginald; Susan Fawkes, daughter of Hubert Clifford; Gael Hammer, cousin of Clara Behrend, and also Clara's great-niece Jean Freeling; Jenny Nickson, granddaughter of 'A. E. H. N.'; Richard Pyke, nephew of Joyce; Anthony Sell, son of Teddy; Graeme Weber, grandson of Clarence; Don Hossack, friend of Eric Westbrook.

Shout-outs to my fellow toilers on the trail of Mollie Dean, Dr Eric Frazer and Travis Sellers. It was likewise gratifying to cross paths and compare impressions with Melita Rowston, Lisa Miller and Katherine

Kovacic, as captivated by Mollie as I have been. I benefited from advice of Margot Tasca, biographer of Percy Leason. And when I had almost despaired, Jenny Martyn accomplished the marvellous feat of translating Hugh Buggy's archaic Pitman shorthand notes into English.

Graeme Haigh of Grajohn Genealogical Services in Sydney traipsed up hill and down dale as I pieced past families together; this is the third book of mine he has aided, and I unhesitatingly recommend his services. Sue and Tom McBeth of Macbeth Genealogical Services in Melbourne helped search property titles here. Acknowledgements for their introduction to the school's holdings of old boy Colin Colahan to Douglas Kennedy, Maria Tallarida and Catherine Hall of Xavier College Archives; for their invaluable guidance about Fritz Hart, Peter Tregear of London University, Anne-Marie Forbes of the University of Tasmania and Stephanie McCallum of the Sydney Conservatorium; for help at Ormond College Archives, Anna Drummond, and at Scotch College Archives, Paul Mishura; for records of the Victoria Police Museum, Caroline Oxley; for direction at the National Film and Sound Archive, Sean Bridgman; for advice about the works of Colin Colahan, Geoffrey Smith of Sotheby's; for their friendly assistance, Margy Burn of the National Library of Australia and Lois McEvey and Sandra Burt at the State Library of Victoria; for answering various of my jumble of inquiries at the University of Melbourne, Dr Jackie Dickenson of the School of Historical and Philosophical Studies, Dr Clare Rhoden of the School of Culture and Communication, Professor Janet McCalman of the Centre for Health & Society and special-collections librarian Leanne McReddin; Marjorie Dalvean and Sue Westwood at the Athenaeum Library; Dr Nancy Underhill, director of the University Art Museum at the University of Queensland; Dr Carolyn Holbrook, Alfred Deakin Research Fellow at Deakin University; Kendrah Morgan, senior curator at Heide

Museum of Modern Art; David Rainey, keeper of the excellent art blog aCOMMENT; and Simon Reeve, consultant with Built Heritage.

Every toiling Australian researcher, of course, owes an undis-chargeable debt to the designers and operators of Trove. In the currency of this book, its longtime steward Marie-Louise Ayres succeeded to the director-generalship of the National Library of Australia, a deserved honour. For services too numerous to mention, including introductions, counsel and other kindnesses, I salute, in no particular order: Philippa Hawker, Amber McMahon, Tritia Evans, Catherine McGregor, Caroline Overington, Geoffrey Blainey, David Studham, Deborah Robertson, Melanie Ostell, Foong Ling Kong, Nick Ryan, Tony Nagy, Dr Barbara Nichol, Angela Meyer, Ruby Crysell, Tony Stephens, Christian Ryan, Russell Jackson and Royce Kurmelov. My wife, Charlotte, and daughter, Cecilia, raised no objection to the other woman in my life, which was typically understanding and tolerant of them.

PRIMARY SOURCES
Public Record Office
Legal and law enforcement
Crown Law department records:
VPRS 12230/P1/1 Index to Opinion Book of the Crown Law Offices
VPRS 266/P0/948, Item 698 Inward Registered Correspondence
VPRS 30/P0/2383, Item 187 Trial briefs (R v Graham 1931)
VPRS 30/P0/2025, Item 585 Trial briefs (R v McMahon 1923)
VPRS 30/P0/2377, Item 79 Trial briefs (R v McMahon 1931)

Divorce proceedings:
VPRS 283/P2/152, item Case No. 1930/217 (Colin and Vi Colahan)
VPRS 283/P2/191, item Case No. 1933/234 (Ellis and Betty Davies)

VPRS 283/P2 unit 187, item Case No. 1933/60 (Gilbert and Monica Boileau)

VPRS 283/P2/235, item Case No. 1936/166 (Louis and Beatrice Lavater)

Police inbound correspondence files:

VPRS 807/P0/879, No. 26490 Indecent assault of Miss Doris Hope Phillips, 31 July 1930

VPRS 807/P0/895, No. 28809 Assault with intent to rob on Miss Beryl Bissett and Mrs Samuel Meyer, 8 November 1930

Education Department

Teacher record books:

VPRS 13579/P1/35, No. 10301–10600 (1884–86): George Dean 10421

VPRS 13579/P1/75, No. 22500–22899 (1922–1922): Mollie Dean 22525

VPRS 13579/P1/76, No. 22900–23299 (1922–23): Edna Johnson 23121

VPRS 13579/P1/79, No. 24100–24499 (1924–25): Sarah Fields 24178

VPRS 13579/P1/85, No. 26250–26449 (1927–1927): Joyce Pyke 26326

VPRS 12230/P1/1: Inspectors' Record Books

Building files:

VPRS 795/P0/1984, item 307: Queensberry Street, North Melbourne, 1928–48

VPRS 795/P0/1972, item 267: Bamfield Street, Sandringham, 1914–35

VPRS 795/P0/2238, item 1479: Brighton Road, St Kilda, 1920–42

Outward letter books:

VPRS 796/P0/8, item 112: Faraday Street, Carlton, 1922–29

VPRS 796/P0/262, item 1479: Brighton Road, St Kilda, 1901–37

VPRS 796/P0/280, item 1542: Wilson Street, Brighton, 1905–13

Central inward primary schools correspondence:

VPRS 640/P0 unit 1026, item 1467: Hawksburn Primary School, 1901–10

VPRS 640/P1 unit 1373, item 1542: Brighton Primary School, 1911–13

VPRS 640/P1 unit 1469, item 1542: Brighton Primary School, 1914–16

VPRS 640/P1 unit 1440, item 267: Sandringham Primary School, 1914–16

VPRS 640/P1 unit 1673, item 1479: St Kilda Primary School, 1921–23

VPRS 640/P1 unit 1699, item 1479: St Kilda Primary School, 1924–26

VPRS 640/P1 unit 1628, item 1479: St Kilda Primary School, 1921–23

VPRS 640/P1 unit 1758, item 112: Carlton Primary School, 1927–29

VPRS 640/P1 unit 1678, item 307: North Melbourne Primary School,
    1924–26

VPRS 640/P1 unit 1763, item 307: North Melbourne Primary School, 1927–29

VPRS 640/P1 unit 1870, item 307: North Melbourne Primary School, 1930–32

Miscellaneous

Kew Asylum:

VPRS 7565/P1/2 Admission warrants, male and female patients, 1895–1901
    (Thomas Beckett)

Wills and Probate

VPRS 28/P23/134 (Sarah Fields)

VPRS 28/P3/2192 (Clarence Weber)

VPRS 28/P1/258 (Adam Graham)

VPRS 7591/P2/967 (Miss J. M. D. Pyke)

VPRS 7591/P2/593 (John J. A. Colahan)

Inquests

VPRS 24/P0/712 (Thomas Beckett)

VPRS 24/P0/924 (Lawrence Bach)

VPRS 24/P0/1532 (Irene Argent)

VPRS 24/Po/1716 (Hugh Stevens)

QSA 36 Inquest no. 648/14 (Richard Pyke)

State Library of Victoria

MS 8273 Papers of Louis Lavater: Letters from Mollie Dean, Box 529/2a

MSS 10070 Papers of Justus Jorgensen: Diaries of Lena Skipper, Item 3

MS 13086 Peter Tregear: *Fritz Hart: An Introduction to His Life and Music*, master's thesis 1993

MS 13637 Papers of Sue Vanderkelen: 'Proem', and 'Cloud Babies', and other stories 1935–52

MS 15592 Scrapbooks of Clarence Weber

National Library of Australia

MS 1174 Papers of Vance and Nettie Palmer

Series 16: Nettie Palmer 1930 diary

Series 17: Typescript draft *Fourteen Years* by Nettie Palmer

MS 2573 Papers of Bernard Cronin

Box 2, File 8: Society of Australian Authors correspondence

MS 2809 Papers of Fritz Hart

Including manuscripts for *Puck and Mr Perkins* (1939), *Alice and a Scruple* (1940), *James Comes Home to Dinner* (1942), *Miss Macchiavelli* (1942), *A Brazen Little Baggage* (1946)

MS 5027 George Johnston Literary Drafts 1951–1970

Series 2, File 3: Outlines, technical breakdowns, summary of scenes, sample dialogues and settings for Charmian Clift's adaptation of *My Brother Jack*, episodes 1–10

MS 6772 Papers of Betty Roland

Box 2, File 6: Three letters from Colin Colahan

Box 3, File 4: 'Molly Dean Murder': items used in the research of *The Eye of the Beholder*

Box 9: 'Proem' by Sue Vanderkelen

Other

Montsalvat

Skipper, Mervyn, *A Pressman's Soul*, unpublished typescript, c1935–40

Weber family

Weber, Lois, *Memoirs*, unpublished, undated

Recordings

National Film and Sound Archive

My Brother Jack, 300 minutes, ABC, 1965

Directed by Gil Brealey

Screenplay by Charmian Clift

Produced by Storry Walton

Starring Ed Devereaux, Nick Tate and Chris Christensen

Tess Mallos as Jessica Wray

David Copping as Sam Burlington

My Brother Jack, 182 minutes, Samson Productions, 2001

Directed by Ken Cameron

Screenplay by John Alsop and Sue Smith

Produced by Sue Milliken and Andrew Wiseman

Starring Matt Day, Simon Lyndon and Claudia Karvan

Lucy Taylor as Jessica Wray

Felix Williamson as Sam Burlington

Headline, 73 minutes, Ealing Studios, 1943
Directed by John Harlow
Screenplay by Maisie Sharman
Produced by Joseph Janni
Starring David Farrar, Anne Crawford and Anthony Hawtrey
Nancy O'Neil as Mollie Dean

Perry family
Colin Colahan interviewed by Eric Westbrook, 21 December 1969
Betty Roland interviewed by Eric Westbrook, undated
Colin Colahan interviewed by Betty Roland, undated
John Farmer interviewed by Michael Jorgensen, 4 November 1981

Lisa Miller
'Molly Dean' by The Dusty Millers
Lisa Miller, vocals/guitar
Loretta Miller, vocals
Tracey Miller, vocals/guitar/ukulele
Produced by The Dusty Millers
Recorded, mixed and mastered by Michael O'Connell, October 2016

SECONDARY SOURCES
Literature
Attiwill, Ken, *Reporter!*, John Long, London, 1933
Bitto, Emily, *The Strays*, Affirm Press, Melbourne, 2014
Bolt, Robert, *A Man for All Seasons*, Heinemann, London, 1960
Boylan, Eustace, *The Heart of the School*, J. Roy Stevens, Melbourne, 1919
Christie, Agatha, *The Murder at the Vicarage*, Collins, London, 1930
Clift, Charmian, *The World of Charmian Clift*, Ure Smith, Sydney, 1970
Cottrell, Dorothy, *The Singing Gold*, Hodder & Stoughton, London, 1928

Cox, Anthony Berkeley, *The Silk Stocking Murders: A Story of Crime*, W. Collins, London, 1928

Cronin, Bernard, *Bracken*, Jarrolds, London, 1931

— *A Sow's Ear,* Endeavour Press, Sydney, 1933

— *The Shadows Mystery*, Frank Johnson, Sydney, 1944

Cusack, Dymphna, *Jungfrau, The Bulletin*, Sydney, 1936

Du Maurier, George, *Trilby*, Osgood McIlvaine, London, 1894

Egan, Reg, *Lottie: A Love Affair with a Man of God and the Cruel Death that Shocked Australia*, Brolga Publishing, Melbourne, 2004

Esson, Louis, *The Time Is Not Yet Ripe*, Fraser & Jenkinson, Melbourne, 1912

Hume, Fergus, *The Mystery of a Hansom Cab*, Jarrolds, London, 1896

Huxley, Aldous, *Point Counter Point*, Chatto & Windus, London, 1928

Johnston, George, *My Brother Jack*, Collins, Sydney, 1964

— *Strong Man from Piraeus and Other Stories*, Penguin, Melbourne, 1986

Keane, Mollie (writing as M. J. Farrell), *Taking Chances,* Elkin Mathews & Marrot, London, 1929

Kovacic, Katherine, *The Portrait of Molly Dean*, Bonnier Publishing, Melbourne, 2018

Lewis, Sinclair, *Main Street*, Harcourt, Brace, New York, 1920

Lindsay, Norman, *A Curate in Bohemia*, Angus & Robertson, London, 1913

McCann, A. L., *Subtopia*, Vulgar Press, Carlton, 2005

McCarthy, Mary, *The Group*, Weidenfeld & Nicolson, London, 1963

Malouf, David, *Johnno*, University of Queensland Press, Brisbane, 1974

Mantel, Hilary, *Wolf Hall*, Fourth Estate, London, 2009

Moore, George, *A Modern Lover,* W. Scott, London, 1886

Murger, Henry, *Scènes de la vie de bohème*, Michel Lévy Frères, Paris, 1890

Neilson, John Shaw, *Ballad and Lyrical Poems*, Webdale, Shoosmith, Sydney, 1923

Nickson, Beryl F. Bennie, *As the Linnets Sing*, Diocesan Book Depot, Melbourne, 1933

Palmer, Vance, *The Man Hamilton,* Ward Lock, London, 1928

— *Men Are Human,* Stanley Paul, London, 1928

Pirandello, Luigi, *Right You Are (If You Think So),* Penguin, Harmondsworth, 1962

Prichard, Katharine Susannah, *Coonardoo,* Cape, London, 1929

Pyke, Lillian, *Three Bachelor Girls,* Ward Lock, Melbourne, 1926

Redhead, Leigh, *Peepshow,* Allen & Unwin, Sydney, 2004

Roland, Betty, *A Touch of Silk,* Melbourne University Press, Melbourne, 1945

Rowston, Melita, *Solitude in Blue,* original script, unpublished, 2002

Shaw, George Bernard, *Pygmalion: A Romance in Five Acts,* Penguin, Harmondsworth, 1941

Simpson, Janice, *Murder in Mt Martha,* Hybrid Publishers, 2016

Stead, Christina, *For Love Alone,* Peter Davies, London, 1945

Swinburne, Algernon, *The Collected Poetical Works,* Heinemann, London, 1917

Thornell, Kristel, *Night Street,* Allen & Unwin, Sydney, 2011

Vanderkelen, Sue (ed. Michael Jorgensen), *The Cruel Man,* Black Jack Press, Carlton North, 2002

Voltaire, *Candide,* Arnold, London, 1960

Waugh, Evelyn, *A Handful of Dust,* Chapman & Hall, London, 1934

Winton, Tim, *Cloudstreet,* McPhee Gribble, Melbourne, 1991

Biography

Blainey, Ann, *I Am Melba: A Biography,* Black Inc, Melbourne, 2008

Burke, Janine, *Australian Gothic: A Life of Albert Tucker,* Penguin Random House, Melbourne, 2011

Clark, Ronald W., *The Life of Bertrand Russell,* J. Cape, London, 1975

Colahan, Colin (ed.), *Max Meldrum: His Art and Views,* Alexander McCubbin, Melbourne, 1919

Davidson, Jim, *Lyrebird Rising: Louise Hanson-Dyer of Oiseau-Lyre, 1884–1962,* Melbourne University Press at the Miegunyah Press, Carlton, 1994

Fitzpatrick, Peter, *Pioneer Players: The Lives of Louis and Hilda Esson*,
    Cambridge University Press, Melbourne, 1995

Hammer, Gael, *Phillip Blashki: A Victorian Patriarch*, P. Blashki & Sons,
    Melbourne, 1986

Hammer, Gael (ed.), *Clara Behrend Remembers*, Hippo Books, Sydney, 2008

Harding, Lesley and Kendrah Morgan, *Modern Love: The Lives of John &*
    Sunday Reed, Heide Museum of Modern Art, Heidelberg, 2015

Hollinrake, Rosalind, *Clarice Beckett: The Artist and Her Circle*, Macmillan,
    Melbourne, 1979

— *Clarice Beckett: Politically Incorrect*, Ian Potter Museum of Art, Melbourne, 1999

Jorgensen, Michael, *The Drawings of Jim Minogue*, privately published,
    Melbourne, 1989

Kinnane, Garry, *George Johnston: A Biography*, Penguin, Ringwood, 1989

— *Colin Colahan: A Portrait*, Melbourne University Press, Carlton South, 1996

Lindsay, Norman, *A Curate in Bohemia*, Angus & Robertson, Sydney, 1913

McInnes, Graham, *The Road to Gundagai*, Hamish Hamilton, London, 1965

Radic, Thérèse, *Bernard Heinze*, Macmillan, Melbourne, 1986

Rankin, Gwen, *Bernard Hall: The Man the Art World Forgot*, NewSouth
    Publishing, Sydney, 2013

Roland, Betty, *The Eye of the Beholder*, Hale & Ironmonger, Sydney, 1984

— *An Improbable Life*, Collins, Sydney, 1989

Rosewood, Jack, *Arnold Sodeman: The True Story of the Schoolgirl Strangler*,
    True Crime by Evil Killers No. 1, Kindle edition, Amazon Digital Services
    LLC, 2015

Serle, Geoffrey, *Percival Serle, Biographer, Bibliographer, Anthologist and Art*
    Curator: A Memoir, Officina Brindabella, Canberra, 1988

Shore, Arnold, *Forty Years Seek and Find,* Australian Galleries, Melbourne, 1957

Skipper, Sonia, *Tales from a Pioneer of Montsalvat*, Black Jack Press, Carlton
    North, 2005

Tasca, Margot, *Percy Leason: An Artist's Life*, Thames & Hudson, Melbourne, 2016

Teichman, Jenny, *Justus Jorgensen: Conversations and a Memoir*, privately
    published, Cambridge, 1976

Thompson, John, *On Lips of Living Men*, Lansdowne, Melbourne, 1962

Thompson, Patricia, *Accidental Chords*, Penguin, Melbourne, 1988

Underhill, Nancy, *Sidney Nolan: A Life*, NewSouth Publishing, Sydney, 2015

Wheatley, Nadia, *The Life and Myth of Charmian Clift*, HarperCollins, Sydney,
    2001

Young, Edith, *Inside Out*, Routledge and K. Paul, London, 1971

Art history

Burn, Ian, *National Life and Landscapes*, Bay Books, Sydney, 1990

Crombie, Isobel and Elena Taylor (eds), *Brave New World: Australia 1930s*,
    National Gallery of Victoria, Melbourne, 2017

Eagle, Mary, *Australian Modern Painting Between the Wars 1919–1939*, Bay
    Books, Sydney, 1989

Hetherington, John, *Australian Painters: 40 Profiles*, Cheshire, Melbourne,
    1963

Jorgensen, Sigmund, *Montsalvat: The Intimate Story of Australia's Most Exciting
    Artists' Colony*, Allen & Unwin, Sydney, 2014

Kovacic, Katherine, *Archie & Amalie Colquhoun*, Castlemaine Art Gallery and
    Historical Museum, Castlemaine, 2010

— *Mediterranean Summers: Australian Artists Along the French and Italian Coast*,
    Castlemaine Art Gallery and Historical Museum, Castlemaine, 2013

Lock-Weir, Tracey, *Misty Moderns: Australian Tonalists 1915–1950*, Art Gallery of
    South Australia, Adelaide, 2008

Lynn, Elwyn and Sidney Nolan, *Sidney Nolan – Australia*, Bay Books, Sydney, 1979

Perry, Peter and John Perry, *Max Meldrum & Associates: Their Art, Lives and
    Influences*, Castlemaine Art Gallery & Historical Museum, Castlemaine, 1996

Stephen, Ann, Philip Goad and Andrew McNamara, *Modern Times: The
    Untold Story of Modernism in Australia*, Miegunyah Press, Carlton, 2008

Taylor, Alex, *Perils of the Studio: Inside the Artistic Affairs of Bohemian Melbourne,* Australian Scholarly Publishing, Melbourne, 2007

General history

Australian Dictionary of Biography, Melbourne University Press, 1966–2012

Blaikie, George, *Remember Smith's Weekly?: A Biography of an Uninhibited National Australian Newspaper, Born 1 March 1919, Died 28 October 1950,* Rigby, Sydney, 1966

Blake, L. J. (ed.), *Vision and Realisation: A Centenary History of State Education in Victoria,* Education Department, Melbourne, 1973

Bongiorno, Frank, *The Sex Lives of Australians: A History,* Black Inc, Collingwood, 2012

Garden, Don, *The Melbourne Teacher Training Colleges: From Training Institution to Melbourne State College, 1870–1982,* Heinemann Educational Australia, Richmond, 1982

Garton, Stephen, *The Cost of War: Australians Return,* Oxford University Press, Melbourne, 1996

Grow, Robin, *Murder of a Messenger,* Brolga Publishing, Melbourne, 2015

Haldane, Robert, *The People's Force: A History of the Victoria Police,* Melbourne University Press, Carlton South, 1995

Hoy, Alice, *A City Built to Music: The History of the University High School, 1910 to 1960,* University High School, Parkville, 1960

Larsson, Marisa, *Shattered Anzacs: Living with the Scars of War,* UNSW Press, Sydney, 2009

Modjeska, Drusilla, *Exiles at Home: Australian Women Writers 1925–1945,* A & R Classics, Sydney, 2001

Morgan, Kevin, *Gun Alley: Murder, Lies and Failure of Justice,* Simon & Schuster, Sydney, 2005

Otto, Kristin, *Capital: Melbourne When It Was the Capital City of Australia 1901–1927,* Text Publishing, Melbourne, 2009

Rhoden, Clare, *The Purpose of Futility: Writing World War 1, Australian Style*, UWA Publishing, Crawley, 2015

Spencer, Baldwin and F. J. Gillen, *Across Australia*, Macmillan, London, 1912

Tregear, Peter, *The Conservatorium of Music, University of Melbourne: An Historical Essay to Mark Its Centenary 1895–1995*, Centre for Studies in Australian Music, Parkville, 1997

Wilmot, R. W. E., *The Melbourne Athenaeum, 1839–1939: History and Records of the Institution*, Stilwell and Stephens, Melbourne, 1939

Miscellaneous

Baumfield, Brian (ed.), *Do Books Matter?*, Working Party on Library and Book Trade Relations, London, 1973

Browne, G. S. (ed.), *Education in Australia: A Comparative Study of the Educational Systems of the Six Australian States*, Macmillan, London, 1927

Elijah, James and John Cole, *The Principle and Technique of Teaching in Elementary Schools*, Whitcombe & Tombs, Melbourne, 1924

Ellis, Havelock, *Women and Marriage*, William Reeves, London, 1888

Ferch, Johann, *Birth Control*, Williams & Norgate, London, 1926

Lindsay, Judge Ben B. with Wainwright Evans, *The Companionate Marriage*, Garden City Publishing, New York, 1927

Nickson, A. E. H., *Christ in Art*, Diocesan Book Depot, Melbourne, 1925

— *The Mind Beautiful* (s.n.), Melbourne, 1927

Russell, Bertrand, *Marriage and Morals*, George Allen & Unwin, London, 1929

Sanger, Margaret, *Family Limitation*, New York Review Publishing Company, New York, 1914

Stashower, Daniel, *The Beautiful Cigar Girl: Mary Rogers, Edgar Allan Poe, and the Invention of Murder*, Dutton, New York, 2006

Stopes, Marie, *Married Love*, Putnam, London, 1919

Sutherland, Halliday, *Birth Control*, Harding & More, London, 1922

Woolf, Virginia, *A Room of One's Own*, Hogarth Press, London, 1929

Newspapers and periodicals

The Age, The Argus, Cairns Post, Evening News, The Herald, The Mail,
   The Observer, Smith's Weekly, Sun News-Pictorial, Sydney Sun, Table Talk,
   Truth (Melbourne, Sydney, Brisbane, Perth editions)

Advance! Australia, Art in Australia, Australian Journal, Australian Woman's
   Mirror, The Bulletin, Home, The New Triad, Pandemonium, People, The Record
   (University High School), *Romance, St Kilda Chronicle, Stead's Review,*
   The Trainee (Melbourne Teachers' College), *The Triad, Verse, Victorian Arts*
   Society Journal, Woman's World

Online resources

Frazer, Dr Eric, 'Mary (Molly) Dean: The Murder, the Inquest, and Abandoned
   Trial', 2017, available at https://www.prov.vic.gov.au/explore-collection/
   provenance-journal/provenance-2016-17/mary-molly-winifred-dean-
   1905-1930

Reeve, Simon, Heritage Alliance, Elwood Heritage Review, Vol. 1: Thematic
   History Citations for Heritage Precincts, prepared for City of Port Phillip,
   2005, available at http://www.portphillip.vic.gov.au/default/Community
   GovernanceDocu ments/Volume_One_Thematic_History_and_Heritage_
   Precincts.pdf

Sellers, Travis, 'The Artist, the Fiancé & Murder at Elwood', History of
   Brighton General Cemetery, available at http://brightoncemetery.com/
   HistoricInterments/Crimes/dean.htm

IMAGE CREDITS

Picture section

Brighton Road State School, Sidney Nolan 1917–1992, Art Gallery of South Australia (2)

Betty, John Longstaff 1861–1941, Art Gallery of Ballarat (4)

Nude, Colin Colahan 1897–1987, Sotheby's Australia (9)

Sleep, Colin Colahan 1897–1987, private collection (10)

State Library Victoria 2 (top), 3, 4 (bottom right), 6, 7 (bottom left and right), 14 (top left and right)

Xavier College Archives 4 (top left and right)

Max Leason 5, 11

Gilda Baracchi 7 (top left and right)

Public Record Office 8, 12 (bottom)

Melbourne Cricket Club 12 (top left and right)

Deanne and Michael Carroll 14 (bottom left and right)

National Library of Australia 1, 13

Jim Tzannes 15

Melita Rowston 16 (top left and right)

Author 16 (bottom)

Text

People 2, 252

State Library of Victoria 24, 63, 79, 99, 225

The Trainee 40

Anthony Sell 51

Xavier College Archives 84